GW01605272

MESSAGE

The history of our glorious ancient India is a history of thousands of years of culture and progress. All of us know about the spiritual heritage of India and we take pride in it, but we are hardly aware of our scientific heritage. We generally accept the West as the forerunner in scientific knowledge and technological development.

We did not lack in scientific heritage but what we lacked is documentation. What we did, we did not record; what we recorded, we did not collect; what we collected, we did not codify and what we codified, we did not make it available to the public. 'Absence of evidence' became the 'evidence of absence'.

Samskrita Bharati has taken this initiative to publish this wonderful collection of writings on the scientific heritage of India. A team of scholars and technocrats have brought us a glimpse of our ancient scientific tradition and knowledge. One can see that our scientific tradition did not leave any field untouched, from abstract mathematics to solid engineering. Our scientific tradition was not against nature, it was in total harmony with nature.

It is a most welcome and refreshing experience to browse through the pages of this book. This experience will fill every reader with a sense of pride that we belong to a culture that had once reached the pinnacles of science and, there is nothing today to stop the march of resurgent modern India to achieve even greater heights in this field. I am sure you and your family will find this book useful and especially the new generation to know about our rich heritage.

Let us all be proud of our India, let us hold our heads high; for we have a rich scientific and spiritual tradition.

(Narendra Modi)
Chief Minister, Gujarat State

PRIDE *Of* INDIA

A Glimpse into India's Scientific Heritage

Published by:

Samskrita Bharati,
Mata Mandir Gali,
Jhandewala,
New Delhi - 110 055.
email: samskritabharatidelhi@rediffmail.com
Website: www.samskrita-bharati.org
Telephone: 011-2351 7689

Compiled by:

Bharatiya Bouddhik Sampada,
'Anand Vilas'
Chitale Road, Dhantoli,
Nagpur - 440 012.
email: ddeepdesh@rediffmail.com

Book Design:

Ram's Creative Chamber,
1, Janaki Avenue,
Abhiramapuram,
Mylapore,
Chennai - 600 004.
email: natesanramanan@gmail.com

Printed in India at :

1st Print, June 2006, MWN Press, Chennai
2nd Reprint, May 2007, MWN Press, Chennai
3rd Reprint Dec. 2007, Span Print, Bangalore.
4th Reprint Aug. 2009, Span Print, Bangalore.
Tel. : 080-2671 8831
Email : spanprint@indiatimes.com

Price: **Rs. 2,000/-**

ISBN 81-87276-27-4

Contents

Why Pride of India ?

The twentieth century has seen unprecedented development in knowledge and technology. Car to spacecraft - all have been invented and commercialised in the lifetime of a person. At the end of this epochal growth, humanity is at crossroads:

- The Green revolution - high yielding varieties of seeds, chemical fertilisers and chemical pesticides - was the blessing, which saved India from ruinous famines and equally ruinous food import bills in the 1960s. Today, the best brains in agriculture and chemical technology, including some who were involved in the green revolution, are searching desperately for ways and means of restoring the soil fertility, which has been completely eroded by the revolution. We are looking for alternatives, which have not emerged yet.

- Allopathy has taken great strides in the last 3 decades. Unknowingly, in this avalanche of development, basic tenets of Allopathy have been lost. "The doctor ties the bandage but it is He who heals the fracture" is the axiom that drove the course of treatment that doctors chose some years ago. This axiom is based on the premise that the body has the potential to heal itself. Today the adverse side effects of allopathic treatment are so acute and widespread that there is a longing for alternate medicines in every part of the world.

The world is compelled to question the appropriateness of the methodologies and technologies that have come into being in the last 100 years. The society needs an alternate worldview - in every area of human life, from the model for the family to system of education to science and technology.

We need an alternate mindset to find innovative solutions. The world is looking to the East, inclusive of India, for such solutions. But, does India have the knowledge base to fill this role?

From time immemorial, this land has been known as 'Bharat', a Samskrit word that denotes a man or a nation immersed in knowledge what is today called a "knowledge society".

In the course of the colonial rule, we have learnt to revere the West and worse discount ourselves. A person who has spent 12 years of his life in learning the Vedas is seen as "uneducated" not only by the society, but also by the person himself.

The only way to reach anything of value to the Indian hearts and minds has been by getting the idea through the West.

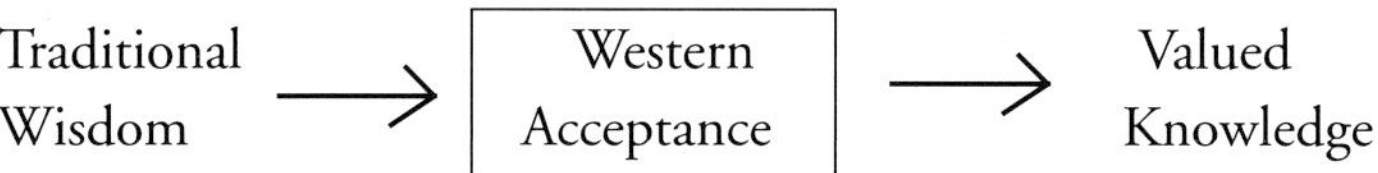

Reiki, Thai massage, child delivery at home, music therapy,..... the list of ideas that have been exported and reimported is long and growing.

Today, the scientific literature in Samskrit available to us is vast and varied, covering subjects as diverse as alchemy and astronomy, mathematics and metallurgy, gemmology and zoology, and many more.

There is knowledge - not merely methodologies but more fundamentally, perceptions and approaches, which have stood the test of time, which could provide the answers. This knowledge, as you will see from this book, is to be found in our sacred (Vedas) as well as secular texts (like Charaka-samhita), in our life style and traditions and in our mythology.

India has the knowledge. But is India conscious of this knowldege?

> India was the cradle of the human race, birth place of human speech, mother of history, grand mother of legend, great grandmother of traditions: the one land all men desire to see and having once seen, by even a glimpse, would not give that glimpse for the show of all the rest of the globe.
>
> **- Mark Twain, an American Novelist (1835-1910).**
>
> I was raised in Tamil Nadu in South India, in the ashram of Sri Ramana Maharshi. My English father and Polish mother were dedicated followers of Sri Ramana Maharshi. After all, how could anyone even an English boy grow up in Tiruvannamalai in the ashram of Sri Ramana Maharshi, and not acquire a pride in his roots? I was surrounded by Indians who were proud of their nationality and heritage. They believed they had a lot to teach us Europeans.
>
> It is therefore with some misgiving that today I find myself dealing with Indians, many of whom do not feel proud of their Indianness. Indians are recognized throughout America as technically superior. Since the day Indians learn pride, India will rapidly move out of its third world status to become one of the world's industrial powers.
>
> **-Adam Osborne, the co-founder (along with Steve Job) of Apple Computers writing for Dataquest magazine.**
>
> How can we lament lack of national pride in Indians without first acquainting them with the country's phenomenal scientific achievements in the dim distant past?
>
> **-D.S.Kothari, Nuclear Physicist in his lecture on "Science and Values" delivered at the Indian National Science Academy.**

Pride of India is an attempt to make Indians conscious of the knowledge heritage of their nation. Out of this awareness, shall emerge pride and self belief.

Self-esteem is one of the important factors in the development of an individual, community or a nation. Enhancement of self-esteem of a nation happens by understanding its past (as well as the present) achievements and strengths and by the transmission of the experience down the generation.

How has the book been structured?

Quotation and meaning

The quotes in Samskrit are followed by transliteration and a literal translation of the quotes. Technical words occurring in the quotes are derived and shown under the head "Etymology". Such a presentation meets the requirement of scientific rigour.

Source

This book contains a small collection from a large reservoir of literature. For each of these quotes, the source is spelt out. E.g., Charaka-samhita, Adhyaya (chapter), Shloka (verse). This has been done to enable an interested reader to reach more material directly.

Current Relevance

Wherever appropriate, the relevance of the idea in today's world is indicated with appropriate authority. This, in addition to establishing the relevance of delving into the past, will enable a reader involved in that subject area, say a doctor, to move from principle to application.

How to read the book?

This is a book on history of science. The book has been presented in such a way that you can understand and appreciate the contents of the book without a background in history or science. Mathematics is the only division where a subject-familiarity could be a prerequisite. You may be a doctor or mechanical engineer, a student of history or philosophy, you could read and will be able to appreciate every single chapter in this book.

You could pick up virtually any page and the content would make sense and stand by itself. You could read quotations and translations and then go to the write-ups or do it the other way around.

How do you benefit from reading this book?

We have several 'convictions' about our civilisation and heritage:

- We are great in philosophy but not much in material sciences
- Samskrit is the language of religion
- Religious texts concern themselves with rituals or philosophy
- There has been so much research and development in "modern medicine" (Allopathy) how could Ayurveda be of any relevance today?

This book would help undo these myths.

For the purpose of understanding the other benefits that could accrue from reading this book, we can categorise the readers as:

- Students and professionals in any area of science and technology
- Samskrit teachers and students.

For Scientists and Technologists

There have been scientists who have spent their entire life studying physics, switched to chemistry at the fag end of their career and managed to win a Nobel prize in their newly chosen field. Newspapers would report this as Mr. X winning a Mathematics Nobel despite being a Physics / Chemistry scholar. In fact, breakthrough thoughts would have occurred only because the person came from a different discipline. **Creativity lies where boundaries of two or more disciplines meet and cross. An exposure to alternate scholarship will widen your perception of your own discipline.**

For professionals who know Samskrit the benefits would be immense.

For the Samskritist

This book will enable you to understand the value of your calling in life more fully.

This book would enable you to identify areas of further study such as

- Encryption
- Manuscriptology
- Research into the content of sacred texts.

Conclusion

With Samskrit ceasing to be a functional language, the knowledge contained in Samskrit texts has become unavailable to the mankind. With Samskrit as the key, we have to unlock this treasure-house of knowledge and become 'Bharat'.

Thanks

The book is what it is today because of the imagination, research and analysis that my friend N.R. Kumar brought to bear on this project in the last several months. A special thanks to him. I also thank the staff of M W N Press for the skill as well as the care that they displayed in printing the book.

Chamu Krishna Shastry
Samskrita Bharati

Chamu Krishna Shastry, All India General Secretary, Samskrita Bharati, New Delhi conceived the idea of bringing to light the science available in ancient Samskrit texts.

The responsibility for selecting the works and quotes suited for this purpose was vested with "Team Nagpur", many of whom have been involved for several years in the publication of "Bharatiya Bouddhik Sampada", a quarterly journal devoted to the exploration of Indian intellectual capital. The action moved from Delhi to Nagpur.

The Team gathered quotes covering the spectrum of science:

Physical Sciences		Natural Sciences
Mathematics		Botany
Astronomy		Zoology
Physics		
Engineering	&	Medicine
Civil		
Mechanical		
Metallurgy		

In each of these disciplines, samples were available in each branch, be it Arithmetic, Algebra, Geometry & Trigonometry in Mathematics or Anatomy to Cardiology in Medicine.

Vrushali Agencies, Nagpur, typeset the material and the bilingual text of Samskrit quotes with English translation reached digital form.

The text and the action moved to Samskrita Bharati, Chennai.

Mr. M.V. Mohan, M.Phil., (Samskrit) Chennai, double-checked and homogenised the translation.

Dr. S.Srivatsan, MBBS., Chennai, scrutinised the medicine part of the compilation.

Samskrita Bharati, Chennai team discovered interesting dimensions in some of these quotes which have been brought to light; such dimensions being:

Revisiting history

- Sushruta (6th Century BCE) defined the function of the heart ahead of Harvey (17th Century AD)

Current Relevance

- Leeches (mentioned in the Vedas) are back in use in US hospitals.

Insight

- Town planning in India was guided by astronomy

Intrigue

- The speed of light occurs in a Vedic hymn used in funeral rites.

Just interesting

- Plastic surgery was born in India.

The compilation of the quotes provided a certain understanding of :

- The vintage of the Indus Valley Civilisation
- The scientific temperament of the community
- The role of Samskrit as a vehicle for thought.

We have captured these various issues in a series of write-ups. The responsibility for this exercise was assumed by Mr. N.R. Kumar, a Management Consultant by profession, who is a Spoken Samskrit enthusiast and a long time volunteer of the Samskrita Bharati.

This exercise also left us with what next issues like:

- Uncovering the manuscript wealth of India
- Reaching Samskrit to the scientist community

which have been presented as write-ups for the readers' reflection.

Editors
12th May 2006

LIST OF CONTRIBUTORS

Project Co-ordinator	**Editors**
Mr. R.M.Pujari, A.M.I.E., Bharatiya Bouddhik Sampada Nagpur.	Dr. Pradeep Kolhe, M.D., Ph.D. (Ayurved), Nagpur. Mr. N.R.Kumar, B.Com., A.C.A., I.C.W.A., Chennai.

Contributors

1. Mathematics	Mr. Shriram Chauthaiwale, M.Sc. (Maths), Yeotmal.
2. Astronomy	Prof. R.Ramachandran, Ph.D. (Samskrit), Chennai. Mr. M.Jayaraman, M.A. (Samskrit).
3. Chemistry	Dr. V.K.Didolkar, Ph.D. (Metallurgy), Nagpur.
4. Life science	Dr. Jayant Deopujari, Ph.D. (Ayurved), Nagpur.
5. Medicine	Dr. Pradeep Kolhe, M.D., Ph.D. (Ayurved), Nagpur. Dr. Prashant Tople, M.D. (Ayurved), Nagpur.
6. Civil Engineering	Dr. R.M.Pujari, A.M.I.E. Nagpur. Prof. P.P.Holay, M.Tech. (Elect. Engg.), Nagpur. Mr. Vinay Tare, M.A. (Samskrit), Nagpur. Mr. A.S.Khadakkar, B.Arch., Nagpur. Dr. A.S.Nene, Ph.D. (Civil Engg), Nagpur.
7. Mechanical Engineering	Prof. P.P.Holay, M.Tech. (Elect. Engg.), Nagpur.
8. Metallurgy	Dr. V.K.Didolkar, Ph.D. (Metallurgy), Nagpur. Mr. M.K.Kawadkar, A.M.I.M.E., Nagpur.
9. Others who facilitated the compilation / translation	Mr. Deepak Deshpande, B.E. (Mech.), DBM Dr. W.B.Rahudkar Ph.D. (Agril.,), Mrs. Durga Parkhi, M.A. (Samskrit) Dr. Ms.Hansashree Marathe, Ph.D. (Samskrit)

SAMSKRITA BHARATI

Today, if a housewife in Tamil Nadu can savour the sweetness of Samskrit in the works of Kalidasa and Jayadeva; if an executive in Kerala can enjoy the subtlety of Bhagvad Gita in its original form; if a pensioner in Punjab can read and understand Valmiki without a translation... Samskrita Bharati has a lot to do with the transformation, the revival of a language that reflects the very soul of India.

Thanks to the innovative, '10-day Spoken Samskrit' classes conducted by Samskrita Bharati across the country, people from different sections of the society are discovering to their delight that Samskrit is a living language, easy to learn and use in everyday life. The activities of Samskrita Bharati include classroom and correspondence courses, teacher training camps, workshops, exhibitions, publications and discussions through e-groups.

Samskrita Bharati, headquartered in Delhi, is staffed by volunteers - men and women who dedicate a part of their life to the propagation of Samskrit.

BHARATIYA BOUDDHIK SAMPADA

There is a wealth of wisdom and a world of knowledge in ancient Indian literature that, if tapped, can lead us to higher levels of learning. But most of these texts are in Samskrit, a language in which today's scientists are not proficient. As it happens, Samskrit scholars are not familiar with the modern sciences and are unable to interpret these texts in a manner required by scientists and technologists. This poses a huge problem to the modern scientist seeking to benefit from the ancient Samskrit works.

Bharatiya Bouddhik Sampada, published from Nagpur, Maharashtra, is a quarterly magazine dedicated to bridging this gap. Bharatiya Bouddhik Sampada has been disseminating traditional knowledge in multiple fields - medicine, metallurgy, agriculture - for the benefit of the scientific community.

Bharatiya Bouddhik Sampada is the mouth piece journal of the G.G. Joshi Shilpa Samshodhan Pratishthan an organisation founded in memory of Mr. G.G. Joshi, an Indologist who spent his lifetime collecting and propogating ancient manuscripts.

PROTOCAL ON THE USE OF SAMSKRIT WORDS

Usage

We have used some words E.g., "Yajna" instead of its equivalent "ritual sacrifice" in this book. The use of Samskrit words has been driven by the following considerations:

- Such words have been used in a context repeatedly such that the words have become definitions.
- Such words are in use in various south and north Indian languages.

In the case of proper nouns, names of places, persons and books, needless to say, the Samskrit word is in use.

Spelling

<table>
<tr><th>In write-ups</th><th>In quotations</th></tr>
<tr><td colspan="2">The first letters of the words have been capitalised E.g., Veda. Where a word consists of two or more words compounded, to facilitate easy reading, we have broken it with a hyphen. E.g., Yajur-veda.</td></tr>
<tr><td>The root of the word has been used in English. E.g.,
- Adhyaya
- Mandala
- Bhasha
this being the standard procedure in Anglicisation of words originating from other languages.</td><td>The words are spelt the way these are terminated in Samskrit. E.g.,
- Adhyāyaḥ
- Maṇḍalam
- Bhāśā</td></tr>
<tr><td>The words have been spelt phonetically. E.g.,
- Shloka
- Shastra</td><td>The words have been spelt with diacritical marks. E.g.,
- Ślokaḥ
- Śāstram
(See the next page for key)</td></tr>
</table>

Meaning

When a word or phrase, E.g., "Chaturdasha-vidya" is used exclusively or mainly in a chapter, the meaning of the word or phrase is explained in situ, in that context itself.

For others, the meaning is provided in the Glossary which is given at the end of the book.

KEY TO TRANSLITERATION

a	rural
ā	father
i	fill
ī	feel
u	full
ū	fool
ṛ	merry
e	prey
ai	high
o	go
au	house
ṁ	amnion
ḥ	wish
k	kind
kh	acknowledge
g	get
gh	yoghurt
ṅ	ink
c	watch
ch	watch here
j	join
jh	jet
ñ	inch
ṭ	tube
ṭh	anthill
ḍ	drum
ḍh	adhere
ṇ	sand
ऽ	a when silent
t	tar
th	thumb
da	thus
dha	those
na	name
p	pen
ph	pump
b	bulb
bh	abhor
m	man
y	loyal
r	run
l	land
v	ivory
ś	shun
ṣ	auction
s	same
h	he

The words in bold are to be pronounced with more aspiration.

DATING PROTOCOL

Pride of India quotes a cross section of texts spread over a long period from the Vedas to the technical literature of 14th century AD.

Traditionally, the 'pre-historic' period of Indian history is classified as:

- The Vedic period
- The Puranic period and
- The Epic period

The phrase - Post Vedic period would refer collectively to epic and puranic period.

Write-ups in Pride of India discuss the dates of the Civilisation, the Vedas and the Mahabharata.

Specific dates of authors and texts of historic period, which are arrived at without much speculation, are mentioned in the source.

TRANSLATOR'S NOTE

Meaning of words

Where a satisfactory word in English is not available, we have used the Samskrit word itself - Vata, Pitta, Kapha - in Medicine or Yajna in the write-up on Vedic texts. In such cases the meaning is explained in situ or in the Glossary found at the end of the book.

The texts contain several technical words. For these, we have shown the derivation of the meaning from the Samskrit word under the head "Etymology" in the respective block.

Sentence Construction

Passive voice is more commonly used in Samskrit than active voice. For E.g., it is quite common to say "The book has been read by me" rather than "I have read the book". In translation, we have stuck to this sentence construction, even though such a sentence construction is not natural to English.

In Samskrit, verbs are subject specific - for I, "gacchaami", for he / she, "gacchati", for they "gacchanti". Because of this, often there is no need to mention the subject in Samskrit sentences. "Gacchaami" would translate to "I go". When the subject is implied, we have shown the subject in bracket in the translation. For E.g., (I) go in the example cited above.

There may be other words, which are implied because of their presence in the previous sentence or the previous verse or paragraph. In the translation, such words are also given in bracket.

In Samskrit literature, authors present their prescriptions in phrases like uchyate (is told), shruyate (is heard), prakirtitaha (is reputed), smaryate (is remembered) etc., The translation faithfully sticks to such usage.

In Samskrit, a series of clauses can be combined in a single sentence, without a loss of clarity with the usage of:

- Participles such as kritva (having done), agatya (having come), parisheelya (having tested)
- Gerunds such as gacchan (while going), agacchan (while coming), parisheelayan (while testing)
- Infinitives such as gantum (for going), agantum (for coming), parishilayitum (for testing).

Translating such sentences into a single English sentence would completely rob the sentence of any clarity. Hence we have presented such sentences in bullet form.

Verses

In Samskrit texts, to facilitate easy recall, technical materials are also presented in verse form. Where a verse delivers an idea completely, which would be true in most occasions, translation has been given individually for each verse. Where an idea runs through two or more verses, translation has been done for the two or more verses together.

The purpose of this rigour in translation has been to ensure, without a shade of doubt, that the English translation is faithful to the original Samskrit text.

Caveat

Each industry has its own technical words; also words discard original meanings and acquire new meanings over a period of time. This book contains quotations from thousand year old texts. Our translation could fall short of the intended meaning in the text on this count.

THIS IS THE LAND OF OURS

"Man must have an original cradle land whence the peopling of the earth was brought about by migration. As to man's cradle land, there have been many theories but the weight of evidence is in favour of Indo-Malaysia."

The Encyclopaedia Britannica

"If there is a country on earth which can justly claim the honour of having been the cradle of the Human race or at least the scene of primitive civilization, the successive developments of which carried into all parts of the ancient world and even beyond, the blessings of knowledge which is the second life of man, that country is assuredly India."

Friedrich Creuzer (1771-1858), German philologist and archaeologist

"... Everything has come down to us from the banks of the Ganges."*

Francois Voltaire (1694-1778), French philosopher

* Voltaire, Lettres sur l'origine des sciences et sur celle des peuples de l'Asie (first published Paris, 1777), letter of 15 December 1775.

A passage in an ancient text The Panchavimshati-brahmana, "The Knowledge - Book of Twenty-five Chapters" states: "The world of heaven is as far removed from this world as thousand GAVA stacked one above the other."*

With the keen interest of the Western world in Eastern culture and traditions, especially in the Vedas from India and the penchant for rendering anything of value into English, there is no dearth of translations of ancient Eastern texts. W. Caland is a Dutch scholar# whose work is among the more respected translations of the Vedas. His translation reads:

"The world of heaven is as far removed from this (earthly) world as a thousand cows standing one above the other."

This meaning as translated defies logic. How come there is a passage which, to put it mildly, is enigmatic and to put it plainly made no sense at all.

How could a text rich in philosophical thoughts, and a society, which produced highly refined ideas in philosophy, not have similar development in the field of material sciences?

There are always superficial but tenable solutions:

Meta-physics is the forte of the East and it is an unlikely place for scientific advancement of the secular kind.

If there was a part of the text which was enigmatic, made no sense and seemed to have little place in a literature of Vedic maturity, such portions have always been set aside as the poetic (by implication meaningless) outbursts of the sages.

Our love for our ancient language - Samskrit - is only matched by our ignorance of the same. When it comes to English, we know it; more importantly English sanctifies what is said in it. We have no difficulty in accepting such translations, convinced that great though our civilisation was, we had no use for physical sciences.

It does not take too much effort to break from this mindset, reach below the surface and discover possible truths for ourselves.

* Panchavimshati Brahmana - Brahmana 16, 8:6

Dr. Subhash Kak, A Thousand Cows Standing the One Above the Other.

The Indian knowledge system encompasses Chaturdasha-vidyas --- the 14 disciplines which consist of:

The "basic" texts	-	The Vedas	4
The supplementary texts	-	The Vedangas	6
The complementary texts	-	The Upangas	4

Of the supplementary 6 texts (Vedangas), the following 4 deal with language:

Shiksha	-	Phonetics
Vyakarana	-	Grammar
Chandas	-	Prosody
Nirukta	-	Etymology

The remaining two, Jyotisha (Astrology) and Kalpa (Rules for rituals), we will get to later.

These supplementary and complementary texts are intended to help reach a proper understanding of the main text viz., the Vedas. So when there is a Rik to be understood, we know the place to go to i.e., the Nirukta, the Veda-specific dictionary.

Nirukta gives two meanings for the word "Gau"*

1. the planet earth and
2. the animal cow

in that order.

I have never had the patience to go through any dictionary - Oxford, Vaman Apte or the Nirukta - in any degree of detail. I tend to settle down quickly for the first mentioned meaning, which should, by definition, meet most needs. Making only this modification, the Dutch translation would read as follows:

"The world of heaven is as far removed from this (earthly) world as 1000 earths stacked one above the other".

This literal translation can be re-stated as follows:

The distance between the Earth and the Heavens = 1000 Earth Diameter

This certainly makes more sense than the chosen translation of 1000 cows stacked one above the other. The correct distance from the earth to the sun is more like 1000 times the Earth's radius than diameter. Or did they not mean the sun at all when they talked of the heaven? We have at least reached a statement on astronomy which qualifies as a starting point for further examination.

This looks elegant and simple. Is this one-off or is it representative?

There are other cases of secular truth - in astronomy and in medicine, which have been brought to the surface from the Vedic ocean.

- Speed of light

    Rig-veda, Mandalam 1, Suktam 50, Mantra 4.

---

* Niruktam, Chapter 2, Paragraph 5, Yaskah (Vedic period)

- Sun as the centre of the universe

  Yajur-aranyakam, Prashna 1, Anuvaka 8, Varga 3.

  Yajur-veda, Taittiriya-samhita, Kanda 3, Prapataka 4, Anuvaka 10, Mantra 3.

- Moon as a satellite of the earth

  Rig-veda, Mandalam 10, Suktam 189, Mantra 1.

  Yajur-veda, Kandam 1, Prapataka 5, Anuvaka 1, Mantra 3 & 4.

- Removal of placenta in child birth

  Atharva-veda, Prathama-kanda, Sukta 11, Shloka 4.

The example of the distance from the earth to the heavens has the classic strength and limitations of an example. It makes a point, but does not reveal the underlying complexities. How did somebody manage to spot this one Rik in the Vedic ocean?

If we are going to look for the needle in the haystack, understanding the haystack - its structure - would be a good starting point.

There are four Vedas

- Rik
- Yajus
- Sama and
- Atharva

Each of these Vedas is in four parts:

- Samhitas
- Brahmanas
- Aranyakas and
- Upanishads

Samhitas are hymns in praise of the various Vedic gods; these are also considered as mantras - the ones with the power to protect. Brahmanas contain directions for using these hymns in rituals.

Rituals are of two kinds:

- Shrauta - sacrifices like Rajasuya and Ashvamedha and
- Smarta - domestic rituals - beginning with naming ceremony at birth, through wedding rituals and finally, the death rites.

Shatapatha-brahmana, of the Shukla-yajur-veda (17 books containing 104 Brahmanas) provides detailed instructions on building sacrificial altars, making bricks for the construction of the altar, the arrangement and maintenance of the various Agnis (ritual sacred fire) and so on.

Similarly Ekagni-kanda of Krishna-yajur-veda contains material on performing wedding rituals.

Because these (the Samhitas and Brahmanas), by and large concern themselves with the conduct of rituals, these are collectively referred to as "The Karma-kanda" - ritualistic part of the Vedas.

It is the later part of the Vedic literature - Aranyakas and Upanishads which concern themselves with religious philosophy. Hence their currency today, 5000 years after their origin.

Our perceived intent and driven by it, the current application of Samhita and Brahmana materials is ritualistic. Once it is a ritual, then, the communication is prescriptive, the adherence is mechanical, the focus is on the form and not the content and the primary requirement is faith and not understanding. Add to this mindset the fact that the text is in Samskrit, which is alien to both the priests and the practitioners of the rituals, the chance of the meanings of the Riks seeping through and reaching the people involved is close to zero, a perfect zero.

The following examples illustrate in what strong ritualistic strait-jackets these materials are presented and preserved.

1. Rig-veda, 1st Mandala, 164th Sukta

This Sukta of 41 Riks is in praise of the sun. The Riks here have repeated reference to the path of the sun, the seven rays of the sun, and the worlds above and below. This Sukta has a Rik which talks about the elliptical path of planets and how they are held together by gravitational forces.

This Sukta is intended for the purification of a Brahmin, who has committed a theft! There are detailed instructions on how the person should recite the Sukta - inaudibly for 3 nights in a row.

2. Rig-veda, 1st Mandala, 164th Sukta, 2nd Rik

Commenting on a Rik in this Sukta, Sayanacharya, the most respected commentator on the Vedas, mentions the speed of light which matches the twentieth century measurement.

This Sukta is prescribed for the final rites of a Nitya Agnihotri (somebody who has performed the fire sacrifice as a daily routine in his lifetime).

While 700 years ago, Sayanacharya was able to perceive, comment upon and declare hard core scientific ideas from these materials, today these Vedic texts yield no meaning of any kind to us.

What really do the Vedas stand for? Let us go back to the origin of the Vedic literature to see whether we can gain an understanding.

Time is cyclical; everyday, there is dawn, noon, dusk and night, day after day. It is cyclical on a monthly basis; the moon waxes and wanes. It is cyclical on an annual basis, there is spring, summer, autumn and winter.

The Indian concept of time is cyclical eternally. There are 4 Yugas - Krita, Treta, Dvapara and Kali. On the completion of the Kali-yuga, the world as it exists comes to an end and is reborn.

While the species are gone, the structure remains or is revived in the old order. All the old knowledge - gravity, speed of light, pulse rate of humans and animals and the Periodic Table of elements continue to be relevant. Hence, knowledge is (the Vedas are) eternal.

Thankfully, the knowledge need not be reacquired. It is revealed to worthy individuals, the sages. To Vishvamitra is revealed the Gayatri-maha-mantra, hence Vishvamitra is the Mantra-drashta and not the Mantra-karta. He is the seer of the Mantra and is not credited with composing it. Since the eternal knowledge is revealed by a higher power to the humans, knowledge is (the Vedas are) "Apaurusheya" not of human origin.

Newton discovered gravity. We have no qualms about calling Isaac Newton the discoverer of gravity. Would "Gravity was revealed to Isaac Newton" be merely another way of stating the same fact?

The Vedic passages were heterogeneous multiple truths which were divined by certain evolved individuals. Vedavyasa, in his time, had arranged these passages. The arrangement was not by discipline but is in terms of the sages who had the revelations and delivered them.

There is a school of thought that at some stage these Vedic passages were woven into the daily rituals of the Hindus so that they were preserved and not lost. **It appears these thoughts are lost in rituals.** Both opportunity and challenge lie in the sifting of these thoughts.

As Dr. Dyer said in his 1990 best seller on transformation: we will see it, if we believe it.

Mathematics in Vedic Literature

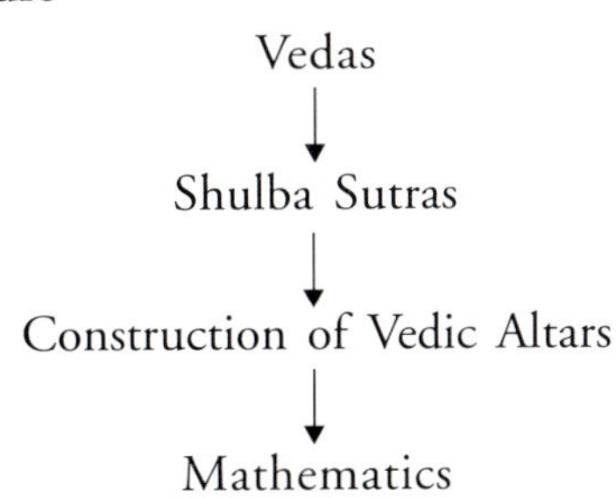

Kalpa is a term given to the group of four Sutra texts. These are:

1. Grhya-sutras which deal with the Vedic duties that are to be performed by a householder.
2. Dharma-sutras which enunciate ethical and moral code.
3. Shrauta-sutras which discuss various aspects of Vedic rituals beginning from the number of officiating priests to the utensils that are to be used in a Vedic sacrifice.
4. Shulba-sutras which concentrate on the construction of the Vedi (sacrificial altar). The term 'Shulba' refers to a measuring cord or a rope. It details the algebraic calculations that are involved in constructing a ritual sacrificial altar.

There is mathematics to be tapped from this part of the Vedas.

Each Vedic Shakha (recension) has its own Kalpa. Various sages have written Kalpas. Ashwalayana, Apasthamba, Bodhayana, Gautama are some among them. Some of these we will look at in the chapter on mathematics.

Encryption - Need

Look at this set of three telegrams apparently in regard to travel arrangements:

Next judiciary council meeting can now be arranged. Confirm convenient date as space must be requested.

Boris

Advise probable travel plans. Your sister's plane arrived late but landed safely. Lost Passport and money. She will be placed in first class Swiss hotel. Will settle account later.

Boris

Your sister will try American embassy to obtain temporary transport. No info available yet on new visa Swiss make Russians seem saints. Will ship sister to you.

Boris

Let us now see how the telegrams would be read by the intended recipient. If every fourth word alone were to be read, it would give the intended message.

Next judiciary council ***meeting*** *can now be* ***arranged.*** *Confirm convenient* ***date*** *as space must be* ***requested.***

Boris

Advise probable travel ***plans.*** *Your sister's plane* ***arrived*** *late but landed* ***safely.*** *Lost Passport and* ***money.*** *She will be* ***placed*** *in first class* ***Swiss*** *hotel. Will settle* ***account*** *later.*

Boris

Your sister will ***try*** *American embassy to* ***obtain*** *temporary transport. No* ***info*** *available yet on* ***new*** *visa, Swiss make* ***Russians*** *seem saints. Will* ***ship*** *sister to you.*

Boris

This is a simple good case of encryption:

- The document (telegram) is accessible to all.
- The document per se makes some sense.
- In the hands of a "competent" recipient, the text delivers its true intent.

The purpose of this encryption is to deliver a confidential message through a public medium.

Venkatesha-ashtottara-shata-namavali

Let us go back a thousand years and look at another example.

There is the Venkatesha-ashtottara-shata-namavali, containing a series of names in praise of Lord Venkatesha, the deity of Tirumala. If one of these names were to be missed the hymn will fall short of the magic number 108.

There is no storyline / meaning which could ensure the utterance of these names in the sequence in which these had been composed. There is a desire on the part of the composer that the hymn is recited as composed.

When the first letters of the names in the hymn are assembled, 4 Shlokas in Anushtup-chandas come into being. If a name were to be missed or the sequence were to be changed, this code would show up the flaw, not unlike the check digit used in coding by software professionals. **The purpose of this coding is to ensure the integrity of the work.**

Let us now look at encodings involving an interplay of alphabets and numbers.

Katapayaadi-sankhya

गोपीभाग्य मधुव्रात शृङ्गीशोदधिसन्धिग।	Gopībhāgya madhuvrāta śṛṅgīśodadhisandhiga ।
खलजीवित खाताव गलहालारसन्धर।।	Khalajīvītakhātāva galahālārasandhara ॥

Oh (Krishna,) the fortune of the Gopis, the destroyer of the demon Madhu, protector of cattle, the one who ventured the ocean-depths, destroyer of evildoers, one with plough on the shoulder and the bearer of nectar, may (you) protect (us).*

This is a Shloka in praise of Lord Krishna.

That is it and nothing more unless you have heard of the protocol called Katapayaadi-sankhya. Under Katapayaadi-sankhya, letters of the alphabets have numerical values ascribed to them. For E.g., Ka, ta, pa, ya mean 1. With this key you can read the same Shloka; out go the alphabets and in come the numbers. The "translation", if you can call it so, is:

3.1415926535897932384626433832792.

You don't have to be a mathematical genius or Samskrit scholar to recognise the number. It is the value of π correct to 31 digits. With an understanding of the encryption tools of Samskrit you will seem like both.

The purpose of this encryption is to recall a number with a large number of digits effortlessly.

Numbers through Symbolism

Numbers are assigned not only for consonants but also for certain words. The deciphering pre-supposes knowledge of Indian literature including mythology, philosophy and natural phenomena and conventions.

Earth, moon	=	1	Rishi, Mountains	=	7
Yugala (twins)	=	2	Vasus, Gaja	=	8
Rama, Agni, Shiva's eyes	=	3	Manus	=	14
Yuga	=	4	Tithis	=	15
Seasons, Gunas (policies of king), Rasas (tastes), enemies (internal)	=	6			

The following list taken from the colophons of various works is a classic example of such usage:

Rāmāgniguṇadharāprame śakahāyane	1633
Kālarṣirasabhūmitame	1676
Vasuvasudhācalavasundharā	1718
Rasādrimanau	1476

* Shri. Bharati Tirtha, Vedic Mathematics, Puri (1884 -1960 AD)

Encryption Capability

There is a recent work (17th century AD) of the name Sri-raghava-yadaviyam. The name is intriguing. Raghava refers to the one born in Raghu-kula viz., Rama the protagonist of the epic Ramayana; Yadava refers to the one born in the Yadhu-kula, Krishna, the protagonist of the other epic Mahabharata.

The 30 Shlokas in the work tell the story of Rama, obviously very very briefly, justifying the first part of the name. How the second part of the name - Yadaviyam? These Shlokas, if read in the reverse, letter by letter, narrate an episode from the life of Lord Krishna - of bringing the Parijata tree from the heavens to the earth.

This interesting though brief work

- Shows the verbal ingenuity of the composer Arasanipalai Venkatacharya and also
- Proves the encryption capability of the Samskrit language.

Encoding & Encryption

The cases cited thus far have some common features. There is play of letters / words in the texts. All the texts have an additional message beyond the apparent meaning. The motive could be to hide (in the case of the telegrams to the Russian spy) or to display (the composer's smartness) as in the case of Raghava-yadaviyam. When the intention is to conceal the second meaning, it is referred to as encryption. The difference between encoding and encryption is really one of objective and not method.

Encryption is a feature of ancient literature. Ancient India placed a lot of emphasis on knowledge reaching only those who could be trusted with the knowledge and not all. Ideas are often conveyed covertly and not overtly in ancient texts. The language and the literary style had more than enough capability to achieve this end.

There are some works, for example, the Sri-vidya literature, which are commonly understood as encrypted. Bhaskararaya (1690 - 1785) defying accepted practices of his time wrote a commentary on Lalita-sahasranama, unlocking some of its hidden thoughts.

Encrypted Science in Rig-veda

How far back does this practice of encryption go? At least one-man - Dr. Subhash Kak, a scientist, historian and indologist felt strongly that there is encrypted truth in the oldest of all literary works - the Rig-veda, backed his instincts and dwelt on the issue. His work* has unveiled the knowledge of astronomy of the Vedic civilisation that lay hidden in the Samhita part of the Rig-veda. Let us look at this now.

Vedas are the earliest extant literary work of the mankind. There are four Vedas. Rik, Yajus, Sama, and Atharva. Each of the Vedas is in four parts.

- Samhita
- Brahmana
- Aranyaka and
- Upanishad.

The Samhita part of Rig-veda contains

---

* Dr. Subhash Kak, The Astronomical Code of Rig Veda, Munshiram Mahoharlal Publishers P. Ltd, Edn. 2000

- Riks (verses with intonation) in praise of various gods and goddesses which are used in rituals and
- Some instructions on conducting ritual sacrifices.

How do you bundle astronomical knowledge in a set of verses?

Vedavyasa has arranged the Riks in the Samhita into ten books.

Book	:	I	II	III	IV	V	VI	VII	VIII	IX	X	Total
No of Riks	:	191	43	62	58	87	75	104	92	114	191	1017

The arrangement embodies several messages. We will look at just one of them. The number of Riks in the 10 books (as arranged by Vedavyasa) in combination, indicates the number of days taken by the 5 planets Mercury, Venus, Mars, Jupiter and Saturn to orbit around the sun measured

- Relative to the Earth (Synodic period)
- Relative to the Stars (Sidereal period)

The Synodic periods of these 5 planets are reflected in the arrangement of Riks into 10 books as shown below:

S.No	Planet	Book Number	Number of Riks in the books	Days	
				Ancient	Current
1	Mercury	III+IV	62+58	120	115.88
2	Venus	I+V+IX+X	191+87+114+191	583	583.92
3	Mars	I+V+VII+VIII+IX+X	191+87+104+92+114+191	779	779.94
4	Jupiter	II+III+V+VIII+IX	43+62+87+92+114	398	398.99
5	Saturn	II+IV+V+VI+IX	43+58+87+75+114	377	378.09

The Sidereal periods have also been made to reflect in the arrangement as shown below:

S.No	Planet	Book Number	Number of Riks in the books	Days	
				Ancient	Current
1	Mercury	Vx1	87x1	87	87.97
2	Venus	IV+VI+VIII	58+75+92	225	224.70
3	Mars	3X+IX	191x3+114	687	686.98
4	Jupiter	IVxVI	58x75	4350	4,332.60
5	Saturn	VIIxVII	104x104	10816	10,759.30

All the values correspond with the correct number with the exception of the number of days that Mercury takes to orbit the planet measured with reference to the earth.

Is this exercise attributing to Vedavyasa an encryption that he did not even attempt? It is unlikely for the following reasons.

1. The Rig-vedic Indians were familiar with these five planets.

   i. These five planets along with the sun and the moon provide the names for the 7 days of the week.

1.	Mercury	Budha	Wednesday
2.	Venus	Shukra	Friday
3.	Mars	Angaraka / Mangala	Tuesday
4.	Jupiter	Guru	Thursday
5.	Saturn	Shani	Saturday

   ii. These planets also figure prominently in the Puranic lore. Guru and Shukra are the teacher - preceptors of the Devas and Asuras respectively.

   iii. The names of the planets suggest that the Vedic Indians knew enough about the size, and orbital movements of the planets as illustrated below:

   - Jupiter is the largest amongst the planets. It has a diameter of 88,736 miles compared with other planets like
     • Mercury - 3032 miles • Venus 7519 miles • Earth - 7926 miles

     The word for Jupiter in Samskrit is Guru, the big one.

   - Saturn's orbit around the sun is 29.5 earth years (10767.5 days). It is the slowest compared with the pace of the other planets.
     • Mercury - 88 days • Venus - 225 days • Earth - 365 days

"Shanaih charathi iti Shanaishchara" the one that move slowly is Shanaishchara (Saturn).

2. Getting 10 connected values (the orbital days of these specific 5 planets) out of a set of 20 numbers, by coincidence, is extremely unprobablistic. The odds are 2.87×10^{-7}

3. One number - Synodic days of Mercury - is off the right value by 5 days. Mercury amongst the 5 planets considered is the most difficult to observe from Earth. The bug, as it were, validates the package.

Therefore we conclude that this is a case of conscious encryption.

The next question is whether, by this exercise, we are attributing to the Rig-vedic Indians a knowledge that they did not possess.

The Knowledge is in the arrangement of the Riks into books and not in the Riks themselves. Therefore it might be fair to conclude that this encryption reflects the knowledge that was available when Vedavyasa organised Rig-veda-samhitas into 10 books.

Conclusion

Three valuable lessons emerge from this exercise of decoding the arrangement of Rig-veda-samhita into 10 books:

- The Indians in Vedavyasa's times (3000 BCE) knew astronomy.
- Patently religious ancient texts also embody secular truths.
- Encryption is practised and therefore every ancient text has to be studied for the gems hidden therein.

MATHEMATICS

$$\sum_{n=1}^{\infty} (n\,\Delta\,x) = \frac{x^2}{2}, \quad \sum_{n=1}^{\infty} (n\,\Delta\,x)^2 = \frac{x^3}{3}$$

and $$\sum_{n=1}^{\infty} (n\,\Delta\,x)^3 = \frac{x^4}{4}$$

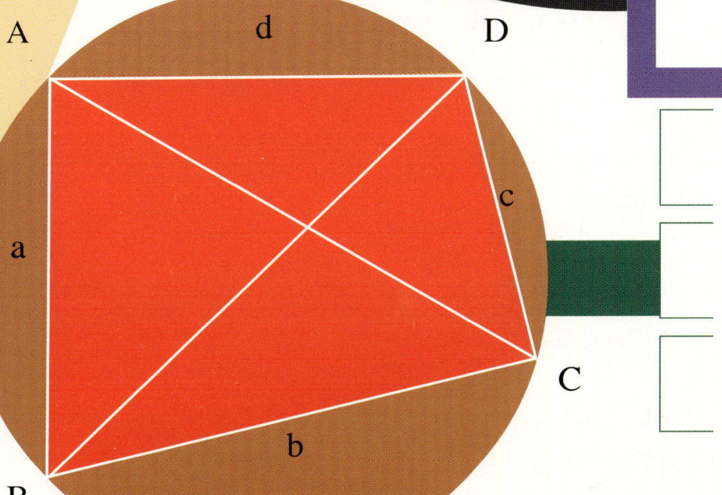

Algebra & Arithmetic

Geometry

Trigonometry

Introduction

Algebra, as a distinct branch of mathematics, originated in the world since Brahmagupta in modern times. In the remote past, Shulba-sutras contain problems and solutions involving quadratic equations of the type $ax^2 + bx = c$.

The sutras also contain rules for the construction of a square n times a given square. The treatment leads to the solution of an indeterminate equation of second degree $x^2 + y^2 = z^2$.

They also contain treatment of surds, quantities like $\sqrt{2}$ etc., Irrational numbers like $\sqrt{3}$ etc., were also treated. Permutations and combination was a favourite mathematical pursuit of Vedic Hindus. The so called Pascal Triangle first appeared in Europe in the work of Apianus (1527 AD). Pingala's Chandas-sutra (200 BCE) preceded him by 1300 years, by the name Meru Prastara.

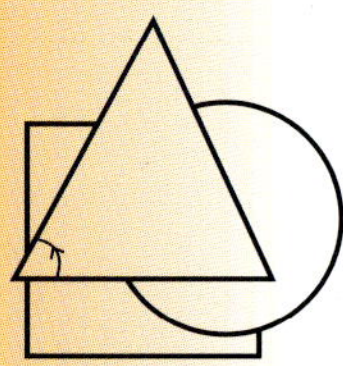

3.1.1 Bhāskara's Cakravāla Method

ह्रस्वज्येष्ठपदक्षेपान् भाज्यप्रक्षेपभाजकान् ।	Hrasvajyeṣṭhapadakṣepān bhājyaprakṣepabhājakān ।

Considering the lesser root, greater root and interpolator as the dividend, augment and divisor,

---

कृत्वा कल्प्यो गुणस्तत्र तथा प्रकृतितश्च्युते ।	Kṛtvā kalpyo guṇastatra tathā prakṛtitaścyute ।
गुणवर्गे प्रकृत्योनेऽथवाऽल्पं शेषकं यथा ।	Guṇavarge prakṛtyone'thavā'lpaṁ śeṣakaṁ yathā ।

the multiplier of it should be so taken as will make the residue of the Prakṛti diminished by the square of that multiplier or the latter minus the Prakṛti the least.

तत्तु क्षेपहृतं क्षेपो व्यस्तः प्रकृतितश्च्युते ।	Tattu kṣepahṛtaṁ kṣepo vyastaḥ prakṛtitaścyute ।

That ratio divided by the (original) interpolator is the interpolator (of a new Varga Prakṛti); it should be reversed in sign in case of subtraction from the Prakṛti.

गुणलब्धिः पदं ह्रस्वं ततो ज्येष्ठमतोऽसकृत् ।	Guṇalabdhiḥ padaṁ hrasvaṁ tato jyeṣṭhamato'ssakṛt ।

The quotient corresponding to that value of the multiplier is the (new) lesser root; then greater root is evaluated.

त्यक्त्वा पूर्वपदक्षेपांश्चक्रवालम् इदं जगुः ।	Tyaktvā pūrvapadakṣepāṁścakravālam idaṁ jaguḥ ।

The same process should be followed repeatedly putting aside (each time) the previous roots and the interpolator. This process is called Cakravāla.

चतुर्द्व्येकयुतावेवमभिन्ने भवतः पदे ।	Caturhyekayutāvevamabhinne bhavataḥ pade ।

By this method, there will appear two integral roots corresponding to an equation with ±1, ±2 or ±4 as interpolator.

चतुर्द्विक्षेपमूलाभ्यां रूपक्षेपार्थभावना ॥	Caturdvikṣepamūlābhyāṁ rūpakṣepārthabhāvanā ॥

In order to derive integral roots corresponding to an equation with interpolator ±1, ±2 or ±4, the bhāvanā principle should be applied.

Explanation

Given equation is

$Nx^2 + 1 = y^2$ --------(A)

Step I: Find initial auxiliary equation

$N (a)^2 + k = (b)^2$ --------(B)

Step II: If k is equal to ±1, ±2 or ±4, then the bhāvanā principle gives the roots of (A).

Step III: Else construct next auxiliary equation of the type

$$N\left(\frac{am + b}{|k|}\right)^2 + \left(\frac{m^2 - N}{|k|}\right)^2 = \left(\frac{bm + Na}{|k|}\right)^2 \text{ ------ (C)}$$

for 'm' to be determined later.

Step IV: Find set of positive values of 'm' for which $|k|$ divides (am + b). Find minimum value of $|m^2 - N|$ and select that m.

Step V: Write equation (C) with selected value of m.

Step VI: Note the value of k in new equation. If k is equal to ±1, ±2 or ±4, Bhāvanā principle gives the roots, otherwise construct equation of type (C) with new value of a, k and b. This is cakravāla.

Bhāskara claims that finite number of 'Cakravāla' will definitely give the roots of (A).

Source

Bīja-gaṇitam, Chapter 6, Ślokaḥ 75-81, Bhāskarācāryaḥ(II) (1150 AD)

Western Reference

Western history reveals that Fermat's problem of solving equation (A) for N=61 resisted the integer solution for nearly 100 years. Finally Eular (1764 AD) and La Grange (1768 AD) solved the problem by different method than Bhaskara. Surprisingly Bhaskara quoted the same problem as illustrative example in Bijaganitam.

They said it

"India was China's teacher in trigonometry, quadratic equations, grammar, phonetics.....".

Mr. Lin Yutang, a Chinese scholar, The Wisdom of India.

3.1.2 Brahmaguptā's Lemmas: (Second Degree Indeterminate Equations)

व्रजाभ्यासौ ज्येष्ठलघ्वोस्तदैक्यं ह्रस्वं लघ्वोराहतिश्च प्रकृत्या ।
क्षुण्णा ज्येष्ठाभ्यासयुग्ज्येष्ठमूलं तत्राभ्यासः क्षेपयोः क्षेपकः स्यात् ॥

Vrajābhyāsau jyeṣṭhalaghvostadaikyaṁ hrasvaṁ laghvorāhatiśca prakṛtyā ।
Kṣuṇṇā jyeṣṭhābhyāsayugjyeṣṭhamūlam tatrābhyāsaḥ kṣepayoḥ kṣepakaḥ syāt ॥

(Find) the two cross products of the two lesser and the two greater roots; their sum is a lesser root. Add the product of the two lesser roots multiplied by the prakṛti to the product of the two greater roots; the sum will be a greater root. In that (equation) the Kṣepaka will be the product of two previous Kṣepakas.

ह्रस्वं व्रजाभ्यासयोरन्तरं वा लघ्वोर्घातो यः प्रकृत्या विनिघ्नः ।
घातो यश्च ज्येष्ठयोस्तद्वियोगो ज्येष्ठं क्षेपोऽत्रापि च क्षेपघातः ॥

Hrasvaṁ vrajābhyāsayorantaraṁ vā laghvorghāto yaḥ prakṛtyā vinighnaḥ ।
Ghāto yaśca jyeṣṭhayostadviyogo jyeṣṭhaṁ kṣepoऽtrāpi ca kṣepaghātaḥ ॥

Again the difference of the two cross products is a lesser root. Subtract the product of the two lesser roots multiplied by the prakṛti from the product of two greater roots; (the difference) will be a greater root. Here also Kṣepaka will be the product of the two (previous) Kṣepakas.

Explanation

$x = a_1$ and $y = b_1$ are solutions of $Nx^2 + k_1 = y^2$ and $x = a_2$ and $y = b_2$ are solutions of $Nx^2 + k_2 = y^2$ (where a_1 and a_2 are lesser roots) then

$$x = a_1b_2 \pm a_2b_1 \text{ and } y = b_1b_2 \pm Na_1a_2$$

are the solutions of the equation

$$Nx^2 + k_1\, k_2 = y^2.$$

As a corollary to this अतुल्य भावना सिद्धान्त (principle of unequal composition), second principle is stated as follows:

If $x = a$ and $y = b$ are the solutions of $Nx^2 + k = y^2$ then $x = 2ab$ and $y = b^2 + Na^2$ are the solutions of $Nx^2 + k^2 = y^2$.

This is called तुल्य भावना सिद्धान्त (principle of equal composition), in which $a_1 = a_2$, $b_1 = b_2$ and $k_1 = k_2$.

Source

Bīja-gaṇitam, Chapter 6, Ślokaḥ 71-72, Bhāskarācāryaḥ (II) (1150 AD)

Western Reference

Eular (1764 AD) and La Grange (1768 AD) rediscovered these two lemmas while attempting to evaluate infinitely many solutions of second degree indeterminate equations.

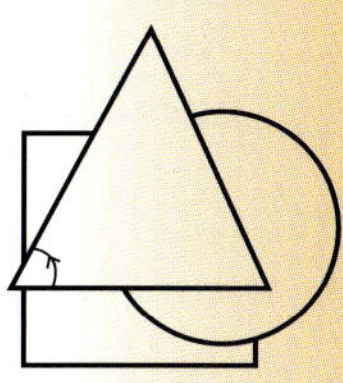

3.1.3 Permutations of Given Things

स्थानान्तमेकादिचयाङ्कघातः सङ्ख्याविभेदा नियतैस्युरङ्कैः । भक्तोऽङ्कमित्याङ्कसमासनिघ्नः स्थानेषु युक्तो मितिसंयुतिः स्यात् ॥	Sthānāntamekādicayāṅkaghātaḥ saṅkhyāvibhedā niyataisyuraṅkaiḥ । Bhaktoऽṅkamityāṅkasamāsanighnaḥ sthāneṣu yukto mitisaṁyutiḥ syāt ॥

At number of places which are filled with equal number of digits, place 1, 2, 3, 4, ------ in increasing order. The product of these (placed) digits is the required number of permutations.

यावत्स्थानेषु तुल्याङ्कास्तद्भेदैस्तु पृथक् कृतैः । प्राग्भेदा विहृता भेदास्तत्सङ्ख्यैक्यं च पूर्ववत् ॥	Yāvatsthāneṣu tulyāṅkāstadbhedaistu pṛthak kṛtaiḥ । Prāgbhedā vihṛtā bhedāstatsaṅkhyaikyaṁ ca pūrvavat ॥

In the given digits, if some digits are repeated then at those number of places find number of permutations assuming different digits. Divide by this number (of permutations), the number of permutations of all given digits, assuming different digits at all places.

Explanation

1. Let 'n' denote number of digits (no two of them are equal) then the product

$$1 \times 2 \times 3 \times 4 \times \text{------} \times n$$

is required number of permutations.

2. If one digit, out of 'n' digits, is repeated 'r' times then total number of permutations are

$$\left\{\frac{1 \times 2 \times 3 \times 4 \times \text{------} \times n}{1 \times 2 \times 3 \times 4 \times \text{------} \times r}\right\}$$

3. Whatever is true for digits holds for any given things that are to be placed.

Source

Līlāvatī, Aṅkapāśaḥ, Chapter 33, Ślokaḥ 1; Chapter 3, Ślokaḥ 4, Bhāskarācāryaḥ (II) (1150 AD)

Notes

This result is a special case of general formula for number of permutations of n things selected r at a time.

3.1.4 Combinations of Given Things

एकाद्येकोत्तरतः पदमूर्ध्वधर्यतः क्रमोत्क्रमशः ।
स्थाप्य प्रतिलोमघ्नं प्रतिलोमघ्नेन भाजितं सारम् ॥

Ekādyekottarataḥ padamūrdhvadharyataḥ kramotkramaśaḥ ।
Sthāpya pratilomaghnaṁ pratilomaghnena bhājitaṁ sāram ॥

Putting numbers starting with one and increasing by one, in the reverse order above, (and) in order below; the product (of those) in the reverse order is divided by the product (of those) in order; (the quotient) is the result.

Explanation

Let 'n' denote the number of things given and 'r' denote the number of things selected. Write first the numbers in reverse order i.e. starting from 'n' upto 'r'. Thus we get

n, n-1, n-2, n-3, ------, n-r+1.

Now write the numbers in order from 1 upto 'r' i.e.

1, 2, 3, 4, ------, r.

$$\text{The quotient} = \frac{\text{The product of numbers in reverse order}}{\text{The product of numbers in order}}$$

$$\therefore \text{Number of combinations} = \frac{n\,(n-1)\,(n-2)\,(n-3)\text{ ------ }(n-r+1)}{1 \times 2 \times 3 \times 4 \times \text{------} \times r}$$

Source

Gaṇita-sāra-saṅgrahaḥ, Chapter 6, Ślokaḥ 218, Mahāvīrācāryaḥ (850 AD)

Western Reference

The general formula for number of combinations, which is propounded by Herigone (1634 AD) is exactly same as Mahaviracarya's result.

They said it

"We owe a lot to Indians, who taught us how to count, without which no worthwhile scientific discovery could have been made. I have made the Gita as the main source of my inspiration and guide for the purpose of scientific investigations and formation of my theories."

Dr. Albert Einstein

Mr. Ravi Kumar, Hindu Genius is Universal, p. 37.

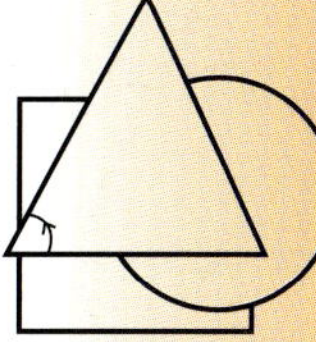

3.1.5 The concept of 'Niruddhaḥ' (L.C.M.)

छेदापवर्तकानां लब्धानां चाहतौ निरुद्धः स्यात् ।
हरहृतनिरुद्धगुणिते हारांशगुणे समो हारः ॥

Chedāparvatakānāṁ labdhānāṁ cāhatau niruddhaḥ syāt ।
Harahṛtaniruddhaguṇite hārāṁśaguṇe samo hāraḥ ॥

The Niruddhaḥ (L.C.M.) is obtained by means of the continued multiplication of (all) the common factors of denominators and their quotients. The (new) numerators and denominators, obtained as products of multiplication of (each original) numerator and denominator by the (quotient of the) Niruddhaḥ divided by the denominator give fractions with the same denominator.

Source

Gaṇita-sāra-saṅgrahaḥ, Chapter 3, Ślokaḥ 56, Mahāvīrācāryaḥ (850 AD)

Indus Inch

Archaeologists also found a ruler made of shell lines drawn 6.7 millimetres apart with a high degree of accuracy. Two of the lines are distinguished by circles and are separated by 33.5 millimetres, or 1.32 inches. This distance is the so called Indus inch. Some speculation: a Sumerian shushi equals half an Indus inch, exactly and adds to the long held suspicion that there was a link between the Sumerian and Indian cultures.

Mr. Dick Teresi, Lost Discoveries, edn.Simon & Schuster (2003), p. 59.

3.1.6 Sum of Squares of 'n' Terms of Arithmetic Progression

द्विगुणैकोनपदोत्तरकृतिहतिषष्ठांशमुखचयहतयुतिः ।
व्येकेपदघ्ना मुखकृतिसहिता पदताडितेष्टकृतिचितिका ॥

Dviguṇaikonapadottarakṛtihatiṣaṣṭhāṁśamukha-
cayahatayutiḥ ।
Vyekepadaghnā mukhakṛtisahitā
padatāḍiteṣṭakṛticitikā ॥

Twice the number of terms is diminished by one and (then) multiplied by square of common difference and is (then) divided by six. (To this) the product of the first term and common difference is added. The resulting sum is multiplied by the number of terms as diminished by one. (To the product so arrived at) the square of first term is added. This sum multiplied by number of terms (given) becomes the sum of squares of all (n) terms in given series.

Explanation

Let 'n' denote the number of terms upto which sum is required. If 'a' is the first term and 'd' is common difference of A.P.,* then sum of squares of 'n' terms is

$$\text{Sum} = \left[\left\{\frac{(2n \sim 1)\, d^2}{6} + ad\right\}(n \sim 1) + a^2\right] \times n$$

Example:

For an A.P., if a = 2 and d = 5 the terms are 2, 7, 12, 17, ------

The sum of squares of n = 10 terms of this A.P. is series

$2^2 + 7^2 + 12^2 + 17^2 + \text{------} + 47^2$

Sum is calculated as

$$\text{Sum} = \left[\left\{\frac{(2 \times 10 - 1)\,(5)^2}{6} + (2 \times 5)\right\} \times (10 - 1) + (2)^2\right] \times 10$$

$$= \left[\left\{\frac{19 \times 25}{6} + 10\right\} \times 9 + 4\right] \times 10$$

$$= \left[\left\{\frac{535}{6} \times 9 + 4\right]\right. \times 10$$

$= 8065$

* A.P.- Arithmetic Progression

Source

Gaṇita-sāra-saṅgrahaḥ, Miśra-kāvya-vyavahāraḥ, Chapter 6, Ślokaḥ 298, Mahāvīrācāryaḥ (850 AD)

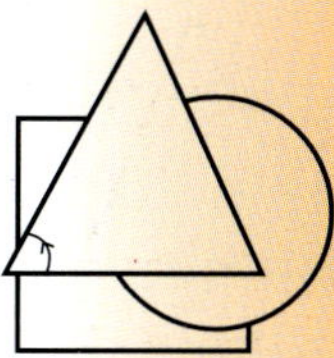

3.1.7 Sum of Cubes of First 'n' Terms of Arithmetic Progression

चित्यादिहतिर्मुखचयशेषघ्ना प्रचयनिघ्नचितिवर्गे ।
आदौ प्रचयादूने वियुता युक्ताधिके तु घनचितिका ॥

Cityādihatirmukhacayaśeṣaghnā pracayanighnacitivarge ।
Ādau pracayādūne viyutā yuktādhike tu ghanacitikā ॥

The sum (of the simple terms of series) is multiplied by first term therein, is (further) multiplied by the difference between the first term and common difference. (Then) square of sum of (simple) series is multiplied by common difference. If the first term is smaller than the common difference, (the first product) is subtracted (from the second product), otherwise added. Thus the required sum is obtained.

Explanation

Consider an A.P., in which first term = a and common difference = d. The sum of first 'n' terms of A.P., is given by

$$S = \frac{n}{2} [2a + (n - 1) d]$$

The value 'S' is called sum of simple terms. The sum of cubes of 'n' terms of A.P., is then given as

$$S_n = S^2 d - S a (a \sim d), \quad \text{if } a < d$$

$$= S^2 d + S a (a \sim d), \quad \text{if } a > d$$

where a ~ d is the difference between a and d, of which positive value is selected.

Special Case:

For a = 1 and d = 1,

$$S = \frac{n (n + 1)}{2}$$

and $S_n = S^2$ [because a ~ d = 0]

Thus $$1 + 2 + 3 + 4 + \text{------} + n = \frac{n (n + 1)}{2}$$

And $$1^3 + 2^3 + 3^3 + 4^3 + \text{------} + n^3 = \left[\frac{n (n + 1)}{2}\right]^2$$

This 'Ghanaciti Rule' is stated earlier by Aryabhata in his work Aryabhatiyam, Chapter 2, Shloka 22.

Example:

1. If a = 2 and d = 5 for an A.P. then the sum of cubes of n = 10 terms is the series

$$2^3 + 7^3 + 12^3 + 17^3 + \text{------} + 47^3$$

This sum is calculated as follows:

First $S = \frac{10}{2} [2 (2) + (9) 5] = 245$

Here a < d and a ~ d = 3

Hence $S_n = (245)^2 (5) - (245) (2) (3) = 298655.$

2. If a = 6, d = 2 and n = 5 then the series is

$$6^3 + 8^3 + 10^3 + 12^3 + 14^3$$

Here $S = \frac{5}{2} [12 + 4 (2) 5] = 50$

Here a > d and a ~ d = 4

Hence $S_n = S^2 d + S (a) (a \sim d)$

$= (50)^2 (2) + 50 (6) (4) = 6200$

Source

Gaṇita-sāra-saṅgrahaḥ, Miśra-kāvya-vyavahāraḥ, Chapter 6, Ślokaḥ 304, Mahāvīrācāryaḥ (850 AD)

Notes

The results contained in 11.6 and 11.7 were also discussed by mathematicians Shridhara (750 AD) and Narayana (1356 AD).

They said it

I shall not now speak of the knowledge of the Hindus,..... Of their subtle discoveries in the science of astronomy - discoveries even more ingenious than those of the Greeks and Babylonians - of their rational system of mathematics, or of their method of calculation which no words can praise strongly enough - I mean the system using nine symbols. If these things were known by the people who think that they alone have mastered the sciences because they speak Greek they would perhaps be convinced, though a little late in the day, that other folk, not only Greeks, but men of a different tongue, know something as well as they.

Monk Severus Sebokht, a Syrian astronomer (writing A.D. 662)

Dr. A.L. Basham, The Wonder that was India, 3rd edition (2003), p. VI

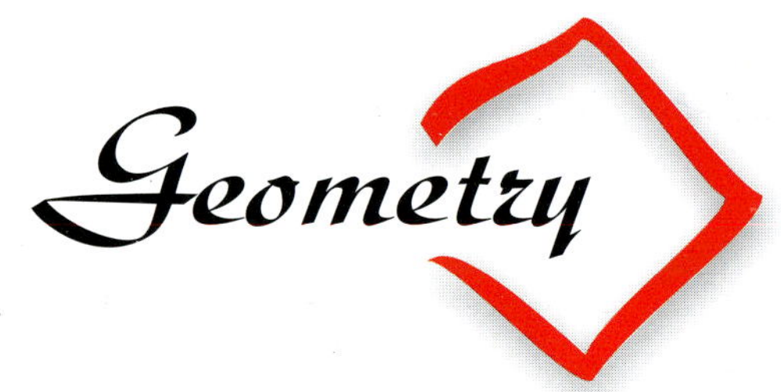

Introduction

Geometry was a highly developed science in ancient India. Vedas contain an important and necessary act of Yajña. The altars, their construction, and measurement involved deep and accurate knowledge of mathematics, particularly geometry.

The Sulba-sutras, containing all these rules, belong to pre-vedic period.

In modern times, we find several mathematicians, such as Bhaskara-I (700 AD), Brahmagupta (600 AD), Mahavira (850 AD) showing deep knowledge of the properties of the triangle, quadrilateral, trapezium, circle, π, etc.

3.2.1 The Śulba theorem or Baudhāyana theorem

दीर्धचतुरश्रस्याक्ष्णया रज्जुः पाश्र्वमानी तिर्यङ्मानी च यत्पृथग्भूते कुरुतस्तदुभयं करोति ।

Dīrghacaturaśrasyākṣṇayā rajjuḥ pārśvamānī tiryaṅmānī ca yatpṛthagbhūte kurutastadubhayaṁ karoti ।

The areas (of the squares) produced separately by the length and breadth of a rectangle together equal the area (of the square) produced by the diagonal.

Explanation

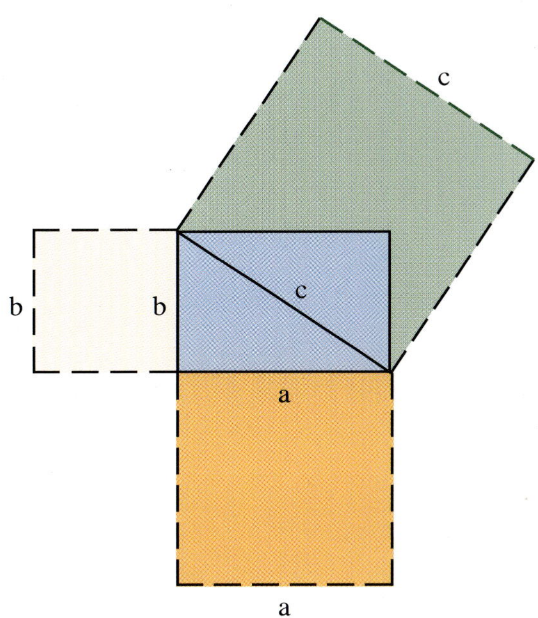

From figure: $a^2 + b^2 = c^2$

Source

Śulba-sūtram, Chapter 1, Ślokaḥ 12, Bodhāyanaḥ (800 BCE)

Western Reference

The theorem is generally attributed to Pythagoras. But Indian scholars applied this theorem and its converse even since the Vedic period.

3.2.2 Brahmaguptā's Theorem

कर्णाश्रितभुजघातैक्यमुभयथान्योन्यभाजितं गुणयेत् ।
योगेन भुजप्रतिभुजवधयोः कर्णौ पदे विषमे ॥

Karṇāśritabhujaghātaikyamubhayathānyonyabhājitaṁ guṇayet ।
Yogena bhujapratibhujavadhayoḥ karṇau pade viṣame ॥

The sums of products of the sides about the diagonal should be divided by each other and multiplied by the sum of the products of opposite sides. The square roots of the quotients are the diagonals in a Viṣama quadrilateral.

Explanation

Let a, b, c and d be the lengths of sides of a cyclic quadrilateral as shown in the figure. Then lengths of diagonals are

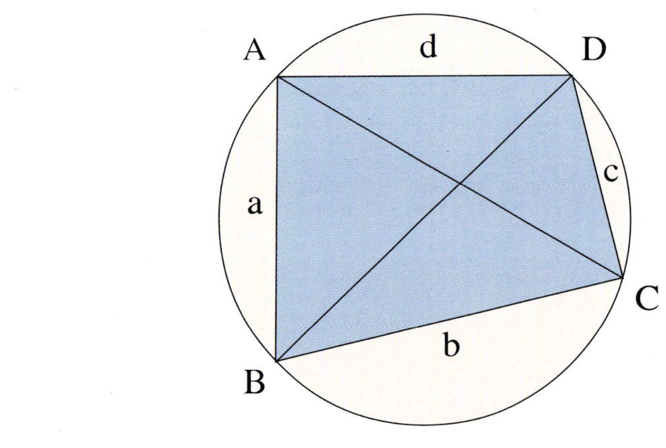

$$l\,(AC) = \sqrt{\frac{ad + bc}{ab + cd} \times (ac + bd)}$$

$$l\,(BD) = \sqrt{\frac{ab + cd}{ad + bc} \times (ac + bd)}$$

Source

Brahma-sphuṭa-siddhāntaḥ, Chapter 12, Ślokaḥ 28, Brahmaguptaḥ (628 AD)

Western Reference

This is one of the significant results discussed by Brahmagupta on cyclic quadrilaterals. Western historians recognized this result as W. Snell's (1619 AD) theorem.

3.2.3 Brahmagupta Quadrilateral

जात्यद्वयकोटिभुजाः परकर्णगुणाः भुजाश्चतुर्विषमे ।
अधिको भूर्मुखं हीनो बाहुद्वितयं भुजावन्यौ ॥

Jātyadvayakoṭibhujāḥ parakarṇaguṇāḥ bhujāścaturviṣame ।
Adhiko bhūrmukhaṁ hīno bāhudvitayaṁ bhujāvanyau ॥

The bases and heights of two right-angled triangles multiplied by each other's hypotenuse are the four sides of quadrilateral of unequal sides: (of these) longest is the base, the least is the face and remaining two sides are the flanks.

Explanation

Consider two right-angled triangles with 3, 4, 5 and 5, 12, 13 as base, height and hypotenuse respectively. Multiply base and height of one triangle with hypotenuse of other. The four values are

$$5 \times 5 = 25,\ 5 \times 12 = 60,\ 13 \times 3 = 39,\ 13 \times 4 = 52$$

Largest value 60 is taken as base, lowest 25 as face and the other two as flanks to construct a quadrilateral which is always cyclic.

1. Lengths of sides AB = 60, BC = 52, CD = 25 and AD = 39 are integers.
2. Length of diagonals AC = 56, BD = 63.
3. Area of cyclic quadrilateral is 1764 Sq. units.
4. Diameter of circumcircle = 65.
5. DM and CN are perpendiculars on AB then length of segment MN (Projection) = 24. Other similar segments also have integral values.
6. DM intersects diagonal AC at G and CN intersects diagonal BD at H then AG = 16, GC = 40, BH = 30 and HD = 33.
7. Diagonals intersect at F then AF = 36, FC = 20, BF = 48 and FD = 15.

Note that all values are integers. Such a quadrilateral is called a Brahmagupta quadrilateral.

Source

Brahma-sphuṭa-siddhāntaḥ, Chapter 12, Ślokaḥ 38, Brahmaguptaḥ (628 AD)

Western Reference

Eular (1707- 1783) is the first western mathematician who discussed construction of such rational quadrilaterals.

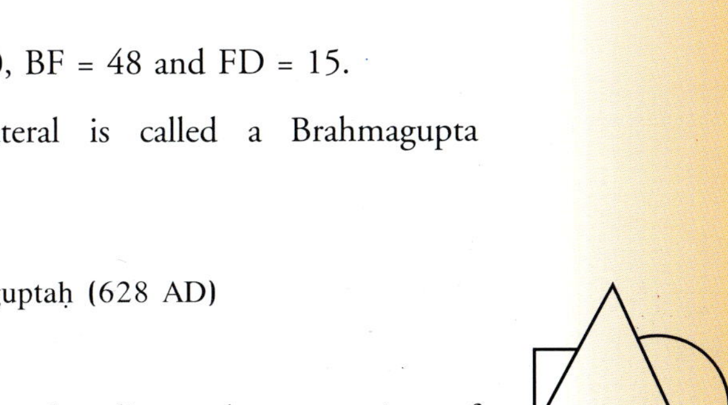

3.2.4 Area of Cyclic quadrilateral and triangle

स्थूलफलं त्रिचतुर्भुजबाहुप्रतिबाहुयोगदलघातः ।
भुजयोगार्धचतुष्टयभुजोनघातात् पदं सूक्ष्मम् ॥

Sthūlaphalaṁ tricaturbhujabāhupratibāhuyogadalaghātaḥ ।
Bhujayogārdhacatuṣṭayabhujonaghātāt padaṁ sūkṣmam ॥

The gross area of a triangle or a quadrilateral is the product of half the sums of the opposite sides; the exact area is the square root of the product of four sets of half the sum of the sides (respectively) diminished by the sides.

Explanation (For exact area only)

1. If a, b, c and d are the lengths of sides of a cyclic quadrilaterals and 2s is perimeter then

   $2s = a + b + c + d$ and

   $$\text{area} = \sqrt{(s-a)(s-b)(s-c)(s-d)}$$

2. If a, b and c are lengths of sides of any triangle and 2s is perimeter then

   $2s = a + b + c$ and

   $$\text{area} = \sqrt{(s-a)(s-b)(s-c)(s)}$$

Source

Brahma-sphuṭa-siddhāntaḥ, Chapter 12, Ślokaḥ 21, Brahmaguptaḥ (628 AD)

Notes

Though Brahmagupta fails to mention that formula (1) is true for cyclic quadrilaterals only, it can be judged by context. Mahavira (850 AD) knows this limitation. Formula (2) is true for any triangle.

Science in the Service of Religion

Vedic Indians solved square roots to build sacrificial altars of the proper size. This was science in the service of religion but science nonetheless.

Mr. Dick Teresi, Lost Discoveries, edn.Simon & Schuster (2003), p no. 26.

3.2.5 Circumradius of Cyclic-quadrilateral

दोष्णां द्वयोर्द्वयोर्घातयुतीनां तिसृणां वधात् ।
एकैकोनेतरत्र्यैक्यचतुष्कवधभाजिते ॥

Doṣṇāṁ dvayordvayorghātayutīnāṁ tisṛṇāṁ vadhāt ।
Ekaikonetaratryaikyacatuṣkavadhabhājite ॥

The three sums of the products of the sides taken two at a time are to be multiplied together and divided by the product of the four sums of the sides taken three at a time and diminished by the fourth.

लब्धमूलेन यद्वृत्तम् विष्कम्भार्द्धेन निर्मितम् ।
सर्वं चतुर्भुजक्षेत्रं तस्मिन्नेवावतिष्ठते ॥

Labdhamūlena yadvṛttam viṣkambhārddhena nirmitam ।
Sarvaṁ caturbhujakṣetraṁ tasminnevāvatiṣṭhate ॥

If the circle is drawn with the square root of this quantity as radius, the whole quadrilateral will be situated on it.

Explanation (For exact area only)

If a, b, c and d are lengths of sides of cyclic quadrilateral as shown in the figure,

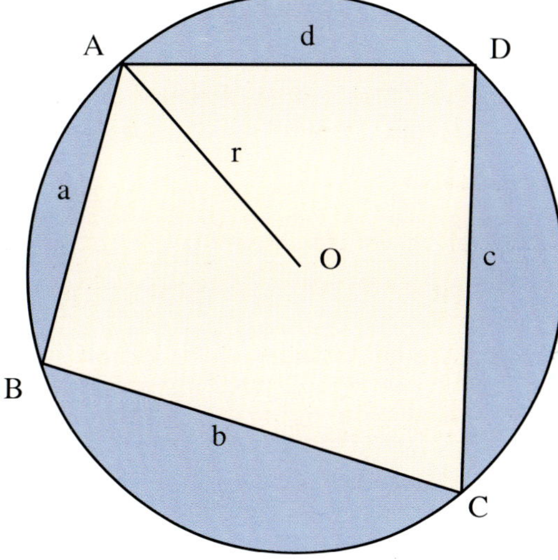

and "O' is center of circumcircle, then circumradius OA = r is

$$r = \sqrt{\frac{(ab + cd)(ac + bd)(ad + bc)}{(a + b + c - d)(b + c + d - a)(c + d + a - b)(d + a + b - c)}}$$

Source

Commentary on Līlāvatī, Ślokaḥ 191, 192, Parameśvaraḥ (1430 AD)

Western Reference

This result is known as Simon A.J. Lhuilier's (1782 AD) theorem. However the result is expressed by using 2S=a+b+c.

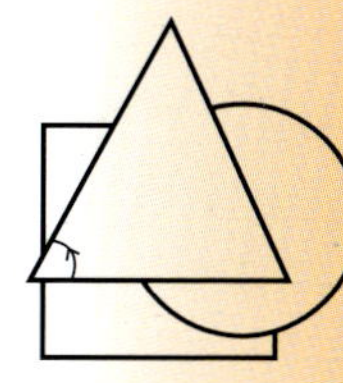

3.2.6 Value of Pi (π)

चतुराधिकं शतमष्टगुणं द्वाषष्टिस्तथा सहस्राणाम् ।
अयुतद्वयविष्कम्भस्यासन्नो वृत्तपरिणाहः ॥

Caturadhikaṁ śatamaṣṭaguṇaṁ dvāṣaṣṭistathā sahasrāṇām ।
Ayutadvayaviṣkambhasyāsanno vṛttapariṇāhaḥ ॥

When 100 plus 4 (is) multiplied by 8 and added to 62,000 (it gives) an approximate value for the circumference of a circle whose diameter is 20,000.

Explanation

Circumference $C = [(100 + 4) \times 8] + 62000$

$= 62832$

Diameter $d = 20{,}000$

and thus $\pi = C/d = 3.1416$ (approximate).

Āryabhaṭa also says that this value is 'āsanna' (approximate).

Source

Āryabhaṭīyam Gaṇitapādaḥ, Chapter 2, Ślokaḥ 10, Āryabhaṭaḥ (499 AD)

Remarks

Values of π: Indian Attempt:

S.No.	Mathematician	Period	Value of π
1.	Mahavira	850 AD	$\sqrt{10}$
2.	Bhaskara II	1150 AD	3927/1250
3.	Nilakantha Somayaji	1444 - 1545 AD	$28{,}27{,}43{,}33{,}88{,}233/9 \times 10^{11}$
4.	Sankara Variyar	1500-1560 AD	104348/33215
5.	Putumana Somayaji	1732 AD	$31{,}415{,}926{,}536/10^{10}$
6.	Sankar Varman	1823 AD	$314{,}159{,}265{,}358{,}979{,}324/10^{17}$
7.	Ramanujan	1887-1920 AD	Ramanujan quoted many amazing expressions for values of π which are correct up to 3,7,8,14,-----31 decimal places.

3.2.7 Three Diagonal Theorem

सर्वचतुर्बाहूनां मुखस्य परिवर्तने यदा विहिते ।
कर्णस्तदा तृतीयः पर इति कर्णत्रयं भवति ॥ १ ॥

Sarvacaturbāhūnāṁ mukhasya parivartane yadā vihite ।
Karṇastadā tṛtīyaḥ para iti karṇatrayaṁ bhavati ॥ 1 ॥

When top side and the flank side of any four sided figure are interchanged, we get a third diagonal called 'para'. Thus there are three diagonals (for quadrilateral).

Based on this concept, Nārāyaṇa states the following theorem for area of cyclic quadrilateral.

द्विगुणव्यासविभक्ते त्रिकर्णघातेऽथवा गणितम् ॥ २ ॥

Dviguṇavyāsavibhakte trikarṇaghāteऽthavā gaṇitam ॥ 2 ॥

Or, when the product of the three diagonals is divided by twice the circumdiameter, we get the area.

Explanation

Consider a cyclic quadrilateral ABCD as shown.

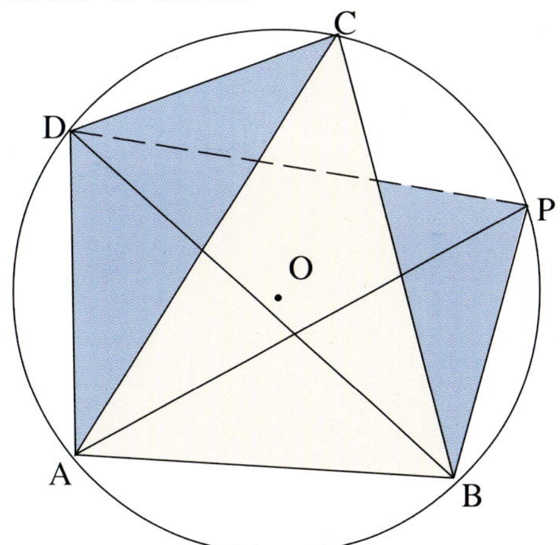

AC and BD are the two diagonals. Select "P' such that BP = CD and BC = DP. Then top side and flank side gets interchanged and AP is the third diagonal.

If "d' is circumdiameter then area of cyclic quadrilateral is

$$\text{area} = \frac{AC \times BD \times AP}{2d}$$

Source

Gaṇita-kaumudī, Kṣetra-vyavahāraḥ 48 & 52, Nārāyaṇaḥ (1356 AD)

3.2.8 Rational Scalene Triangle

जन्यभूजार्धं छित्वा केनापिच्छेदलब्धजं चाभ्याम् ।
कोटियुतिर्भूः कर्णौ भुजौ भुजा लम्बका विषमे ।।

Janyabhūjārdhaṁ chitvā kenāpicchedalabdhajaṁ cābhyām ।
Koṭiyutirbhūḥ karṇau bhujau bhujā lambakā viṣame ।।

Half of the base of the derived rectangle is first divided by the optional divisor. The quotient and divisor are used to obtain another rectangle. The sum of the uprights is the base, two diagonals are the sides and the base of the rectangle is altitude of required scalene triangle.

Explanation

Let m and n be any two rational numbers. The rectangle generated out of these numbers is ABCD (say) with base AB = 2mn, upright BC = $m^2 - n^2$ and diagonal AC = $m^2 + n^2$.

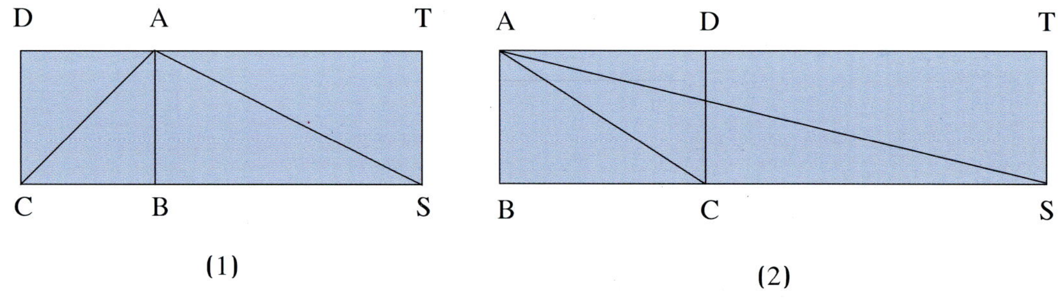

(1) (2)

Let p and q be any two numbers such that mn = pq. The second rectangle ABST so generated has base AB = 2pq, uprights BS = $p^2 - q^2$, and diagonal AS = $p^2 + q^2$. When we juxtapose two rectangles so that they do not overlap as shown in the figure (1), the sides of the rational scalene triangle ACS are:

Base CS = $[(m^2 - n^2) + (p^2 - q^2)]$, Side AC = $m^2 + n^2$ and Side AS = $p^2 + q^2$.

When rectangles overlap, the rational scalene triangle ACS is as shown in figure (2) where

Base CS = $[(m^2 - n^2) + (p^2 - q^2)]$ etc.

Source

Gaṇita-sāra-saṅgrahaḥ, Chapter 7, Ślokaḥ 110, Mahāvīrācāryaḥ (850 AD)

3.2.9 Pairs of Rational Isosceles Triangles

रज्जुकृतिघ्नान्योन्यधनाल्पाप्तं षड्द्विघ्नमल्पमेकोनम् ।
तच्छेषं द्विगुणाल्पं बीजे तज्जन्ययोर्भुजादयः प्राग्वत् ॥

Rajjukṛtighnānyonyadhanālpāptaṁ
ṣaḍdvighnamalpamekonam ।
tacchesaṁ dviguṇālpaṁ bīje
tajjanyayorbhujādayaḥ prāgvat ॥

The square (of the ratio value) of the perimeters are multiplied by that of areas crosswise. After dividing larger product by smaller one, the quotient is multiplied by six and separately by two. The smaller product is diminished by one. [The larger product and the diminished smaller product constitute the two bījās (i.e. first pair required). 1 is added and 2 is subtracted from the 4 times the quotient of larger and smaller products. That constitute the second pair of the required bījās.] From these two pairs the sides and other things (relating to the required triangle) are to be obtained as (explained) before.

Explanation

Let S_1 and S_2 be perimeters and A_1 and A_2 be areas of two rational isosceles triangles, such that $S_1 : S_2 = m : n$ and $A_1 : A_2 = p : q$.

Let $n^2p > m^2q$ then quotient 't' is

$$t = \frac{n^2p}{m^2q} \quad \text{Otherwise } t = \frac{m^2q}{n^2p}$$

Hence first pair of bījās is $(6t, 2t - 1)$ and second pair is $(4t + 1, 4t - 2)$.

Now the dimensions of isosceles triangle formed by the first are:

(Equal) Sides $= m\,[(6t)^2 + (2t - 1)^2]$,

Base $= 24mt\,(2t - 1)$,

Altitude $= m\,[(6t)^2 - (2t - 1)^2]$.

Similarly, dimensions of isosceles triangle by second pair are:

(Equal) Sides $= n\,[(4t + 1)^2 + (4t - 2)^2]$,

Base $= 4n\,(4t + 1)\,(4t - 2)$,

Altitude $= n\,[(4t + 1)^2 - (4t - 2)^2]$.

Source

Gaṇita-sāra-saṅgrahaḥ, Chapter 7, Ślokaḥ 137, Mahāvīrācāryaḥ (850 AD)

Western Reference

The particular case of rational isosceles triangle is found discussed by F.S. Younger (1657 AD) and J.H. Rahn (1677 AD). However the general rule is not available.

3.2.10 Construction of Rational Right-angled Triangle

यद्यत्क्षेत्रं जातं बीजैस्संस्थाप्य तस्य कर्णेन ।
इष्टं कर्णं विभजेल्लाभगुणाः कोटिदोः कर्णाः ॥

Yadyatkṣetraṁ jātaṁ bījaissaṁsthāpya tasya karṇena ।
Iṣṭaṁ karṇaṁ vibhajellābhaguṇāḥ koṭidoḥ karṇāḥ ॥

Each of the various figures that are derived with the aid of given (bījās) is written down. The given diagonal is divided by the diagonal of the known bījās (elements). The perpendicular side, the base side and the diagonal (of given figure) as multiplied by the quotient (here obtained), give rise to the perpendicular side, the base and the diagonal (required).

Explanation

Brahmagupta [628 AD - the earlier mathematician] had stated that, for any integers m and n, sides of the right-angled triangle are as follows:

The perpendicular side = $m^2 - n^2$

The base = 2mn

The hypotenuse = $m^2 + n^2$

(m is not less than or equal to n and that both are non-zero integers is obvious.)

These values are considered as bījās.

Let the length of given diagonal be p (integer), then

$$\text{quotient} = \frac{p}{m^2 + n^2}$$

Thus for different values of m and n the various triangles can be constructed as follows:

$$\text{The perpendicular side} = p \times \left(\frac{m^2 - n^2}{m^2 + n^2}\right)$$

$$\text{The base} = p \times \left(\frac{2mn}{m^2 + n^2}\right)$$

The hypotenuse = p

For given value of p, the proper choice of m and n will generate different rational right-angled triangles.

Example:

Let hypotenuse = p = 65.

We can construct different rational right-angled triangles as shown in the below figure.

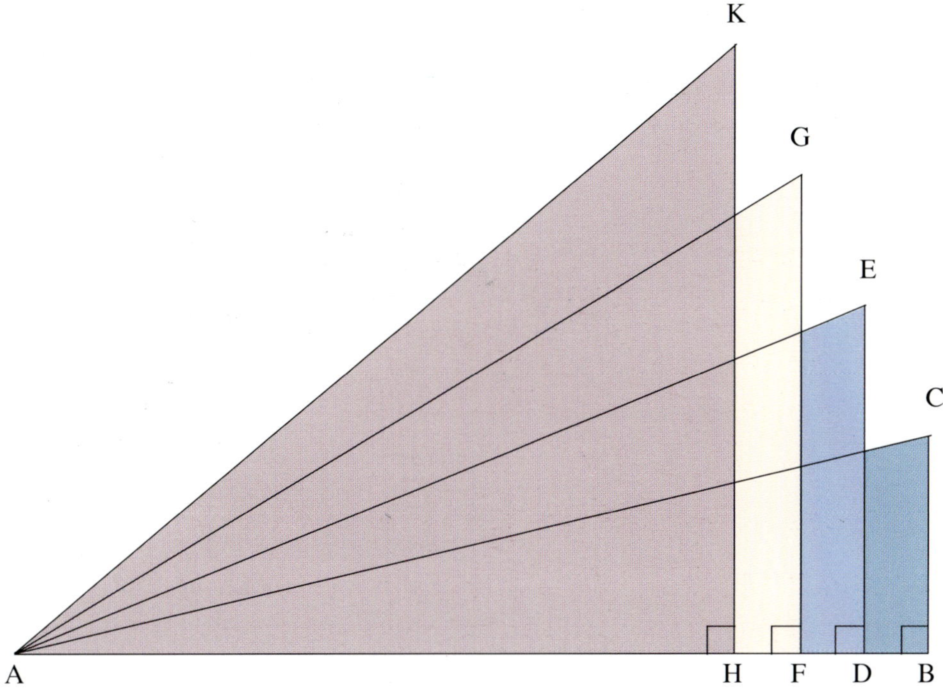

Δ ABC, Δ ADE, Δ AFG and Δ AHK are all right-angled triangles with following dimensions:

	Triangle	Base	Perp.-side	Hypotenuse	Area
1.	ABC	63	16	65	504
2.	ADE	60	25	65	750
3.	AFG	56	33	65	924
4.	AHK	52	39	65	1014

(1 unit = 0.2 cm)

For every right-angled triangle circumdiameter = 65.

Source

Gaṇita-sāra-saṅgrahaḥ, Chapter 7, Ślokaḥ 122, Mahāvīrācāryaḥ (850 AD)

Western Reference

Leonardo Fibonacci (1202 AD) is the first among Western mathematicians to discuss the method of constructing rational right-angled triangle.

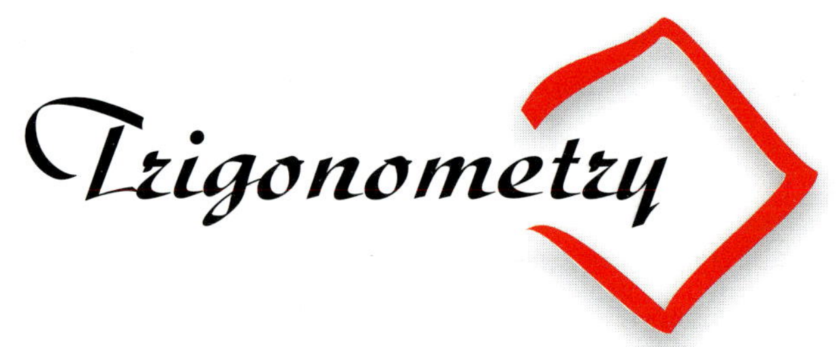

Introduction

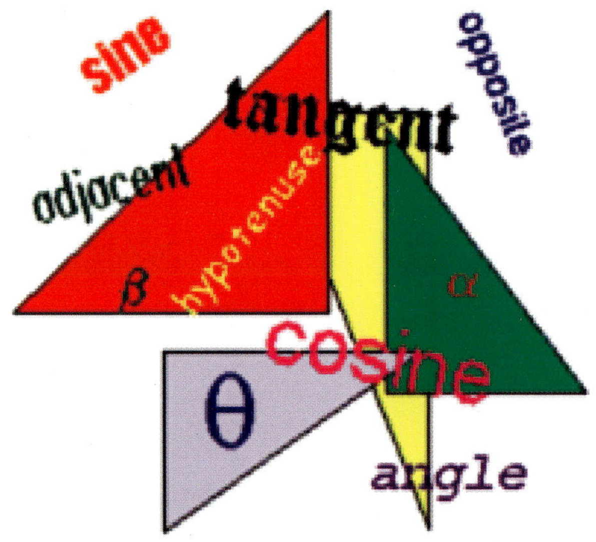

Bhaskaracharya II was a genius (of modern times) who must be called the father of modern calculus. He had developed his science many centuries before Leibnitz and Newton. It is regrettable that the world is not aware of Bhaskaracharya's contribution.

Though Trigonometry originated in India long before Bhaskaracharya, he made significant contribution even in that subject. Aryabhata I, Aryabhata II, Lalla, Brahmagupta all contributed to its development. However none was the originator of this. Its origin goes back to an earlier date, but it probably had to do with astronomy which was a developed subject since long.

3.3.1 Mādhava's sine and cosine series

निहत्य चापवर्गेण चापं तत्तत् फलानि च ।
हरेत् समूलयुग्वर्गैस्त्रिज्यावर्गाहतैः क्रमात् ।
चापं फलानि चाधोऽधौन्यस्योपर्युपरि त्यजेत् ।
जीवाप्त्यै सङ्ग्रहोऽस्यैव विद्वान् इत्यादिना कृतः ॥ १ ॥

Nihatya cāpavargeṇa cāpaṁ tattat phalāni ca ।
Haret samūlayugvargaistrijyāvargāhataiḥ kramāt ।
Cāpaṁ phalāni cādhoऽdhaunyasyoparyupari tyajet ।
Jīvāptyai saṅgrahoऽsyaiva vidvān ityādinā kṛtaḥ ॥ 1 ॥

One should multiply the arc and the resulting products by the square of the arc, and these should be divided in order by the square of the even numbers combined with their roots, and multiplied by the square of the radius. The arc and these products should be placed one beneath the other in order and the lower one should be subtracted from the upper ones for getting the sine-chord.

निहत्य चापवर्गेण रूपं तत्तत् फलानि च ।
हरेत् विमूलयुग्वर्गैस्त्रिज्यावर्गाहतैः क्रमात् ।
किन्तु व्यासदलेनैव द्विघ्नेनाद्यं विभज्यताम् ।
फलान्यधोऽधः क्रमशोन्यस्योपर्युपरि त्यजेत् ॥ २ ॥

Nihatya cāpavargeṇa rūpaṁ tattat phalāni ca ।
Haret vimūlayugvargaistrijyāvargāhataiḥ kramāt ।
Kintu vyāsadalenaiva dvighnenādyaṁ vibhajyatām ।
Phalānyadhoऽdhaḥ kramaśonyasyoparyupari tyajet ॥ 2 ॥

One should multiply one and the resultant products by the square of arc and divide in order by the squares of the even numbers diminished by their roots, and multiplied by the square of radius. But let the first be divided by the radius multiplied by two only. These terms should be placed one beneath the other in order and the lower ones should be subtracted in order from the one above them in order to get the arrow (part of chord of a circle).

Explanation

1. If a is the arc and r is the radius then

First term = a

$$a \times \frac{a^2}{(2^2+2)\,r^2} = \frac{1}{3!}\,\frac{a^3}{r^2} \qquad \text{where } 3! = 3 \times 2 \times 1.$$

$$\frac{1}{3!}\,\frac{a^3}{r^2} \times \frac{a^2}{(4^2+4)\,r^2} = \frac{1}{5!}\,\frac{a^5}{r^4}$$

$$\frac{1}{5!}\,\frac{a^5}{r^4} \times \frac{a^2}{(6^2+6)\,r^2} = \frac{1}{7!}\,\frac{a^7}{r^6} \qquad \text{and so on.}$$

Hence sine-chord $= a - \left(\frac{1}{3!}\right)\frac{a^3}{r^2} + \left(\frac{1}{5!}\right)\frac{a^5}{r^4} - \left(\frac{1}{7!}\right)\frac{a^7}{r^6} + ---$

2. First term $= \frac{a^2}{2r} = \frac{a^2}{1 \times (2^2 - 2)} \times \left(\frac{1}{r}\right)$

$$\frac{a^2}{2r} \times \frac{1}{4^2 - 4} \times \frac{a^2}{r^2} = \frac{1}{4!}\frac{a^4}{r^3}$$

$$\frac{1}{4!} \times \frac{a^4}{r^3} \times \frac{1}{6^2 - 6} \times \frac{a^2}{r^2} = \frac{1}{6!}\frac{a^6}{r^5}$$ and so on.

∴ Versed sine or śara of sine-chord $= \left(\frac{1}{2!}\right)\frac{a^2}{r} - \left(\frac{1}{4!}\right)\frac{a^4}{r^3} + \left(\frac{1}{6!}\right)\frac{a^6}{r^5} - ---$

Thus cosine-chord $= r - \left(\frac{1}{2!}\right)\frac{a^2}{r} + \left(\frac{1}{4!}\right)\frac{a^4}{r^3} - \left(\frac{1}{6!}\right)\frac{a^6}{r^5} + ---$

Substitute $a = r\,\theta$, sine-chord $= r \sin \theta$ and cosine-chord $= r \cos \theta$, we get

1. $\sin \theta = \theta - \frac{\theta^3}{3!} + \frac{\theta^5}{5!} - \frac{\theta^7}{7!} + ---$

2. $\cos \theta = 1 - \frac{\theta^2}{2!} + \frac{\theta^4}{4!} - \frac{\theta^6}{6!} + ---$

Source

Yuktibhāṣaḥ, Chapter 6, Ślokaḥ 12-13, Jyeṣṭhadevaḥ (1500-1610 AD)

Western Reference

Newton (1642-1727) and Brook Taylor (1685-1731) formulated similar sine and cosine series but with a different approach.

3.3.2 Mādhava's first tangent series

इष्टज्यात्रिज्ययोर्घातात् कोट्याप्तं प्रथमं फलं ।
ज्यावर्गं गुणकं कृत्वा कोटिवर्गं च हारकम् ॥

Iṣṭajyātrijyayorghātāt koṭyāptaṁ prathamaṁ phalam ।
Jyāvargaṁ guṇakaṁ kṛtvā koṭivargaṁ ca hārakam ॥

The product of the given sine-chord and the radius, divided by the cosine-chord, is the first result. Then series of results are to be obtained.

प्रथमादिफलेभ्योऽथ नेया फलकृतिर्मुहुः ।
एकत्याद्योजसङ्ख्याभिर्भक्तेष्वेतेष्वनुक्रमात् ॥

Prathamādiphalebhyo'tha neyā phalakṛtirmuhuḥ ।
Ekatyādyojasaṅkhyābhirbhakteṣveteṣvanukramāt ॥

From this first result and the succeeding ones by making the square of the sine-chord the multiplier, and the square of cosine-chord the divisor.

ओजानां संयुतेस्त्यक्त्वा युग्मयोगं धनुर्भवेत् ।
दोः कोट्योरल्पमेवेष्टं कल्पनीयमिह स्मृतम् ॥

Ojānāṁ saṁyutestyaktvā yugmayogaṁ dhanurbhavet ।
Doḥ koṭyoralpameveṣṭam kalpanīyamiha smṛtam ॥

When these are divided in order by the odd numbers 1, 3 etc., the sum of the even place is to be subtracted from the sum of the terms in the odd places to get the arc. The smaller of the sine and cosine chords is to be used for this calculation.

Explanation

If s and c are sine and cosine chords,

$$\text{arc} = \frac{s}{c}r - \frac{1}{3}\frac{s}{c}r\frac{s^2}{c^2} + \frac{1}{5}\frac{s}{c}r\frac{s^4}{c^4} - \frac{1}{7}\frac{s}{c}r\frac{s^6}{c^6} + \cdots$$

$$\text{arc} = \frac{s}{c}r - \frac{1}{3}\frac{s^3}{c^3}r + \frac{1}{5}\frac{s^5}{c^5}r - \frac{1}{7}\frac{s^7}{c^7}r + \cdots$$

For $r = 1$ and $\tan\theta = \frac{s}{c}$, we get

$$\text{arc} = \tan\theta - \frac{1}{3}\tan^3\theta + \frac{1}{5}\tan^5\theta - \frac{1}{7}\tan^7\theta + \cdots$$

Source

Kriyākramakārī, Chapter 2, Ślokaḥ 40, Putumana Somayājī (1350-1410 AD)

Western Reference

James Gregory (1638 AD) and G.W. Leibnitz (1644 AD), developed tangent series with calculus approach.

3.3.3 Mādhava's infinite series for π

व्यासे वारधिनिहिते रूपहृते व्याससागराभिहते ।
त्रिशरादिविषमसङ्ख्याभक्तं ऋणं स्वं पृथक्क्रमात् कुर्यात् ॥

Vyāse vāradhinihite rūpahṛte vyāsasāgarābhihate ।
Triśarādiviṣamasaṅkhyābhaktaṁ ṛṇaṁ svaṁ pṛthakkramāt kuryāt ॥

Muliply the diameter by 4 and divide by 1 (for first term), decrease and increase the terms obtained by multiplying diameter by 4 (each) time, and divide by odd numbers starting from 3 and then 5, 7, 9, ... termwise to get circumference.

Explanation

If 'C' is the circumference and 'd' is diameter then

$$\text{First term} = \frac{4d}{1}, \text{ Second term} = \frac{4d}{3}, \text{ Third term} = \frac{4d}{5} \text{ and so on.}$$

and

$$C = 4d - \frac{4d}{3} + \frac{4d}{5} - \frac{4d}{7} + \text{--- ---} \qquad \text{—(1)}$$

$$\text{From (1), } \frac{C}{d} = \pi = 4\left(1 - \frac{1}{3} + \frac{1}{5} - \frac{1}{7} + \text{------}\right) \qquad \text{—(2)}$$

(2) is Mādhava's infinite series for π. Mādhava has given three correction terms for series (1)

$$R_1(n) = \frac{1}{4n}, \qquad R_2(n) = \frac{n}{4n^2 + 1} \qquad \text{and} \qquad R_3(n) = \frac{n^2 + 1}{n\,[4\,(n^2 + 1) + 1]}$$

Thus (1) is written as

$$C_i(n) = 4d - \frac{4d}{3} + \frac{4d}{5} + \text{------} + (-1)^{n-1}\frac{4d}{2n-1} + (-1)^n\, 4d\, R_i(n) \qquad \text{—(3)}$$

where i = 1, 2 or 3.

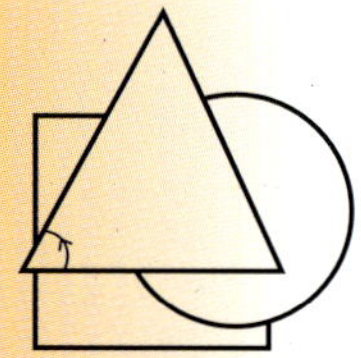

With the help of (3) more and more correct values of π can be derived. Based on this basic series Nīlakaṇṭha obtained many infinite series for π, three of which are listed below.

$$1.\quad C = 8d\left(\frac{1}{2^2 - 1} + \frac{1}{6^2 - 1} + \frac{1}{10^2 - 1} + \cdots\right)$$

$$\therefore \frac{\pi}{8} = \frac{1}{2^2 - 1} + \frac{1}{6^2 - 1} + \frac{1}{10^2 - 1} + \cdots\cdots$$

$$= \frac{1}{1\cdot 3} + \frac{1}{5\cdot 7} + \frac{1}{9\cdot 11} + \cdots\cdots$$

$$2.\quad C = 4d - 4d\left(\frac{1}{3} - \frac{1}{5}\right) - 4d\left(\frac{1}{7} - \frac{1}{9}\right) - \cdots\cdots$$

$$\therefore \frac{4 - \pi}{8} = \frac{1}{4^2 - 1} + \frac{1}{8^2 - 1} + \frac{1}{12^2 - 1} + \cdots\cdots$$

$$= \frac{1}{3\cdot 5} + \frac{1}{7\cdot 9} + \frac{1}{11\cdot 13} + \cdots\cdots$$

$$3.\quad C = \sqrt{12d^2} - \frac{\sqrt{12d^2}}{3\cdot 3} + \frac{\sqrt{12d^2}}{3^2\cdot 5} - \frac{\sqrt{12d^2}}{3^3\cdot 7} + \cdots\cdots$$

$$\therefore \pi = \sqrt{12}\left[1 - \frac{1}{3\cdot 3} + \frac{1}{3^2\cdot 5} - \frac{1}{3^3\cdot 7} + \cdots\cdots\right]$$

From this result Mādhava gave rational approximation to π as follows:

$$\pi = 2{,}827{,}33{,}388{,}233/9^{11} \quad = 3.14159265359$$

This value of π is correct upto 11 decimal places.

Source

Tantra-saṅgrahaḥ, Nīlakaṇṭhaḥ (1445-1545 AD)

Western Reference

Infinite series for π are discussed by John Wallis (1655 AD), Abraham sharp (1717 AD) etc. Later, Ramanujan (1887 - 1920) suggested many incredible infinite series for π, thanks to his inimitable style.

References

1. Aryabhatiya of Aryabhata: Ed. K.S. Shukla, INSA, New Delhi, 1976.
2. Brahmasphutasiddhanta: Ed. Acarya Ram Swarup Sharma, Indian Institute of Astronomical and Sanskrit Research, Delhi, 1966.
3. Sri Mahaviracharya's Ganitasarasangraha: Ed. Dr. Padmavathama, Sri Hombuja Jain Math, 2000.
4. Lilavati Punardarshan: N.H. Fadake, Pune, 1971.
5. Bijaganita: Tr. Pt. V.P. Khanapurkar, Aundh (Maharashtra), 1913.
6. History of Hindu Mathematics (Vol.1,2): Bibhutibhushana Datta and Avadhesh Narayan Singh, Bharatiya Kala Prakashan, Delhi Edition 2001.
7. Geometry in Ancient and Medieval India: T.A. Sarasvati Amma, Motilal Banarasidas, Delhi, Edition 1999.
8. The Golden Age of Indian Mathematics: Dr. S. Parameswaran, Swadeshi Science Movement Kerala, Kochi, 1998.

Deductive Reasoning

What Pythagoras arguably did that impressed Bronowski and others - and justifiably so - was to construct a geometric proof of the theorem. The concept of the proof as more important than the theorem itself was promulgated two centuries later by Euclid. Thus, non-western mathematics has been viewed as second rate because it is empirically based rather than proof based. Both methods are useful. The Euclidian geometry most of us learned is axiomatic. It begins with an axiom, a law assumed to be true, and deduces theorems by reasoning downward. It is deductive and assumptive.

Mr. Dick Teresi, Lost Discoveries, edn. Simon & Schuster (2003), p. 18.

PHYSICS

Mechanics

Matter

Magnetism

Optics

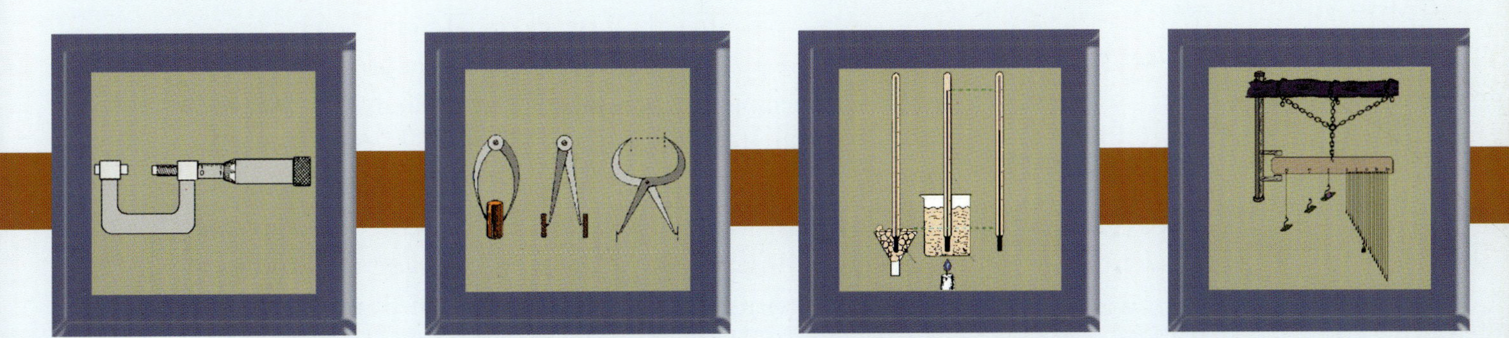

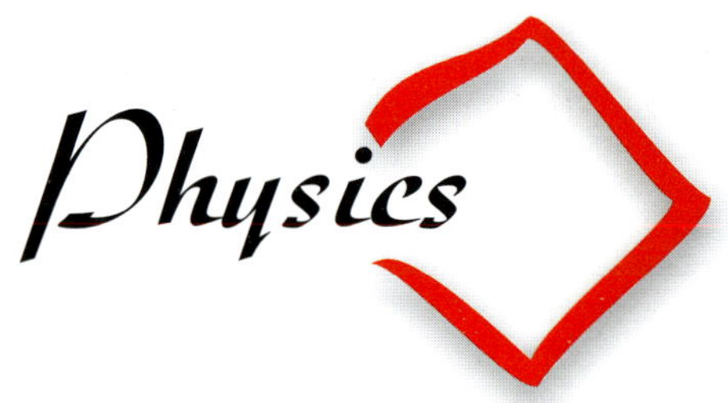

Introduction

Metaphysics ———> Physics

"Science, like Vedantic philosophy, uses analogy to comprehend phenomena, as logic had its own limitations and left the scientist in the lurch after taking him up to a certain point."

Dr. Erwin Schrodinger, Nobel laureate who worked on wave equation that placed the revolutionary quantum concept (as opposed to the Newtonian mechanistic interpretation) on a firm scientific basis in an essay "Seek For The Road", written in 1925.*

"After the conversations about Indian Philosophy, some of the ideas of Quantum Physics, that had seemed so crazy, suddenly made much more sense."

German Physicist W. Heisenberg (1901-1976), a 1932 Nobel laureate who worked on sub-atomic particles.*

What did Oppenheimer have in his mind?

Only seven years after the first successful atom bomb blast in New Mexico, Dr. Robert Oppenheimer (1904-1967) scientist, philosopher, bohemian, and radical, a theoretical physicist and the Supervising Scientist of the Manhattan Project, who was familiar with ancient Samskrit literature, was giving a lecture at Rochester University. During the question and answer period, a student asked a question to which Oppenheimer gave a strangely qualified answer:

Student: Was the bomb exploded at Alamogordo during the Manhattan Project the first one to be detonated?

Dr. Oppenheimer: "Well -- yes. In modern times, of course".#

* Md. Vazeeruddin, Who remembers ancient India's scientific wealth? - Syndicate Features, Vol.5 No.361 (19/04/2006).

\# http://www.hinduwisdom.info/Vimanas.htm

4.1 Mechanics - Motion

उत्क्षेपणापक्षेपणाकुञ्चनप्रसारणगमनानि पञ्च कर्माणि ।	Utkṣepaṇāpakṣepaṇākuñcanaprasāraṇa-gamanāni pañca karmāṇi I

The five kinds of action (movement) are upward, downward, contraction, expansion and locomotion.

Source

Tarkasaṁgrahaḥ, Chapter 1, Section 1, Sūtra 7, Annambhaṭṭaḥ (18th Century AD)

4.2 Matter - Elasticity

ये घना निबिडाः अवयवसन्निवेशाः तैः विशिष्टेषु स्पर्शवत्सु द्रव्येषु वर्तमानः स्थितिस्थापकः स्वाश्रयमन्यथा कथमवनामितं यथावत् स्थापयति पूर्ववदृजुः करोति ।	Ye ghanā nibiḍāḥ avayavasanniveśāḥ taiḥ viśiṣṭeṣu sparśavatsu dravyeṣu vartamānaḥ sthithisthāpakaḥ svāśrayamanyathā kathamavanāmitaṁ yathāvat sthāpayati pūrvavadṛjuḥ karoti I

Elasticity is a property in the bodies having densely populated elemental parts; when sheared by (external) deforming forces, it helps the body recover its original state.

Source

Nyāyakandalī, Śrīdharācāyaḥ (991 AD)

Etymology

Sthiti + sthāpakaḥ = original state + bring back = elasticity.

4.3 Magnetism - Magnets

भ्रामकं चुम्बकं चैव कर्षकं द्रावकं तथा ।
एवं चतुर्विधं कान्तं रोमकान्तं च पञ्चमम् ॥
एकद्वित्रिचतुःपञ्चसर्वतोमुखमेव तत् ।
पीतं कृष्णं तथा रक्तं त्रिवर्णं स्यात् पृथक् पृथक् ॥

Bhrāmakaṁ cumbakaṁ caiva karṣakaṁ drāvakaṁ tathā I
Evaṁ caturvidhaṁ kāntaṁ romakāntaṁ ca pañcamam I
Ekadvitricatuḥpañcasarvatomukhameva tat I
Pītaṁ kṛṣṇaṁ tathā raktaṁ trivarṇaṁ syāt pṛthak pṛthak I

Magnets are of 5 varieties - Bhramakam, Chumbakam, Karshakam, Dravakam and Romakantam. They again are single-faced, double-faced, three-faced, four-faced, five-faced and multi-faced. Each is again in three colours-yellow, black or red.

Source

Rasārṇavam, Pāṭalaḥ 6, Adhyāyaḥ 40, Ślokaḥ 21 (12th century AD)

Notes

Basic property 5
Profile 6
Colour 3
Thus 90 varieties of magnets are enumerated.

4.4 Optics - Lens & Rainbow

अप्राप्यग्रहणं कायाभ्रपटलस्फटिकान्तरितोपलब्धेः ॥

Aprāpyagrahaṇaṁ kāyābhrapaṭalasphaṭikāntaritopalabdheḥ II

That which cannot be perceived (with naked eye) can be perceived with (lens made of) glass, mica or crystal.

सूर्यस्य विविधवर्णाः पवनेन विघट्टिताः कराः साभ्रे ।
वियति धनुः संस्थानाः ये दृश्यन्ते तदिन्द्रधनुः ॥

Sūryasya vividhavarṇāḥ pavanena vighaitāḥ karāḥ sābhre I
Viyati dhanuḥ saṁsthānāḥ ye dṛśyante tadindradhanuḥ II

The multi-coloured rays of the sun being dispersed by wind in a cloudy sky are seen in the form of a bow which is Rainbow.

Source

Nyāya-darśanam, Adhyāyaḥ 3, Sūtram 46, Kaṇādaḥ (800 BCE)
Bṛhat-saṁhitā, Ślokaḥ 35, Varāhamihiraḥ (6th Century AD)

Etymology

Indra + dhanuḥ = rain + bow.

ASTRONOMY

History

Rotation of the Earth

Gravity of the Earth

The Heliocentric Theory

The Speed of light

Lunar Eclipse

Moon a Satellite of the Earth

Planetary Motion

History

A lot of the astronomical knowledge goes all the way back to the Vedic literature -

- To the Samhitas
- To the Brahmanas and
- To the commentaries on the Samhitas.

The period ranges from 6000 BCE for a direct Rig-vedic quote to 14th century AD for Sayanacharaya's commentary. How so much of astronomical knowledge came into being at such ancient times is a matter to be reflected upon, individually, personally and not a matter for assertion in terms of when or how the knowledge came into being.

Post-Vedic period, the big names in Indian astronomy are:

- Aryabhata I 5th Century AD
- Brahmagupta 7th Century AD
- Bhaskara I 7th Century AD and
- Bhaskara II 12th Century AD

In respect of each of these astronomers we know their time, correct to their dates of birth and place, correct to their villages, because, as good astronomers, they have documented these information in the opening or closing Shlokas of their works.

Aryabhata (476 - 550 AD)

Aryabhata was born in 476 AD in Kerala and migrated to Kusumapura in the Magadha empire, not far away from the

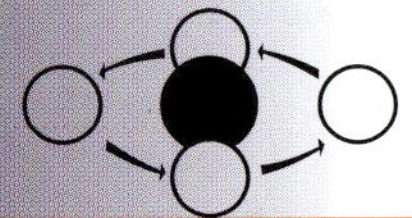

celebrated Nalanda University. This place is in the present-day Bihar state in Northern India. There is a speculation that Aryabhata was a chancellor of the Nalanda University as he is referred to as Kulapa by some of his commentators. It is possible that Aryabhata's family had moved to Kusumapura from somewhere south because, they have also been referred to as Ashmakas - those that had come from the south.

Aryabhata had produced two works:

- Aryabhatiya
- Aryabhata-siddhanta

One measure of the importance of Aryabhata's work is the length of time it has dominated the astronomical discourse in this country and also the number of commentaries and commentaries on commentaries it has engendered. Starting with Bhaskara's commentary in 629 AD (Vallabhi in Saurashtra), there has been a series of scholarly works on Aryabhatiya. The presence of several works in Tamil, Telugu and Malayalam also vouch for the nation widespread of his ideas.

The calendric system in this country was based on Aryabhatiya untill the switch over to the Gregorian calendar in the last century.

This is what Dick Teresi a science historian has to say on Aryabhatiya:

"The Aryabhatiya is a summary of Hindu mathematics up to his time, including astronomy, spherical trigonometry, arithmetic, algebra, and plane trigonometry. In it, one of Aryabhata's main goals was to simplify the ever more complex computational mathematics of Indian astronomy. He had a practical purpose for this: to fix the Hindu calendar for easier forecasting of eclipses and movements of celestial bodies".*

Ujjain Observatory (17th Century AD)

The twentieth century has recognised Aryabhata's contribution to the science; the first satellite launched by India on 19th April 1975 was named after Aryabhata and the International Astronomical Union has named a crater of the moon after Aryabhata.#

* Mr. Dick Teresi, Lost Discoveries, edn.Simon & Schuster (2003), p.133.

\# http://www.lunarrepublic.com/gazetteer/crater_a.shtml

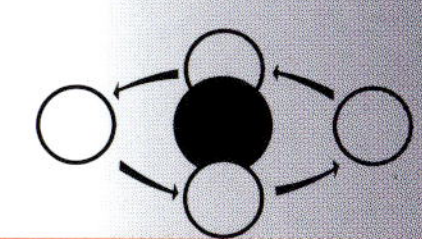

Brahmagupta (598 - 668 AD)

A centre of excellence for astronomy besides Nalanda was the observatory in Ujjain - in the present-day Madhya Pradesh - better known for King Bhoja and his "Nava-ratnas" which included the celebrated poet Kalidasa.

Brahmagupta is revered both for his mathematical genius and his accomplishments as an astronomer. His works include:

- Brahmagupta-siddhanta (substantially based on Aryabhatiya) and
- Khanda-khadyaka (literally Sweetmeat because it is an user-friendly version of Aryabhatiya)

Khanda-khadyaka, was written in two parts, the second part being devoted to where Brahmagupta differed from Aryabhata.

Both Brahmagupta-siddhanta and Khanda-khadyaka were translated into Arabic (Zij-al-Arkand and AZ-Zij Kandakatik al-arabi) by Persian scholar Al-Biruni. These were later translated into Latin in 1126 AD from the Arabic version by Ya'qub ibn Tariq.

Kepler's theory of Parallax is a repeat of Khanda-khadyaka.

Bhaskara II (1114 - 1185 AD)

Bhaskara is also from the Ujjain school and is also a commentator of Aryabhata. Bhaskara's principal work is Siddhanta-siromani, which is in two parts:

- Gola-adhyaya (Astronomy)
- Graha-ganita (Mathematics of the planets)

365-Day Year

Aryabhata's value for the length of the year at 365 days, six hours, twelve minutes and thirty seconds, however is a slight overestimate: the true value is fewer than 365 days and 6 hours.

Mr. Dick Teresi, Lost Discoveries, edn.Simon & Schuster (2003), p. 133.

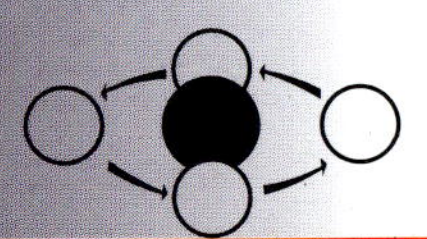

5.1 Rotation of the Earth (1)

अनुलोमगतिनौस्थः पश्यत्यचलं विलोमगं यद्वत् ।
अचलानि भानि तद्वत् समपश्चिमगानि लङ्कायाम् ॥

Anulomagatirnausthaḥ paśyatyacalaṁ vilomagaṁ yadvat | Acalāni bhāni tadvat samapaścimagāni laṅkāyām ||

Just as a person in a boat moving forward sees the stationary objects (on the bank) as moving backwards, the stationary stars are seen in Lanka (at the equator) as moving towards the west.

Source

Āryabhaṭīyam, Golapādaḥ, Chapter 4, Ślokaḥ 9, Āryabhaṭaḥ (499 AD)

Etymology

Bhāsate ----> Bam ----------------> Bani

Shines ----> That which shines - Star ----> Stars

Notes

- At that point in time, the Indian astronomers worked with reference to a Hindu Equator running through Lanka. Hence the reference to Lanka.
- For this work of Aryabhata, Someswara, one of his students has written a commentary. That commentary says "The place Lanka, is mentioned as an illustration. This principle is applicable universally".
- Aryabhata shows by a simple example that it is the earth that moves and that the stars are fixed and stationary.
- In Samskrit there are no nouns as commonly understood. Each noun is derived from the function of the subject being described. The Samskrit word for the earth is jagath - the one that moves. The understanding of the rotation of the earth or its orbiting the sun must be at the root of this coinage.

Western Reference

Léon Foucault demonstration in 1851 AD of the diurnal motion of the earth by the rotation of the plane of oscillation of a freely suspended, long and heavy pendulum in the Panthéon in Paris, caused a sensation in both the learned and popular worlds, for it was the first dynamical proof of the earth's rotation.

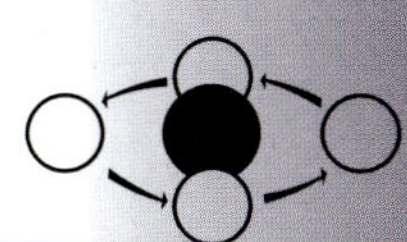

5.2 Rotation of the Earth (2)

भूमिर्भ्राम्यति बुद्ध एव मरुत: प्रत्यग्भ्रमोऽस्त्यद्भुतो
भ्राम्यन्त्येव सहाश्रयेण यदि वा ज्योतीषि सर्वाण्यपि ।
आवर्तयोऽयमपाम्भ्रम: परिचिता मूर्तिर्हरस्याष्टमी
या सास्त्यप्पयदीक्षितो जयति सा मूर्तिर्निरस्तभ्रमा ॥

Bhūmirbhrāmyati buddha eva marutaḥ
pratyagbhramoऽstyadbhuto bhrāmyantyeva
sahāśrayeṇa yadi vā jyotīṁṣi sarvāṇyapi ।
Āvartayoऽyamapāmbhramaḥ paricitā mūrtirha
rasyāṣṭamī yā sāstyappayadīkṣito jayati sā
mūrtirnirastabhramā ॥

It is well known that the earth indeed rotates with the inward rotation of air and with its base and all the celestial lights. This rotation is known even as that of the water. That form of Appayyadikshita shines, which is known as the eighth form of Shiva.

Source

Śivotkarṣa-mañjarī, Ślokaḥ 52 Nīlakanṭha-dīkṣitaḥ (16th Century AD)

Notes

Śiva+Utkarṣa+Mañjarī--->translates into A bouquet in praise of Shiva.

The last shloka is traditionally used to provide the identity of the author and in extremely brief form the benefits of reciting the work - E.g., prosperity or often greater devotion to the Lord. In this work, Nilakanta Dikshita (a Minister of King Thirumalai Naicker) pays homage to his grand-uncle Appayya Dikshita by describing him as an incarnation of the Lord Shiva himself.

This quote merely indicates that the rotation of the earth was common knowledge in Dikshita's time in 16th century AD.

Western Reference

Léon Foucault demonstration in 1851 AD.

That's Accuracy

It was generally believed that the earth was stationary and was the centre of the universe and all heavenly bodies revolved round the earth. But Aryabhata-I differed from the other astronomers and held the view that the earth rotates about its axis and the stars are fixed in space. The period of one siderial rotation of the earth according to Aryabhata-I is 23 hours, 56 minutes 4.1 seconds. The corresponding modern value is 23 hours, 56 minutes 4.091 seconds.

Aryabhata, Aryabhatiya, Gitika-pada.

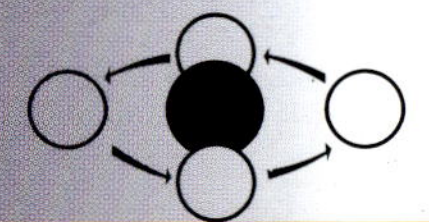

5.3 Gravity of the Earth

तथा पृथिव्यामभिमानिनी या देवता प्रसिद्धा सैषा पुरुषस्य अपानवृत्तिमवष्टभ्याकृष्य वशीकृत्याध एव अपकर्षेण अनुग्रहं कुर्वती वर्तत इत्यर्थः । अन्यथा हि शरीरं गुरुत्वात् पतेत् सावकाशे वोद्गच्छेत् ।

Tathā pṛthivyāmabhimāninī yā devatā prasiddhā saiṣā puruṣasya apānavṛttimavaṣṭabhyākṛṣya vaśikṛtyādha evāpakarṣeṇānugrahaṁ kurvatī vartata ityarthaḥ ||

Anyathā hi śariram gurutvāt patet sāvakaśe vodgacchet ||

Similarly the deity that is earth exists by favouring, attracting, controlling by pulling down the vital function called Apana of the human. Else the body would fall due to its weight or would fly into the sky if left free.

Source

Śaṅkara's commentary (8th century AD) on Praśnopaniṣad (Vedic Period), Chapter 3, Mantra 8

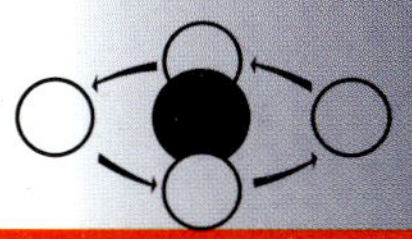

5.4 The Heliocentric theory

नैवास्तमनमर्कस्य नोदयः सर्वदा सतः । उदयास्तमनाख्यं हि दर्शनादर्शनं रवेः ॥	Naivāstamanamarkasya nodayaḥ sarvadā sataḥ । Udayāstamanākhyaṁ hi darśanādarśanaṁ raveḥ ॥

There is, in truth, neither rising nor setting for the sun, for it is always there, and these terms (of rising and setting) merely imply his presence and disappearance.

दाधर्थ पृथिवीमभितो मयूखैः ।	Dādhartha pṛthivīmabhito mayūkhaiḥ ।

(The sun) holds the earth from all sides with (his) rays.

मित्रो दाधार पृथिवीमुतद्याम् । मित्रः कृष्टीः ।	Mitro dādhāra pṛthivīmutadyām । Mitraḥ kṛṣṭīḥ ॥

The sun holds the earth and the celestial region. The sun is the attracting power.

Source

Viṣṇu-purāṇam, Book 2, Chapter 8, Ślokaḥ 15, Vyāsaḥ (Post-Vedic period)

Yajur-āraṇyakam, Praśnaḥ 1, Aṇuvākaḥ 8, Vargaḥ 3 (Vedic period)

Yajur-veda, Taittirīya-saṁhitā, Kāṇḍaḥ 3, Prapāṭakaḥ 4, Anuvākaḥ 10, Mantraḥ 34 (Vedic Period)

Western Reference

Copernicus (1473 - 1543), a Polish astronomer, published in his book "De reveloutionibus Orbium Coelestium" in 1543 AD, the theory that the sun is the centre of the universe and that the earth and other planets revolve around it. This is considered a defining moment in the history of science.

The Big Guy and the Small Guy

Aryabhata uses the Aphorism "Laghava-gaurava-nyaya" (the logic of the big and small) to put in perspective the place of the earth vis-a-vis the sun.

This logic would make:

- Sun larger than the earth
- Earth would orbit the sun and not the other way about.

Deivatthin Kural (Tamil), Volume II, p. 572 Of His Holiness Shri. Chandrashekharendra Saraswati Swami of Kanchi, Tamilnadu, India.

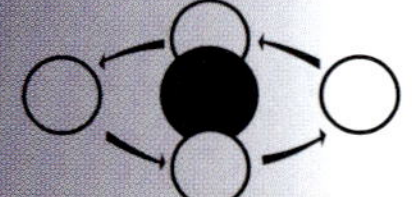

5.5 The Speed of Light

तरणिर्विश्वदर्शतो ज्योतिष्कृदसि सूर्य । विश्वमाभासि रोचनम् ।	Taraṇirviśvadarśato jyotiṣkṛdasi sūrya I Viśvamābhāsi rocanam I

Oh Sun! (You) overwhelm all in speed, visible to all, source of light. (You) shine pervading the Universe.

तथा च स्मर्यत योजनानां सहस्रं द्वे द्वे शते द्वे च योजने । एकेन निमिषार्धेन क्रममाण नमोऽस्तु ते ॥	Tathā ca smaryate yojanānāṁ sahasraṁ dve dve śate dve ca yojane I Ekena nimiṣārdhena kramamāṇa namoऽstu te II

It is remembered (that) Salutations to Thee (sun), the traveller of 2,202 yojanas in half a nimisha.

Source

Ṛg-veda-saṁhitā, Maṇḍalam 1, Sūktam 50, Mantraḥ 4 (6000 BCE)

Sāyaṇācārya's commentary (14th century AD)

Notes

1. The commentary on the Rig-veda by Sayana (c. 1315-1387), a minister and scholar par excellence in the court of King Bukka I of the Vijayanagar Empire in South India is well known.
2. Sayana's computation of Speed of Light:

Distance travelled	= 2202 Yojanas
1 Yojana	= 9 miles, 110 Yards = 9.0625 miles
	= 21,144.705 miles
Time taken	= 1/2 nimisha = 1/8.75 = 0.114286 second.
Speed of light	= 185,016.169 miles / second.
Modern Value	= 186,282.397 miles / second.

3. This Sukta is attributed to the son of Kanva Maharshi and is prescribed for use in two different occasions - in Suryeshti sacrifice (a ritual to please the Sun God) and in Chaturmasya-yajna (a Vedic ritual).

Western Reference

1. The speed of light was first determined in 1676 AD by a Danish astronomer Olaus Roemer who looked at the difference in the times that light from Io, one of the moons of Jupiter, takes to reach earth based on whether it is on the near side of Jupiter or the far side. Until then light was taken to travel with infinite velocity. Even Newton assumed so.
2. In 1887 AD, Michealson and Morley established the velocity of light as 1,86,300 miles / sec.

5.6 Lunar Eclipse

छादयति शशी सूर्यं शशिनं महती च भूच्छाया ।	Chādayati śaśī sūryaṁ śaśinaṁ mahatī ca bhūcchāyā ।

The moon covers the sun and the great shadow of the earth covers the moon.

Source

Aryabhaṭīyam, Golapādaḥ, Chapter 4, Ślokaḥ 37, Āryabhaṭaḥ (499 AD)

Notes

1. Eclipses undoubtedly fascinated all ancient civilisations.

- The oldest known record of a lunar eclipse took place at Ur in Mesopotomia around 2000 BCE.
- In 1300 BCE, Chinese began a long series of observation of eclipses. Chinese astronomers recorded 900 solar and 600 lunar eclipses over a period of 2600 years.
- The Babylonians used their long record of eclipses to see regular patterns of eclipses. By 700 BCE they could predict lunar eclipses.

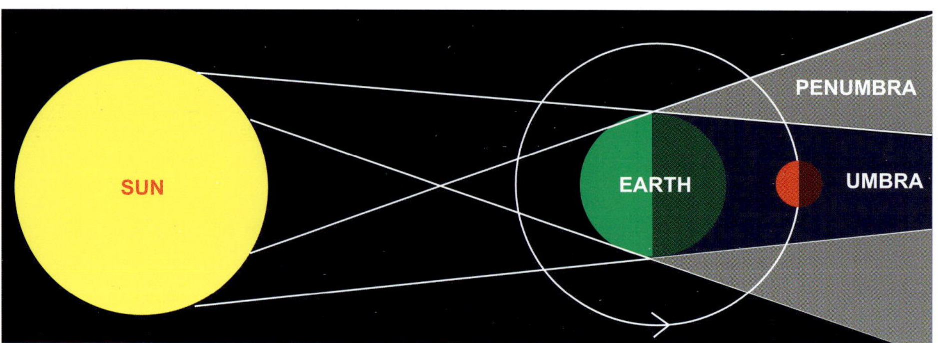

2. Aryabhata went beyond observation and explained the cause of eclipse.
3. The snake Rahu devouring the moon and people having a sanctifying bath after the eclipse to mourn the death of the moon, is the ritual which has unfortunately been taken as the understanding of the civilisation of the eclipse. Knowledge, very clearly, as can be seen from this quote and the rituals do not bind each other.

Western Reference

Although not as well known, Halley also made important scientific contributions in his studies of eclipses. He is credited with the first eclipse map showing the path of the Moon's shadow across England during the upcoming total eclipse of 1715 AD.

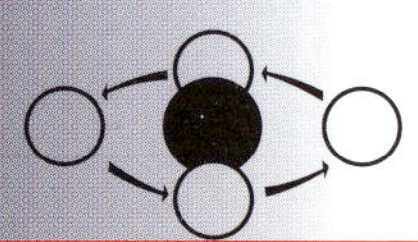

5.7 Moon - A Satellite of the Earth

आयङ्गौः पृश्निरक्रमीदसदन्मातरं पुरः ।	Āyaṅgauḥ pṛśnirakramīdasadanmātaraṁ puraḥ I
पितरञ्च प्रयन्त्स्वः ।	Pitarañca prayantsvaḥ I

The moon, being a satellite of the earth, revolves around its mother planet and follows it in its revolution round the self-luminous father planet (the sun).

Source

Ṛg-vedaḥ, Maṇḍalam 10, Sūktam 189, Mantraḥ 1 (6000 BCE)

Notes

The Vedic metaphor is indicative of a certain heirarchy:

Sun
|
Earth
|
Moon

which is substantially true.

24 hours and 50 minutes

The Purusha Hymn of the Rigvedà says that the mind is born of the moon. Recently, by research on volunteers, who stayed in underground caves for months without any watches or other cues about time, it was found that the natural cycle for the mind is 24 hours and 50 minutes. The period of the moon is also 24 hours and 50 minutes

Dr. Subhash Kak, Interview on The Rediff (18/11/1999).

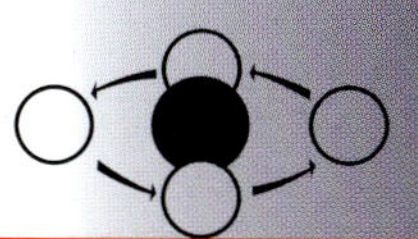

5.8 Orbiting Planets - Concept of Gravity

आकृष्टिशक्तिश्च मही तया यत्	Ākrṣṭiśaktiśca mahī tayā yat
खस्थं गुरु स्वाभिमुखं स्वशक्त्या ।	khasthaṁ guru svābhimukhaṁ svaśaktyā ।
आकृष्यते तत्पततीव भाति	Ākrṣyate tatpatatīva bhāti
समे समन्तात् क्व पतत्वियं खे ॥	same samantāt kva patatviyaṁ khe ॥

The attracting (gravitational) force (is) the earth. That (earth) with that gravitational force of hers attracts towards herself the large objects in the sky. It seems as though she is falling. In space, with matching forces where will she (earth) fall.

Source

Siddhānta-śiromaṇiḥ, Bhuvanakośaḥ 6, Bhāskaraḥ II (1150 AD)

Notes

This quote very clearly talks about the gravitational force of not only earth, but of other heavenly bodies as well.

Western Reference

The universal law of gravitation was propounded by Issac Newton (1642-1727) 500 years after Bhaskara.

Johannes Kepler (December 27, 1571 – November 15, 1630), a key figure in the scientific revolution, was a German mathematician, astronomer, and an early writer of science fiction stories. He is best known for his laws of planetary motion, based on his works Astronomia nova (1609), Harmonice Mundi (1619) and the textbook Epitome of Copernican Astronomy.

Takshila

Takshila university was established in 700 BC. More than 10,500 students from all over the world studied more than 60 subjects. The campus accommodated 10,500 students who came from as far as Babylonia, Greece, Syria, Arabia, and China and offered over sixty different courses in various fields, such as science, mathematics, medicine, politics, warfare, astrology, astronomy, music, religion, and philosophy.

http://www.quotesandsayings.com/gindia.htm

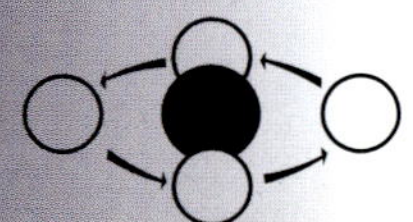

5.9 Planetary Motion

कक्ष्या प्रतिमण्डलगा भ्रमन्ति सर्वे ग्रहा: स्वचारेण ।
मन्दोच्चादनुलोमं प्रतिलोमञ्चैव शीघ्रोच्चात् ॥

Kakṣyā pratimaṇḍalagā bhramanti sarve grahāḥ svacāreṇa I Mandoccādanulomaṁ pratilomañcaiva śīghroccāt II

The mean planets move on their orbits and the true planets on their eccentric circles. All the planets whether moving on their orbits or on the eccentric circles move with their own (mean) motion, anticlockwise from their apogees and clockwise from their perigees.

Source

Āryabhaṭīyam, Kalākriyā-pādaḥ, Chapter 3, Ślokaḥ 17, Āryabhaṭaḥ (499 AD)

Etymology

Manda = upper apsis of planet

Uccha = apex of an orbit of a planet

Śīghra = the lower apsis (as opposed to manda)

Thus, Manda+uccha = apogee

Śīghra+uccha = perigee

Pratiloma = contrary to the natural order = anti-clockwise.

Notes

Aryabhata stated this law in the 5th Century AD much before the first law of Planetary motion given by the German astronomer Johannes Kepler in 1609 AD.

Mean Planet - Natural Satellite

True Planet - The Main Planet

Apogee - a heavenly body's point of greatest distance from the earth

Perigee - the point of the moon's orbit at which it is nearest to the earth.

Nalanda

The Nalanda University once housed 9 million books. It was the centre of education for scholars from all over Asia. Many Greek, Persian and Chinese students studied here. The university was burnt down by pillaging Muslim invaders who overran India in the 11th century

http://www.indpride.com/didyouknow.html

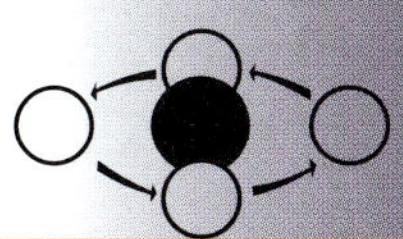

5.10 The Elliptical Path of Planets

त्रिनाभिचक्रमजरमनर्वं यत्रेमा
विश्वा भुवनानि तस्थुः ।

Trinābhicakramajaramanarvaṁ yatremā viśvā
bhuvanāni tasthuḥ ।

The elliptical path through which all the celestial bodies move, is imperishable and unslackened.

Source

Ṛg-veda-saṁhitā, Maṇḍalam 1, Sūktam 164, Mantraḥ 2 (6000 BCE)

Notes

This quote is excerpted from the part describing the performance of the final rites of an Agnihotri - a person who has been doing the fire sacrifice as a daily ritual. This and the other quotes from the Vedas demonstrate how the ritualistic prescriptions are littered with secular knowledge.

The Samskrit word for the Universe is Brahmanda - the very large egg. The elliptical shape of the movement of all planets is possibly the reason for the coinage.

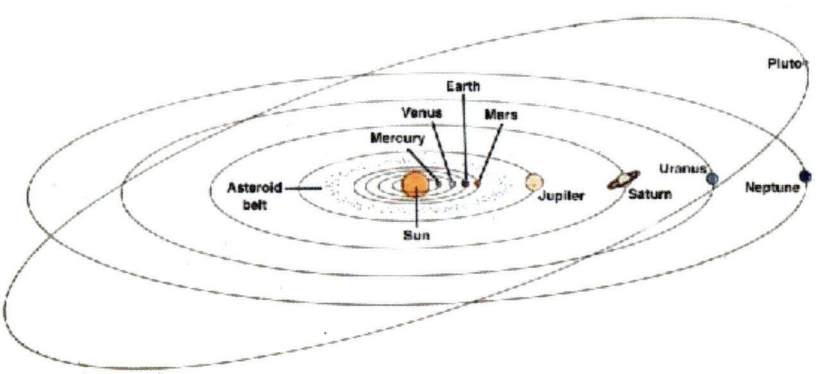

Western Reference

In the western astronomical tradition upto the age of Copernicus (1473-1543), it was believed that the planets and other celestial bodies had circular orbits. Later Johannes Kepler (1571-1630) proposed in 1609 that, the path of all the planets and other celestial bodies is elliptical.

Smart Bhaskaracharya

Bhaskaracharya calculated the time taken by the earth to orbit the sun hundreds of years before the astronomer Smart. Time taken by earth to orbit the sun: (5th century) 365.25756484 days

www.vepachedu.org

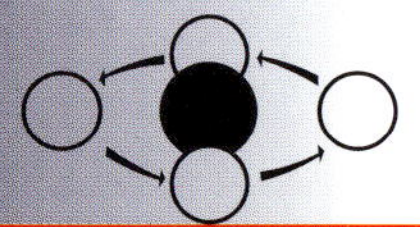

108

108 is a number of great sanctity in Hindu religious practices. It occurs repeatedly

- Reciting the names of gods is a prescribed path for deliverance."Kalau nama-sankirtanam". In the Kali yuga it is the recitation of the Lord's name, as the other prescriptions like sacrifices would be difficult to practise. There are several works in praise of the several gods in the Hindu pantheon of gods. Most of these are a collection of 108 (Ashtottara-stotharam) names of the chosen gods. There are a few which are a collection of 1000 names.
- Physical effort is another form of worship. Jatra (a distorted version of the Samskrit word Yatra meaning travel) is another important tradition particularly in Western India. It is amazing to see individuals who lead sedate lives in metros like Mumbai and Chennai go on Yatra - in Mumbai to Shiridi and in Chennai to Shabari malai. Mahatma leveraged this faith with remarkable success in his Dandi Yatra. Another form of this physical effort is circumambulation of the deities in temples. My mother would, on special occasions, do 108 times circumambulation of the deity in the nearby temple.
- Any number of domestic rituals are prescribed for the Hindu, starting from the daily sun worship (Sandhya-vandana) to several rituals of fortnightly, monthly and annual cycles. All these rituals would include the recitation of prescribed mantras (like Gayatri); while the family purohit may give a choice 10, 28 and 108, to suit the hustle and bustle of the day, the default setting is 108.
- For the Vaishnavites (worshippers of Vishnu), the Divya Kshetras (temples sanctified by their savants, the Alwars) are 108.

The obvious is seldom understood; it is so common it is not questioned, it is taken for granted.

Esoteric explanation for the Hindu 108 are not wanting. Here is one:

1 = The Ultimate

0 = Maya (Illusion of duality)

8 = 5 sense organs and mind, intellect and ego.

Human beings are expected to use these 8 tools to reach the ultimate, piercing the "Maya". Interesting, but is there more to it?

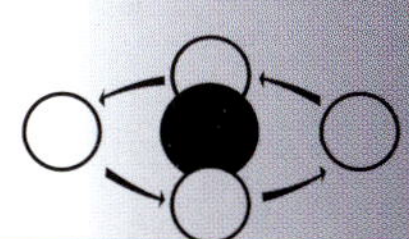

Here is something more concrete:

	Moon (Miles)	Sun (Miles)
Diameter	2,160	8,64,000
Distance from Earth	2,34,000	9,35,00,000
Ratio	108.33	108.22

The religious practice of 108, is a number of unique astronomical relevance.

Is this a coincidence or is this by design? This question can be split into two separate issues to reach a possible answer:

- Is it likely that the ancient Indians knew of the astronomical significance of the number 108?
- If yes, is it likely that they wove this number deliberately into their religious practices?

We will attempt to answer each of these two questions.

Aryabhata (500 AD) is reputed to have written two books Aryabhatiya and Aryabhata-siddhanta. The first book is really two books Dasa-gitika-sutra and Aryabhata-sutra as evidenced by two sets of Dhyana Shlokas and concluding Shlokas. That leaves the second book with 108 Shlokas. In the case of Aryabhata, it would be fair to assume that the number of shlokas in the Magnum Opus, was by intention.

Surya Siddhanta, (400 AD) an ancient astronomy text talks of the distance between the earth and the moon as 2,53,000 miles, which is close to the currently verified value of 2,52,710 miles.

Yajnavalkya (1800 BCE) actually talks of 108 times the respective diameters as the distance from the earth of both the sun and the moon.

The first question, whether the ancient Indians knew of this astronomical ratio, the answer would be, yes for at least the last about 4,000 years.

Astronomical knowledge has been brought into play in all walks of life, sacred as well as secular, from the construction of the sacrificial altars to town planning. Therefore this 108 as a value in religious routine is very likely to be intentional.

108 is an everyday occurrence in the Hindu way of life. It is so amazing that there is science behind such routines.

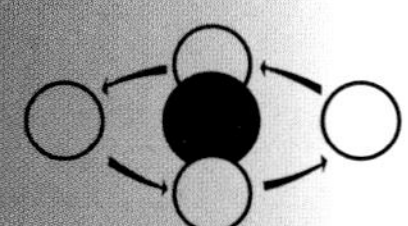

The Indus Valley civilisation was stumbled upon as late as the early 20th century by a British officer in India. The civilisation spread across parts of Punjab, Uttar Pradesh, Gujarat, Baluchistan and Sind. Some of the main centres of the civilisation have been discovered at Harappa, Mohenjo Daro, Lothal, Ropar and Kalibangan.

The primary reason why the Indus Valley civilisation has been so widely acclaimed is that it was an urban civilisation. The civilisation was town based and there were granaries that stored the grain that was believed to have been brought in from the adjoining agricultural lands. Most city dwellers may have been traders or artisans, reflecting a high degree of occupational specialisation for a culture that developed so early. Art and culture were fairly well developed, as may be judged from the exquisite sculpture of the bronze dancing girl of Mohenjo Daro.

Town planning was one of the key achievements of the Indus Valley people. Roads were straight and cut at right angles, something that is a rare sight even in cities of today. Cities were planned systematically, with residential, governance and administrative quarters clearly demarcated. All houses, offices, granaries etc. were built with baked bricks of the same size. Sophisticated sewerage were in place, with an elaborate system of covered drains. The Indus civilisation is home to the world's first urban sanitation system, again one that is far superior to what is seen in most parts of the country today.

A second astounding aspect of the Indus Civilisation was the standardisation of weights and measures. The much-spoken-of seals are a striking achievement of the Indus people that allowed for authentication of goods that were traded. The sheer quantity of seals discovered suggests that each merchant or mercantile family owned its own seal. These seals are in various quadrangular shapes and sizes, each with a human or an animal figure carved on it. Trade was extensive, and Indus seals have been found in Persian Gulf and Sumer.

The fact that the script used by the Indus people has still not been deciphered would imply that there is a lot more to the civilisation that remains unknown to us.

"Pride of India" is a book on the history of Indian Science. In a history book, it is important to get the dates right.

The starting point for the dating of the Indus Valley civilisation is the excavation in the 1920s, of the Mohenjo Daro and Harappa sites in the Gangetic plains. The archaeological find was rich:

- Multi level housing
- Broad, well laid-out streets
- A comprehensive drainage system
- Public utilities like bathhouses
- The Indus seals

A mature, prosperous civilisation. Archaeologists, through carbon dating, established the recoveries as belonging to 3500 BCE.

This Harappan civilisation seemed to have ended abruptly, which warranted an explanation. It was proposed that, in the absence of evidence of natural calamities - flood, earthquake, volcanic eruption - to account for the cessor of the civilisation, there must have been a human factor in the shape of an invasion by an alien force. It was proposed that a Central Asian warring tribe had entered the country though the present day Afghanistan, occupied the Gangetic plains and driven south the Harappan inhabitants.

The corollaries of this "Aryan invasion" theory are:

- India is not even *a* civilisation. It is really two - the original Harappan which became Dravidian with its southward migration and the invading Aryan which occupied the Gangetic plains.

- The Indian civilisation is transplanted and is not native to this land. Its roots are in Central Asia. The present residents of this land are as much colonisers as are the residents of the present America and Australia.

  This premise could be supported by philological, archaeological and literary evidences:

- Linguistic studies* conducted by R.D. Gray and Q.D. Atkinson of the University of Auckland, New Zealand, show that the oldest Indo-European language, which is over 10,000 years old, bears close affinity to the Rig-vedic-Samskrit. It was conceivable that Samskrit was born from a European language brought in by the invading army of Central Asia.

- Horses are an important part of the Vedic rituals (as in Ashvamedha, the horse sacrifice performed by emperors). The Harappan sites had no horse skeletons whereas Arabia is the land of horses. It is conceivable that the Vedas are a product of Arabians who settled in the Indus valley.

---

* Language-tree divergence times support the Anatolian theory of Indo-European origin, Nature Journal (27/11/2003)

- There is the Vedic lore of Indra, the king of the Devas, destroying Shatapuras, hundred cities which possibly refers to the Harappan cities being destroyed by the (superior) Aryan invaders.

The theory sat well with the mental models of that era. The western scholars did not have to reckon with the discomfiture of a literature, which predated the Old Testament (500 BCE)and a civilisation that pre-dated the Greek (1100 BCE) substantially.

However the theory did not find universal acceptance. There have been several infirmities.

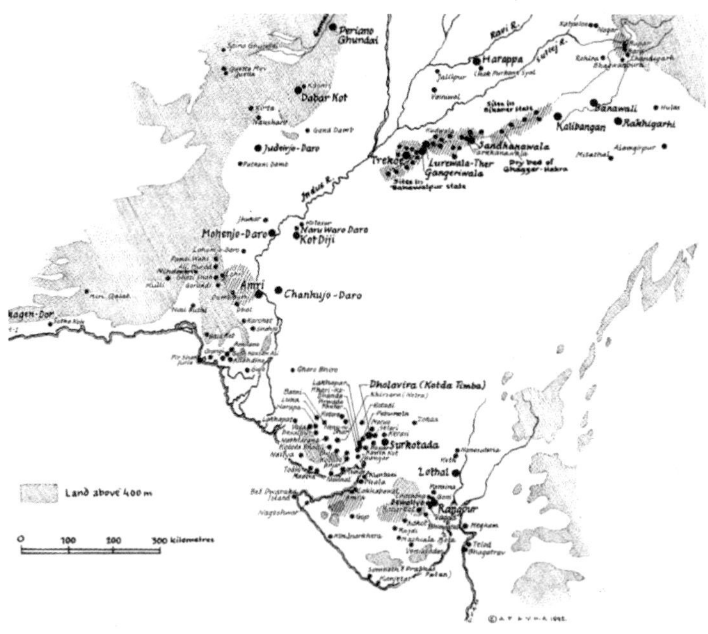

1. Aryans away from the river

All ancient civilisations were founded on river banks be they

- The Egyptian on the banks of Nile (7000 BCE),
- The Mesopotamian (the present day Iraq) on the banks of Tigris and Euphrates (4500 BCE),
- The North American Mayan civilisation in the Mackenzie River valley. (2000 BCE) or
- The Greek on the banks of Arta and Acherons (1100 BCE).

How could the Harappan Civilisation owe its origin to the central Asian region, which had no perennial river?

2. Harappan sites away from the river

Over 40% of the Harappan sites (175 out of 435) were far away from the banks of the Indus River. Why would an agrarian people build cities so far away from the riverbank?

3 Skeletal Remains

The Aryan Invasion theory = the invasion and destruction of the Harappan cities. An examination of the skeletal remains of these locations with current and better equipment has completely ruled out the possibility of invasion / war.

- A large number of skeletons found in *a* place would be indicative of a battle / an invasion and the loss of a lot of lives. But Prof. G.F. Dales of the Berkeley University* has shown that the human skeletons at Mohenjo Daro come from different mud layers, which got repeatedly deposited due to repeated floods in the river and were not the result of a single event.
- Prof. Kennedy of Cornell University, who is a renowned anthropologist and who has recently closely studied the skeletons, which are attributed to 'invasion' and 'massacre', has convincingly shown that none of these skeletons bears any sign of injury from any kind of weapon, which may have resulted in the death of the slain or injured.
- As many as 325 skeletons found in the excavations have been examined by anthropologists. They concluded that the skeletons do not belong to any of the postulated racial types such as Mongoloid, Nordics and Mediterranean. "The cephalic index shows that the skeletons found in Mohenjo Daro (Sindh) are like those of modern residents of Sindh and those in Lothal (Gujarat) are like those of modern residents of Gujarat".

Notwithstanding an *apparent* agreement on the Aryan Invasion theory, these lacunae lead to research and studies continuously re-examining this premise.

Sir Auriel Stein (1862 -1943)

A geologist Sir Auriel Stein, who had surveyed the ancient Sarasvati's course, concluded that there was a Sarasvati river, which had dried up with the shift in the course of Sutlej, its main tributary#. Somehow this down to earth survey which showed an alternative cause for the *apparent cessor* of the Harappan civilisation did not acquire currency.

What the geological survey could not achieve, an aerial survey did. A 1990 picture taken by the American satellite Landsat, showed a 1000 miles dried up tract of the "mythological" river Sarasvati, from Himalayas to South Rajasthan towards Somnath, ending on the Sourashtrian coast.

This NASA image completely changed the terms of reference of enquiry for all scholars.

A reconstruct could be formulated *without stretching one's imagination:*

1 Sarasvati originates from the Himalayas
2 Sarasvati flows as a copious river
3 Sarasvati dries up
4 The inhabitants on the banks of the river migrate.

---

* Prof. G. F. Dales, former head of Department of South Asian Archaeology and Anthropology, Berkeley University, USA, The Mythical Massacre at Mohenjo-daro Expedition, Vol. VI, 3 (1964)

An Archaeological Tour along the Ghaggar - Hakra River", Geographical Journal, Vol. 99, pp 173-82

1. **Sarasvati originates from the Himalayas**

i Current Evidence

- In 1996, the Indian Space Research Organisation (ISRO) did a follow up (aerial) survey of the NASA discovery with its own remote sensing satellite. In 1998, the Central Ground Water Commission dug 24 wells in the dry bed identified by ISRO; all but one yielded potable water.
- In 1998, post Pokhran atomic test, The Baba Atomic Research Centre (BARC) drew sub-soil water from a depth of 70 meters to confirm that the aquifers have not been affected by radioactive material. The analysis showed the water samples to be Himalayan glacial water of 8000 : 14000 years vintage!*

These two water samples confirmed the Himalayan origin of Sarasvati.

ii Historic Evidence

The discovery of Sarasvati also helped resolve a century-old puzzle. In 1869, archaeologist Alex Rogue found Himalayan alluvial deposits in the Gulf of Cambay. Neither Sabarmati nor Narmada, which flow into Cambay, has their origin in the Himalayas. Did at any time a Himalayan river flow into Cambay was the question that went abegging.*

2. Sarasvati flows as a copious river

i. Current Evidence

The colour images from the Indian remote sensing satellite (ISRO) clearly showed marks of palaeochannel as wide as 3 km to 12 km in the same stretch.

ii. Historic Evidence

In 1844, Major F. Makenson conducted a survey to connect Sindh with Delhi. He found a riverbed, which could conveniently accommodate an 8-lane highway from Sindh to Delhi.

iii. **Puranic Corroboration**

Not only did the events of the recent past acquire meaning, a number of mythological episodes also fitted into the jigsaw:

- Chandra, the moon god, is married to the 27 principal stars. Chandra is partial to the beautiful Rohini, earns the wrath of his father-in-law Daksha Prajapathi who curses him to wane. Chandra redeems himself from the curse by bathing in the Sarasvati.
- Traditions are like pickles - made long ago, but currently in use.
    - ❖ For centuries, devout Hindus have been going on pilgrimage to Prayag (Near Allahabad in present day Uttar Pradesh) to bathe in the confluence of Ganga, Yamuna and the "mythical" Sarasvati. The practice of dipping into the confluence and the name "Triveni-sangamam" (confluence of three streams) have endured despite the drying up of one of the three rivers.

---

* The Week (18/8/2002), Rebirth of Sarasvati, Dr. Karthikeya Sharma.

- Surnames in this country are based on location - Madgaonkar, Belgumwala, occupation - Palkiwala, Vaidya, education - Mukhopadhyaya, Bandhopadhyaya or their anglicised versions Mukherjee and Bannerjee, the part of Vedas followed - Shukla. An ascetic, as the Samskrit word Sanyasin makes it clear, is somebody who has renounced everything and somebody who is not attached to anything. If he has renounced everything, then what does he belong to, what belongs to him? He belongs to the culture with no reference to sub-sect of any kind. Our scriptures prescribe 10 names as appropriate for ascetics. Chiefs amongst this list of ten, which are in vogue even today, are Bharati, Sarasvati and Theerta. At some point in time were the words Bharati and Sarasvati being used as synonyms? This tradition of surnames of ascetics is another reservoir where Sarasvati has been preserved.

The two queries on the Aryan Invasion theory turned out to be valid:

- How come this civilisation originated in Central Asia and not on a river bank?	- The civilisation was born of river Sarasvati.
- How come 40% of the Harappan sites were far away from the Indus river?	- These sites were bang on the banks of the river Sarasvati.

Having seen the evidence for the river actually flowing, let us see whether there are reasons and evidences to support the next two events

3. Sarasvati dries up

Sarasvati possibly originated in the non-glacial part of the Himalayas. It was fed by Sutlej and Yamuna. A tectonic uplift diverted the course of Yamuna and Sutlej denying Sarasvati the flow of water. This would have caused a partial drying up of the river. There was a period of global aridity between 2000 BCE and 1800 BCE which completed the drying up of the river.

Puranic Corroboration

- Geologists tell us that post a tectonic upheaval, Sutlej not only changed course to become a tributary of the Sindhu, but also braided into several channels. My grandmother told me the story of Sage Vasishta who on the death of his son, attempting suicide by jumping into the Sarasvati River and the river, to save the sage, splitting into a hundred rivulets, thus acquiring the name "Sutudri" the one that split into hundred.*
- Rishi Kavasa-ailusa, a great scholar and a man of great penance, was excommunicated by the other Rishis, because he was a Dasi-putra (the son of a servant woman). In retaliation, the angry Ailusa walked away with Sarasvati. This is the final word in our Puranas on the drying up of Sarasvati.

4. The inhabitants on the banks of the river migrate

The drying up of Sarasvati caused the Harappans to move south-westwards. There is enough and more archaeological evidence to vouchsafe the relocation of the civilisation through migration. Sarasvati ceased to be a seagoing river around 3000 BCE, explaining why the 3rd millennium settlements on the banks of the Sarasvati river end in the Bahawalpur region of the Punjab and do not reach the sea.

---

* Vedavyasa, Mahabharata, Chaitraratha-parva, chapter 179.

ii. Historic Evidence

In 1940 Sir Auriel Stein looking for the Central Asian silk route stumbled on late Harappan sites on the dry bed of a river in Gujarat / Rajasthan. This shows that the Harappans had, at some stage, taken for granted the complete drying up of the river, ruled out its resurgence and built cities *on* the riverbed.

There are Harappan sites all the way to Cambay.

iii. Puranic Corroboration

There are episodes from the Mahabharata which appear to take off from this migration:

- There is the story of the king Yayati expelling his sons, and their migrating westward[*]
- Did Lord Krishna move from Mathura (near the present Delhi) with the entire Yadava clan to Dvaraka[#] (the present Western Gujarat) merely to avoid a conflict with the powerful Jarasanda or was it the compulsion of the drying Sarasvati also?

The Revised Postulate

The Indus Valley Civilisation did not come to an end by an alien invasion, but it re-located itself. The drying up of the river was the natural cause for the decline and the demise of the Harappan civilisation. "The abrupt end to the civilisation theory" has come to an abrupt end and the invaders from Central Asia invented to fill this gap no longer have a role to play. In one stroke, scores of books on Indian history have become, to put it mildly, obsolete and to put it plainly, wrong, as to the pre-historic period of Indian history.

The fact that nobody went looking for proof on the existence of Sarasvati and Sarasvati showed herself up entirely through serendipitous discoveries lends credence to the discovery of Sarasvati in a field in which scholarship is often vitiated by passion.

Therefore 3500 BCE, the date of the Harappan finds, marks not the beginning of the "Aryan Civilisation" but the point of maturity of the Harappan Civilisation.

The Past and The Future

To end with my first question, what quality or qualities would you say define India for you?

Melinda Gates: I think it's the amazing human spirit here; people want to lift themselves up.

Bill Gates: In some ways you think of it in terms of historical things and then in terms of new approaches for IT or embracing the future in this big way... in some ways it's the most futuristic and in some ways most historical country in the world and this aspect has a certain beauty to it because you don't want to really give up either one of those things.

The Hindu (10/12/05), Bill Gates and Melinda Gates in an interview during their visit to India.

---

* Bhagavata, Skanda 9, Chapter 18 & 19.

\# Bhagavata, Skanda 10, Chapter 52, Shloka 13.

We now come to the main concern of this book - the dating of the Vedas.

The Vedas are not a book like the Old Testament or the New Testament or the Zend-avesta, but a virtual library. The Vedas are not the product of a person or a period. They represent the contributions of many; they came into existence over a period of years.

- The three Vedas had preceded the Atharva-veda possibly by a thousand years.
- In each Veda, the Brahmanas and Aranyakas precede the Upanishad. While the body of Vedas is devoted to rituals and prayer, the Upanishads encapsulate philosophical thoughts of the greatest subtlety. The Rishis belonging to specific Shakhas of the Vedas added the Upanishads to their respective Shakhas, thus letting the Vedas grow. The ripening of thoughts between the Brahmana and Aranyaka and the Upanishad is there for all to see. The Samhitas must have preceded the Upanishad portion of the Vedas by several hundred years.

In this study, when we talk about the date of the Vedas, we are referring to the earlier parts of the work.

Based on the premise of the "Aryan Invasion", the Harappan 3500 BCE marked the beginning of the settlement. The alien invaders had to settle down in the new location, imbibe the local milieu and produce their literature - the Vedas. This easily could warrant two millennia. Therefore, it was surmised, reasonably, that the Vedas were "revealed" in 1500 BCE, give or take 500 years. In addition to Indologists like Max Muller, respected historians like A.L. Basham have gone by this 1500 BCE as the age of the Vedas and by implication the Vedic Civilisation.

Max Muller (1823 –1900)

Vedas and the Harappan Civilisation

"This great Vedic literature requires a great urban culture to explain it; just as the great Harappan urban culture requires a literature to explain it. Both come from the same region and cannot be separated."

-David Frawley

Young students of Samskrit are always cautioned against "Dooranvayam" the practice of bringing together two words, which are not adjacent to each other to obtain a (desired) meaning. This principle of simplicity in construct is relevant in reconstruction / theorising on history. The Harappan civilisation and the Vedas, both of which were found in the Gangetic plains, have been linked through a Central Asian tribe. The Aryan Invasion theory was a stretch, a stretched imagination of what could have happened 3500 years ago. Fortunately, the discovery of "Sarasvati" has undone this fiction.

From the date of the civilisation to that of its literature - the Vedas, in all fairness, one question need be raised and answered -**Whether the Vedas were produced during the Harappan days or after the southwestward migration.**

We will examine this case, following the method of the ancient preceptors; we will first look at the possibility of the "Poorva-paksha", the anti-thesis. Let us presume that the Vedas were produced not during the Harappan days, but during the post Harappan days, which would let the dating of the Vedas at 1500 BCE stand despite the invalidation of the Aryan Invasion theory.

If we assume, for a moment, that the Vedas had been composed in 1500 BCE, from then on till 500 BCE (the recorded advent of Buddhism), the following events had to be filled in

- The Puranic events of the pre-Ramayana period
- The Ramayana
- The Mahabharata and
- The decline of Vedic ritualism and the advent of Buddhism.

Thousand years is too small a period to fit in all these epochal events. The period from the Ramayana to the Mahabharata itself is estimated to be thousand years. Therefore it stands to reason that at least the early parts of the Vedic literature would have been composed in the banks of the river Sarasvati prior to the migration. **One date we can put on the Vedas is that they were certainly produced earlier to 3500 BCE.**

If the Vedas had been composed on the banks of the river Sarasvati, we still need answer the question; at what stage would the composition have taken place. In the Rig-veda-samhita, the oldest part of the Vedic literature, there is reference to Sarasavati.

प्रक्षोदसा धायसा सस्त्र	Pra kṣodasā dhāyasā sasra
एषा सरस्वती धरुणमायासी पूः।	eṣā sarasvatī dharuṇamāyasī pūḥ ।
प्रबाबधाना रथ्येव याति	Prabābadhānā rathyeva yāti
विश्वा अपो महिना सिन्धुरन्याः।।	viśvā apo mahinā sindhuranyāḥ ।।

Rig-veda, Mandala 7, Adhyaya 95, Anuvaka 6, Mantra 1

"This Sarasvati comes falling, crushing, nourishing, supporting and cleansing. She moves like a juggernaut. (This) supreme revered water goes to the other ocean".

The mighty Sarasvati River and its civilisation are referred to in the Rig-veda more than fifty times. It stands to reason that Sarasvati acquired this state of reverence during its hay days and not after it started drying.

Mahabharata to the Vedas

The Period of Mahabarata is established with a fair degree of certainty at 3000 BCE. From the Mahabarata to the Vedas we can work back through

- A dynasty of kings and
- A Lineage of Teachers

Dynasty of Kings

In the Mahabharata, the genealogy of kings upto Dharmaputra (the eldest of the Pandavas) is listed. Considering the period of Mahabharata as 3000 BCE, we can reach the period of Ramayana, the beginning of the Puranic period and from thereon to the Vedic period.

No	King	Generations	At 25 yrs King(BCE)	At 20 yrs King(BCE)	Event
1	Krishna		3000	3000	Mahabharata, the beginning of the Kaliyuga
2	Rama to Krishna	54	1350	1080	
3	Rama		4350	4080	Beginning of the Dwapara yuga
4	Bhagiratha to Rama	20	500	400	
5	Bhagiratha		4850	4480	Change in Ganga's course
6	Bhagiratha to Puranic Kings	25	625	500	
7	First of the Puranic Kings		5475	4980	

Lineage of Teachers

The Brihadaranyaka-upanishad talks of a lineage of 60 teachers from the Upanishadic period to Mahabharata.

Mahabharata	3000 BCE
Number of teachers	60
Upanishadic period	
- At 30 years / generation	4800 BCE
- At 35 years / generation	5100 BCE

The Rishis and teachers fought but mental battles and therefore enjoyed much longer tenures than the poor kings who provided them their patronage.

Since the Upanishads came into being 1000 years after the Samhitas, for the Samhita part of the Vedas, we reach a date of 6000 BCE.

The Astronomical Markers

Independent of history, astronomy can help place events of great vintage, specific to even a day, depending upon the uniqueness of the astronomical marker used.

The Vedas contain descriptions of unique astronomical events of their period. Since it is agreed that the knowledge to work back the positions of a time gone by was not available, the descriptions should relate to the Vedic period. It is conceivable that some dramatic astronomical events are remembered for decades by the community, narrated to each other and retained in memory. The description in the Vedas could, in which case, follow the astronomical events by a few decades, not much more.

To reach any kind of conclusion on the basis of astronomical evidence, the event should be so unique that the conjunction of planets described should not be capable of occurring over a span of four thousand years, as the range of time within which the Vedic period is debated is truly that long.

There are multiple astronomical markers which answer this requirement of uniqueness which place the Vedas at 6000 BCE or earlier.

Conclusion

Weighing the evidence on hand, 6000 BCE or earlier is the date that one is able to place on Vedic literature. I am certain we would be assailed for underestimating the antiquity of the Vedas, which would only be matched by the ferocity of the criticism that we have imported on to the Vedas an antiquity which is not there. We have attempted to approach this delicate task objectively and present our understanding in an easy-to-fathom fashion.

Caveat

When you are trying to figure out "what happened when, thousands of years ago", one mistake that you could make is to imagine that you have got it right this time. New evidences would be found; there would be more appropriate interpretations of new and existing evidences. The only thing that we can aspire for is to sift the available data and reach fair conclusions, which we have attempted.

The Traditional Perspective

Traditionally, the Vedas are believed to be of divine origin and also eternal, which would suggest that the Vedas have been there since the birth of the present universe. The traditional belief as to the age of the universe (43,20,000 years) happens to match with current "scientific understanding" as well.

The law givers - Manu and Kautilya

Inequality of birth was given religious sanction, and the lot of the humble was generally hard. Yet our overall impression is that in no other part of the ancient world were the relations of man and man, and of man and the state, so fair and humane. In no other early civilization were slaves so few in number, and in no other ancient lawbook are their rights so well protected as in the Arthasastra. No other ancient lawgiver proclaimed such noble ideals of fair play in battle as did Manu . In all her history of warfare, Hindu India has few tales to tell of cities put to the sword or of the massacre of non-combatants. To us the most striking feature of ancient Indian civilizaton is its humanity.

Dr. A.L Basham, The Wonder that was India, (2000) p. 8.

CIVIL ENGINEERING

Building Construction

Temple Architecture

Town Planning

Building Construction

Introduction

Quality of housing is a measure of development of early civilisations. Samskrit literature has several references to planning and construction of buildings - residential, royal, military and religious. The Atharva-veda, in the "Shala-nirmana-sukta" and the "Shala-sukta", contains several hymns on permanent constructions. That is how far we go back in terms of house construction.

In this segment, some examples are given on the different stages of construction, from testing the soil to erecting pillars.

Khajuraho Temple (9th century AD)

9.1.1 Building Construction - Soil Testing

पूर्वं भूमिं परिक्षेत पश्चात् वास्तु प्रकल्पयेत् ।।

Pūrvaṁ bhūmiṁ parikṣeta paścāt vāstu prakalpayet ।।

First test the earth (site); after that plan the construction.

वल्मीकेन समायुक्ता भूमिरस्थिगणैस्तु या ।।
रन्ध्रान्विता च भूर्वर्ज्या गतीघेश्च समन्विता ।।

Valmīkena samāyuktā bhūmirasthigaṇaistu yā ।।
Randhrānvitā ca bhūrvarjyā gatīgheśca samanvitā ।।

Land with anthills, skeletons, full of pits and craters should be avoided.

वर्णगन्धारसाकारादिशब्दस्पर्शनैरपि ।
परिक्ष्यैव यथायोग्यं गृह्णीयाद् द्रव्यमुत्तमम् ।।

Varṇagandhārasākārādiśabdas-parśanairapi ।
Parikṣyaiva yathāyogyaṁ gṛhṇīyād dravyamuttamam ।।

After examining the colour, smell, taste, shape, sound and touch (of the soil) buy the best material as found suitable.

यावत्तत्र जलं दृष्टं खनेत्तावत्तु भूतले ।।

Yāvattatra jalaṁ dṛṣṭaṁ khanettāvattu bhūtale ।।

Till water is seen there, (one) should dig the ground.

रत्निमात्रमधे गर्ते परीक्ष्य खातपूरणे ।।
अधिके श्रियमाप्नोति न्यूने हानिं समे समम् ।।

Ratnimātramadhe garte parīkṣya khātapūraṇe ।।
Adhike śriyamāpnoti nyūne hāniṁ same samam ।।

It (soil) should be tested by digging a pit of 1 arm length and refilling it (with the same soil). If (soil is) more, one will beget prosperity; if short, one will beget loss; if equal, it is normal.

Source

Matsya-purāṇam, Adhyāyaḥ 253, Ślokaḥ 11 (Puranic period)

Vāstu-śāstram, Ślokaḥ 5 Viśvakarmā (6th century AD)

Bhṛgu-saṁhitā, Adhyāyaḥ 4 (Post-vedic period)

Kāśyapa-śilpaḥ, Adhyāyaḥ 4 (Post-vedic period)

Notes

If some soil is left after filling the pit (in digging which, the soil was found), it shows the scope for compaction of the sand and such a soil is considered desirable. This testing procedure mentioned in the 5th Century BCE text is in vogue to this day.

9.1.2 Building Construction - Making of Bricks

(इष्टकासङ्ग्रहणम्) ऊषरं पाण्डुरं कृष्णचिक्कणं ताम्रपुल्लकम् ॥ मृदश्चतस्रस्तास्वेव गृह्णीयात् ताम्रपुल्लकम् ।	(Iṣṭakāsaṅgrahaṇam) Ūṣaram pāṇḍuraṁ kṛṣṇacikkaṇaṁ tāmrapullakam ॥ Mṛdaścatasrastāsveva gṛhṇīyāt tāmrapullakam ।

(The making of bricks)

Salty, off-white, black and smooth, red and granulated, these are the four kinds of clay.

अशर्कराश्ममूलास्थिलोष्टं सतनुवालुकम् ॥ एकवर्णं सुखस्पर्शमिष्टं लोष्टेष्टकादिषु ।	Aśarkarāśmamūlāsthiloṣṭaṁ satanuvālukam ॥ Ekavarṇaṁ sukhasparśamiṣṭaṁ loṣṭeṣṭakādiṣu ।

Clay suitable for making bricks and tiles must be free from gravel, pebbles, roots and bones and must be soft to touch.

मृत्खण्डं पूरयेदग्रे जानुदघ्ने जले ततः ॥ आलोड्य मर्दयेत् पद्भ्यां चत्वारिंशत् पुनः पुनः ।	Mṛtkhaṇḍaṁ pūrayedagre jānudaghne jale tataḥ ॥ Ālodya mardayet padbhyāṁ catvāriṁśat punaḥ punaḥ ।

Then fill the clods of clay in knee-deep water; then having mixed, pound with the feet forty times repeatedly.

क्षीरद्रुमकदम्बाम्राभयाक्षत्वग्जलैरपि ॥ त्रिफलाम्बुभिरासिक्त्वा मर्दयेन्मासमात्रकम् ।	Kṣīradrumakadambāmrābhayākṣa-tvagjalairapi ॥ Triphalāmbubhirāsiktvā mardayenmāsamātrakam ।

After soaking in the sap of fig, kadamba, mango, abhaya and aksha and also in the water of myrobalan for three months, pound (the clay).

IS 1077

The area covered by the Harappan culture therefore extended from some 950 miles from north to south, and the pattern of its civilisation was so uniform that even the bricks were usually of the same size and shape from one end of it to the other.

Dr. A.L. Basham, The Wonder that was India (2003), p. 14.

Most interesting are their dimensions; while found in 15 different sizes, their length, width and thickness are always in the ratio of 4:2:1

Mr. Dick Teresi, Lost Discoveries, edn.Simon & Schuster (2003), p. 60.

चतुष्पञ्चषडष्टाभिमात्रैस्तद्धिद्विगुणायताः ॥	Catuṣpañcaṣaḍaṣṭābhirmātraistaddhidviguṇāyatāḥ ॥
व्यासार्धार्धत्रिभागैकतीव्रा मध्ये परेऽपरे ।	Vyāsārdhārdhatribhāgaikatīvrā madhye pare'pare ।
इष्टका बहुशः शोष्याः समदग्धाः पुनश्च ताः ॥	Iṣṭakā bahuśaḥ śoṣyāḥ samadagdhāḥ punaśca tāḥ ॥

These (bricks) are in four, five, six and eight unit (widths) and twice that in length. Their depth in the middle and in the two ends (is) one fourth or one-third the width. Again these bricks should normally be dried and baked.

एकद्वित्रिचतुर्मासमतीत्यैव विचक्षणः ।	Ekadvitricaturmāsamatītyaiva vicakṣaṇaḥ ।
जले प्रक्षिप्य यत्नेन जलादुद्धृत्य तत् पुनः ॥	Jale prakṣipya yatnena jalāduddhṛtya tat punaḥ ॥

The experts, only after one, two, three or four months, again throwing (the baked bricks) in water, and extracting (them) from the water with effort, (will put the brick to use).

Source

Maya-matam, Kalā-mūla-śāstram, Ślokaḥ 114-120 Kapila-vātsyāyanaḥ (6th Century AD)

5000 Year Warranty

The altars were built of bricks. It is no great surprise, that the Vedic Indians built bricks which could last not years but thousands of years.

The ruins of Harappa contributed to a hundred mile railway line between Multan and Lahore in the nineteenth century. The British dug up Harappa for its bricks, which they used as ballast on the rail bed. The bricks speak a story greater than ballast. The Harappans learned to exploit the annual flooding of their farmland to grow crops without need for plowing, fertilization, or irrigation. To do so they had to control the flooding with flood walls, so they developed kiln fired bricks, less permeable to rain and floodwater than mud bricks. Harappan bricks contain no straw or binding material and are still in usable shape after five thousand years.

Mr. Dick Teresi, Lost Discoveries, edn. Simon & Schuster (2003), p. 60.

9.1.3 Building Construction - Mortar

पञ्चांशं माषयूषं स्यान्नवाष्टांशं गुडं दधि ॥ आज्यं द्व्यंशं तु सप्तांशं क्षीरं चर्म षडंशकम् ।	Pañcāṁśaṁ māṣayūṣaṁ syānnavāṣṭāṁśaṁ guḍaṁ dadhi ॥ Ājyam dvyaṁśam tu saptāṁśam kṣīram carma ṣaḍaṁśakam ।

There should be 5 parts extract of beans, nine and eight parts molasses* and curd* (respectively). Clarified butter (ghee) 2 parts, 7 parts milk, hide (extract) 6 parts.

* Molasses - A thick treacle that drains from sugar

* Curd - Milk thickened or coagulated by acid

त्रैफलं दशभागं स्यान्नालिकेरं युगांशकम् ॥ क्षौद्रमेकांशकं त्र्यंशं कदलीफलमिष्यते ।	Traiphalaṁ daśabhāgaṁ syānnālikeraṁ yugāṁśakam ॥ Kṣaudramekāṁśakaṁ tryaṁśaṁ kadalīphalamiṣyate ।

There should be 10 parts of myrobalan*. Coconut two parts, honey one part. Three parts plantain are desired.

*Myrobalan - The astringent fruit of certain Indian mountain species of Terminalia (combretaceae): a variety of Plum.

लब्धे चूर्णे दशांशे तु युञ्जीतव्यं सुबन्धनम् ॥ सर्वेषामधिकं शस्तं गुडं च दधि दुग्धकम् ।	Labdhe cūrṇe daśāṁśe tu yuñjītavyaṁ subandhanam ॥ Sarveṣāmadhikaṁ śastaṁ guḍaṁ ca dadhi dugdhakam ।

In the powder (thus) obtained, 1/10th lime should be added. Larger quantity than others of molasses, curd and milk is best.

चूर्णद्व्यंशं करालं मधुघृतकदलीनालिकेरं च माषं । शुक्तेस्तोयं च दुग्धं दधिगुडसहितं त्रैफलं तत् क्रमेण ।	Cūrṇadvyaṁśaṁ karālaṁ madhughṛtakadalīnālikeraṁ ca māṣaṁ Śuktestoyaṁ ca dugdhaṁ dadhiguḍasahitaṁ traiphalaṁ tat krameṇa ।

In two parts of lime, (add) karaka, honey, clarified butter, plantain, coconut and bean. When dry (add) water, milk, curd, myrobalan along with molasses gradually.

लब्धे चूर्णे शतांशेऽंशकमिदमधुना चानुवृद्धिं प्रकुर्या- देतद् बन्धं दृषत्सादृशमिति कथितं तन्त्रविद्भिर्मुनीन्द्रैः ॥	Labdhe cūrṇe śatāṁśeऽṁśakamidamadhunā cānuvṛddhiṁ prakuryādetad bandhaṁ dṛṣatsādṛśamiti kathitaṁ tantravidbhirmunīndraiḥ ॥

Now in the powder (thus) obtained, grow one in hundred part. It (the compound) is said by leading thinkers who know the technology as rocklike.

Source

Maya-matam, Kalā-mūla-śāstram, Kapila-vātsyāyanaḥ (6th Century AD)

9.1.4 Building Construction - Assembling Pillars

स्तम्भसन्धयः
मेषयुद्धं त्रिखण्डं च सौभद्रं चार्धपाणिकम् ।
महावृत्तं च पश्चैते स्तम्भानां सन्धयः स्मृताः ॥

Stambhasandhayaḥ
Meṣayuddhaṁ trikhaṇḍam ca saubhadram cārdhapāṇikam ।
Mahāvṛttam ca pañcaite stambhānām sandhayaḥ smṛtāḥ ॥

Assembly of Pillars: It is said that there are five types of assemblies suitable for pillars; these are Meṣayuddha, Trikhaṇḍa, Saubhadra, Ardhapaṇi and Mahāvṛtta.

स्वव्यासकर्णमध्यर्धद्विगुणं वा तदायतम् ।
त्र्यंशैकं मध्यमशिखं मेषयुद्धं प्रकीर्तितम् ॥

Svavyāsakarṇamadhyardhadviguṇam vā tadāyatam ।
Tryaṁśaikaṁ madhyamaśikhaṁ meṣayuddhaṁ prakīrtitam ॥

When there is a central tenon* (with a width) a third (that of the pillar) and a length twice or two and half times its width, this is Mesa-yuddha (mortise* and tenon) assembly.

* Tenon - The projection at the end of a piece of wood etc

* Mortise - A hole to receive a tenon.

स्वस्त्याकारं त्रिखण्डं स्यात् सत्रिचूलि त्रिखण्डकम् ।
पार्श्वे चतुःशिखोपेतं सौभद्रमिति संज्ञितम् ॥

Svastyākāraṁ trikhaṇḍaṁ syāt satricūli trikhaṇḍakam ।
Pārśve catuḥśikhopetam saubhadramiti saṁjñitam ॥

In the Trikhaṇḍa assembly, there are three mortises and three tenons arranged as a Svastikā. The assembly called Saubhadra comprises four peripheral tenons.

अर्धं छित्वा तु मूलेऽग्रे चान्योन्याभिनिवेशनात् ।
अर्धपाणिरिति प्रोक्तो गृहीतघनमानतः ॥

Ardham chitvā tu mūleSgre cānyonyābhiniveśanāt ।
Ardhapāṇiriti prokto gṛhītaghanamānataḥ ॥

An assembly is called Ardhapaṇi (scarf joint) when half the lower and half the upper pieces are cut to size according to the thickness chosen (for the pillar).

अर्धवृत्तशिखं मध्ये तन्महावृत्तमुच्यते ।
वृत्ताकृतिषु पादेषु प्रयुञ्जीत विचक्षणः ॥

Ardhavṛttaśikham madhye tanmahāvṛttamucyate ।
Vṛttākṛtiṣu pādeṣu prayuñjīta vicakṣaṇaḥ ॥

When there is a semicircular section tenon at the centre, the assembly is called Mahāvṛtta, the well advised man employs this for circular section pillars.

स्तम्भानां स्तम्भदैर्घ्यार्धादधः सन्धानमाचरेत् ।
स्तम्भमध्योर्ध्वसन्धिश्चेद् विपदामास्पदं सदा ॥
कुम्भमण्ड्यादिसंयुक्तं सन्धानं सम्पदां पदम् ।
सालङ्कारे शिलास्तम्भे यथायोगं तथाचरेत् ॥

Stambhānām stambhadairghyārdhādadhaḥ sandhānamācaret ।
Stambhamadhyordhvasandhiśced vipadāmāspadam sadā ॥
Kumbhamaṇḍyādisaṁyuktam sandhānam sampadām padam ।
Sālaṅkāre śilāstambhe yathāyogam tathācaret ॥

The assembling of (the different parts of) a pillar should be done below the middle and any assembling done above will be a source of accident; (however) the assembly which brings together the bell-capital and the abacus gives the certainty of success. When a stone pillar, with its decoration, (is to be assembled) this should be done according to the specific case.

स्थितस्य पादपस्याङ्गप्रवृत्तिवशतो विदुः ।
ऊर्ध्वमूलमधश्चाग्रं सर्वसम्पद्विनाशनम् ॥

Sthitasya pādapasyāṅgapravṛttivaśato viduḥ ।
Ūrdhvamūlamadhaścāgram sarvasampadvināśanam ॥

It should be known that the assembling of the vertical pieces is done according to the disposition of the different parts of the tree; if the bottom is above and the top is below, all chance of success is lost.

Source

Maya-matam, Kalā-mūla-śāstram Ślokaḥ 29-37, Kapila-vātsyāyanaḥ (6th Century AD)

Temples of Tamilnadu

The hall forming part of the Thiruveezhimizhalai temple in Tamilnadu has an arch of approximately 50 feet width. This arch is a standing (pun intended) witness to the construction capability of our ancestors.

In Kodangai in Tamilnadu in South India, there is a temple for the god named Aavudayar. In that temple, you can see a rock ground finely like a sheet of paper. This temple is another evidence of not only the skills but also the tools that people had years ago in temple construction.

Deivatthin Kural (Tamil), Volume 1, p. 458 Of His Holiness Shri. Chandrashekharendra Saraswati Swami of Kanchi, Tamilnadu, India.

Temple Architecture

Introduction

Temples and stupas from Sanchi in Bihar to Tanjore in Tamilnadu vouch for the heights ancient India had scaled in architecture. Several references to architecture are found in Samskrit literature - Vastu-shastra texts like Maya-mata, Manasara, Samarangana-sutradhara, Puranas like Matsya-purana, Agni-purana and secular literature like Brihat-samhita and Arthashastra.

In this segment, a few examples are given on:

- Selecting of stone for the construction of temples and monuments
- Materials and specification of idols and
- The tools used in construction

9.2.1 Temple Architecture - Selection of stone

शिला तद्देशे लोकज्ञाने षड्धा प्रथिता, हिरण्यरेखिका, समवर्णा, ताम्रा, धातुपुटिता, वज्रलब्धा सैकतालिकेति ।

Śilā taddeśe lokajñāne ṣaḍdhā prathitā, hiraṇyarekhikā, samavarṇā, tāmrā, dhātupuṭitā, vajralabdhā saikatāliketi ।

In this land, six types of stones are in common knowledge, being

Hiraṇya-rekhikā	=	Of golden lines
Sama-varnā	=	Of uniform colour
Tāmrā	=	Copper coloured
Dhatu-puṭitā	=	Mineral layered
Vajra-labdhā	=	Diamond like
Saikatālikā	=	Sand stone.

यदा हिरण्यरेखा कुटिला सोऽवलक्षणः । सा प्रतिमार्थहीना विरूपं प्रददाति । तद्दर्शनेन विकल्पभावः प्रभवति । दर्शनादेता अर्थहीना उच्यन्ते, वदन्ति, भवन्तीति ।

एतदर्थं प्रतिमावैलक्षण्यं भवति ।

Yadā hiraṇyarekhā kuṭilā so'valakṣaṇaḥ ।
Sā pratimārthahīnā virūpaṁ pradadāti ।
Taddarśanena vikalpabhāvaḥ prabhavati ।
Darśanādetā arthahīnā ucyante, vadanti, bhavantīti ।
Etadarthaṁ pratimāvailakṣaṇyam bhavati ।

When the golden lines are crooked, it (the stone) is ugly. It is unfit for idols. It gives disfigurement. Its sight causes distorted imagination. By visual inspection, these (stones) are talked of as and are purposeless. Therefore, the idol acquires disfigurement.

समवर्णा यदा पूर्णशैलमेकवर्णं कृष्णं कृष्णपिङ्गलं हारिद्रं वा मुख्यप्रतिमार्थं ध्येयं सा समवर्णा ।

Samavarṇā yadā pūrṇaśailamekavarṇaṁ kṛṣṇaṁ kṛṣṇapiṅgalaṁ hāridraṁ vā mukhyapratimārthaṁ dhyeyaṁ sā samavarṇā ।

When a Samavarṇā stone is entirely of a single colour, be it black, dark brown or turmeric yellow, that stone should be thought of for the principal idol.

कठिनतमगाढपिङ्गलशिला न ध्येया ।

यदा शैलं भित्त्याकृतेरपृथक् प्रतिमाशालार्थं तद् ध्येयम् । शैलं पृथक्त्वेन हीनं भवति ।

यत्र केवलं लीलाविग्रहा निवसन्ति भित्त्यङ्गे, इति ।

Kaṭhinatamagāḍha-piṅgalaśilā na dhyeyā ।

Yadā śailaṁ bhittyākṛterapṛthak pratimāśālārthaṁ tad dhyeyam । Śailaṁ pṛthaktvena hīnaṁ bhavati ।

Yatra kevalaṁ līlāvigrahā nivasanti bhittyaṅge, iti ।

Very hard stone of copper-red colour should not be considered. When the stone is not severed from the rock, it can be used for sculpture halls. When the stone is separated, it becomes deficient. When only mythological scenes exist in the walls (these stones can be used).

शिला धातुपुटिता धूम्रवर्णा व्रणोपेता रूपार्थं घोरेति ।

Śilā dhātupuṭitā dhūmravarṇā vraṇopetā rūpārthaṁ ghoreti ।

Dhātupuṭitā stone, smoke coloured or with pores is awful for idol making.

शैलान्तरे स्तराभ्यन्तरे कोमलरसबद्धा रेखाः सन्ति याः पीतप्रभाः सदाधमा भवन्ति श्रेष्ठैः शिल्पकारैः ।

Śailāntare starābhyantare komalarasabaddhā rekhāḥ santi yāḥ pītaprabhāḥ sadādhamā bhavanti śreṣṭhaiḥ śilpakāraiḥ ।

According to good sculptors, stones which are bright yellow and have in them or between their layers soft mineral lines, become inferior.

सैकतालिकशिला यूपयोनिमिथुनस्तम्भ वृषस्तम्भाकुण्डार्थं विशिष्टा, सा रूपार्थं ग्राह्या, तज्ज्ञानलब्धस्थापकाः समुपतिष्ठन्ति जनलोके सम्पन्ना महीयन्ते ।

Saikatālikaśilā yūpayonimithunastambha vṛṣastambhākuṇḍārthaṁ viśiṣṭā, sā rūpārthaṁ grāhyā, tajjñānalabdhasthāpakāḥ samupatiṣṭhanti janaloke sampannā mahīyante ।

Sandstone is especially good for sacrificial posts, altars, double-pillars and furnaces. It is (also) to be taken for making images. The sculptors who possess this knowledge are found among people and are greatly honoured as accomplished.

Source

Vāstusūtra-upaniṣad, Śaila-bhedanam, Sūtram 9 (Post-vedic period)

Etymology

Rasabaddha-rekhikā = Lines bound by minerals = Mineral lines.

9.2.2 Temple Architecture - Idols

सौवर्णी राजती वापि ताम्री रत्नमयी तथा ।
शैली दारुमयी चापि लोहसधमयी तथा ॥
रीतिका धातुयुक्ता वा ताम्रकांस्यमयी तथा ।
शुभदारुमयी वापि देवतार्चा प्रशस्यते ॥

Sauvarṇī rājatī vāpi tāmrī ratnamayī tathā ।
Śailī dārumayī cāpi lohasadhamayī tathā ॥
Rītikā dhātuyuktā vā tāmrakāṁsyamayī tathā ।
Śubhadārumayī vāpi devatārcā praśasyate ॥

The worship of idols made of gold, silver, copper, gems, stone, wood, metal, or alloys, alloys with iron, of copper and brass, and of bronze is praised.

प्रतिमामुखमानेन नवभागान् प्रकल्पयेत् ।
चतुरङ्गुला भवेद्ग्रीवा भागेन हृदयं पुनः ॥
नाभिस्तस्मादधः कार्या भागेनैकेन शोभना ।
निम्नत्वे विस्तरत्वे च अङ्गुलं परिकीर्तितम् ॥

Pratimāmukhamānena navabhāgān prakalpayet ।
Caturaṅgulā bhavedgrīvā bhāgena hṛdayaṁ punaḥ ॥
Nābhistasmādadhaḥ kāryā bhāgenaikena śobhanā ।
Nimnatve vistaratve ca aṅgulaṁ parikīrtitam ॥

Make idols in nine parts starting with the face. The neck should be 4 fingers width; then the chest a part. Below that the beautiful navel famous for its depth and expansiveness of a finger width should be made with one part.

नाभिरधस्तथामेढं भागेनैकेन कल्पयेत् ।
द्विभागेनायतावूरू जानुनी चतुरङ्गुले ॥
जङ्घे द्विभागे विख्यति पादौ च चतुरङ्गुलैः ।
चतुर्दशाङ्गुलस्तद्वन्मौलिरस्य प्रकीर्तितः ॥

Nābhiradhastathāmeḍham bhāgenaikena kalpayet ।
Dvibhāgenāyatāvūrū jānunī caturaṅgule ॥
Jaṅghe dvibhāge vikhyati pādau ca caturaṅgulaiḥ ।
Caturdaśāṅgulastadvanmaulirasya prakīrtitaḥ ॥

Build the genitals below the navel in one part. The thigh and the knee come in two parts in four fingers width. The legs are known in two parts, the feet in 4 fingers width. Similarly the crown of 14 fingers is well known.

Source

Matsya-purāṇam, Pratimā-nirmāṇa-varṇanam, Ślokaḥ 26-29 (5th century BCE)

9.2.3 Temple Architecture - Chisels and carving

खनित्रपञ्चकं श्रेष्ठम् ॥

भेदास्तु लाञ्जी, लाङ्गली, गृध्रदन्ती, सूचीमुखा वज्रा इति, सर्वे आयसा द्विविधा भवन्ति क्षीणाः प्रशस्ताश्च, मुषलधरुभे मुषलदण्डेन खनित्रं घातयन्ति प्रयोजयन्ति शिलाभेदने तत् । सर्वास्त्राणि तीक्ष्णानि गवाम्बुपुटितानि । ततः इङ्गिडालेपितानि चर्मशाणितानि च ।

Khanitrapañcakaṁ śreṣṭham ॥

Bhedāstu lāñjī, lāṅgalī, gṛdhradantī, sūcīmukhā, vajrā iti, sarve āyasā dvividhā bhavanti kṣīṇāḥ praśastāśca, muṣaladharubhe muṣaladaṇḍena khanitraṁ ghātayanti prayojayanti śilābhedane tat । Sarvāstrāṇi tīkṣṇāni, gavāmbupuṭitāni । Tataḥ iṅgiḍālepitāni carmaśāṇitāni ca ।

Five types of chisels are good. The different varieties being lāñjī (biting), lāṅgalī (plough like), gṛdhradantī (like vulture teeth), sūcīmukhā (needle tipped) and vajra (diamond like), all of steel and each one of two types narrow and broad.

(Men) beat the chisel on the long mallet, with the short mallet*(such chisel, people) use for breaking stone. All instruments are sharpened, dipped in cow's urine and then smeared with ingida (asafetida) oil and whetted in leather.

* Mallet - A small wooden hammer

शिल्पकाराः प्रलेपयन्ति द्रावकरसम् ॥

शङ्खद्राव–कुष्ठरस–सैन्धवखर्पर–उकत्सवल्कलचूर्णेन सहितं शिलाद्रवणार्थमेवं रसचतुष्टयम् अनेन मन्त्रेण दशाह–मर्दनान्ते वैताने खनित्रं प्रयोजयन्ति खननमाचरन्ति भद्रेण स्थापकाः ।

Śilpakārāḥ pralepayanti drāvakarasam ॥

Śaṅkhadrāvakuṣṭharasa-saindhavakharpara-ukatsavalkalacūrṇena sahitaṁ śilādravaṇārtha-mevam rasacatuṣṭayaṁ anena mantreṇa daśāhamardanānte vaitāne khanitraṁ prayojayanti khananamācaranti bhadreṇa sthāpakāḥ ।

Sculptors apply a softening mixture. Shell-solvent, Kuṣṭharasa, sea salt and the powder of the bark of the ukatsa tree are thus the four fluids for the softening of stones. With this plan, after immersing (the chisel) for 10 days, sculptors use the chisel in sacrificial rites and also dig with ease.

Source

Vāstusūtra-upaniṣad, Sūtram 6, 8, Śaila-bhedanam (Post-vedic period).

Notes

Kusta-rasa = Costus specious or arabicus.

In the forests of the Mahendra mountain a tree is found whose bark is called stone-breaking i.e. Prastara-bhedi.

Introduction

There are several aspects of town planning - construction of roads in towns and in mountainous terrain, planning the course of roads and regulating the construction of houses - like mandatory spacing between houses. There are examples of each of these in ancient Samskrit literature.

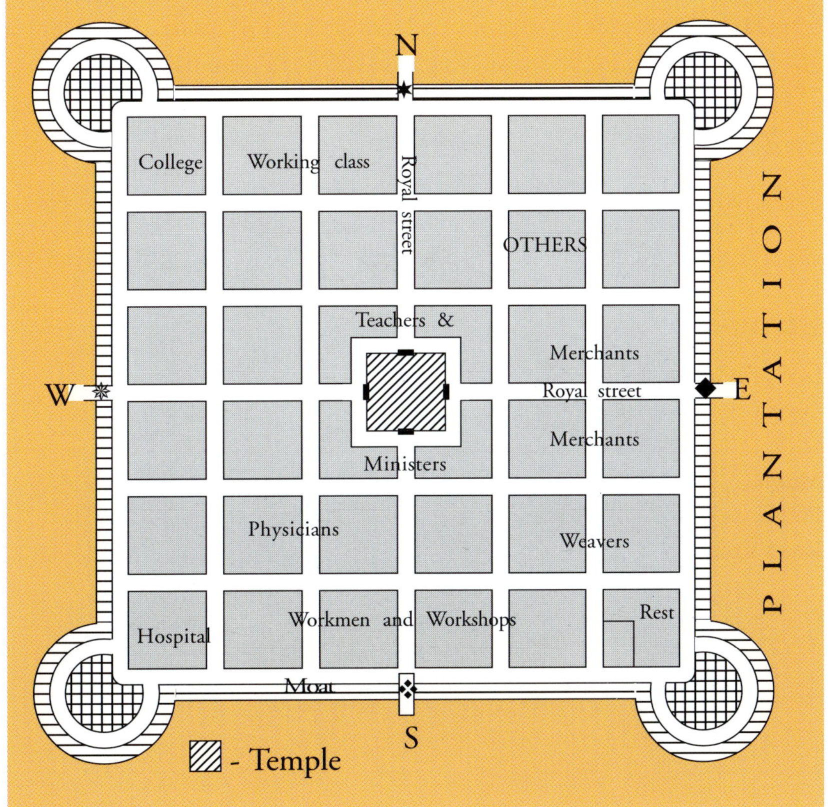

9.3.1 Town Planning - Roads

कूर्मपृष्ठा मार्गभूमः कार्यग्राम्यैः सुसेतुका ।
कुर्यान्मार्गान् पाश्र्वखातान् निर्गमार्थे जलस्य च ।

Kūrmapṛṣṭhā mārgabhūmiḥ kāryagrāmyaiḥ susetukā ।
Kuryānmārgān pārśvakhātān nirgamārthe jalasya ca ।

The surface of a road should be made like the back of a tortoise, along with culverts by the villagers. The kings should dig drains in the sides for the drainage of the water.

मार्गान्सुधाशार्करैर्विघट्टितान् प्रतिवत्सरम् ।
अभियुक्ता निरुद्योगैः कुर्याद् ग्राम्यजनैर्नृपाः ॥

Mārgānsudhāśarkarairvighaṭṭītan prativatsaram ।
Abhiyuktā nirudyogaiḥ kuryāt grāmyajanairnṛpāḥ ॥

Diligent kings should, every year, with unemployed villagers, break the roads and bind them with lime and gravel.

चतुर्दण्डान्तरा रथ्याः । राजमार्ग-द्रोणमुख-स्थानीय-राष्ट्रविवीतपथाः संयानीय-व्यूह-श्मशान-ग्राम-पथाश्चाष्टदण्डाः । चतुर्दण्डः सेतुवनपथः । द्विदण्डो हस्तिक्षेत्रपथः । पञ्चारत्नयो रथपथश्चत्वारः पशुपथो द्वौ क्षुद्रपशु-मनुष्यपथः ।

Caturdaṇḍāntarā rathyāḥ । Rājamārga-droṇamukha-sthānīya-rāṣṭra-vivītapathāḥ saṁyānī-vyūha-śmaśāna-grāma-pathāścāṣṭadaṇḍāḥ । Caturdaṇḍaḥ setuvanapathaḥ । Dvidaṇḍo hastikṣetra-pathaḥ । Pañcāratnayo rathapathaścatvāraḥ paśupatho dvau kṣudrapaśu-manuṣyapathaḥ ।

Roads for carts (should be of) 4 dandas width. Royal path, national, state and local highways, roads (leading to) pastureland, roads for groups carrying dead bodies to the cremation ground (should be of) 8 dandas. Bridges and forest paths 4 dandas. Paths for chariots 5 aratni. Paths for cattle 4 aratni. Paths for small animals and men 4 aratni.

Source

Śukra-nītiḥ, Adhyāyaḥ 1, Ślokaḥ 165-166, Śukrācāryaḥ (Post-vedic period)

Arthaśāstram, Adhikaraṇam 2, Prakaraṇam 20, Adhyāyaḥ 4, Kauṭilyaḥ (4th century BCE)

Etymology

Droṇa-mukha-patha:

Droṇa	=	A lake of 400 poles area
Mukha	=	entry point
Patha	=	roads.

Road from several (400) towns = highway.

9.3.2 Town Planning - Ghat Road

प्रतोली मानगणना द्विगुणं त्रिगुणं तु वा । कुल्या वेतुयुतं वापि महासेतुयुतं क्वचित् ॥	Pratolī mānagaṇanā dviguṇam triguṇaṁ tu vā । Kulyā vetuyutaṁ vāpi mahāsetuyutaṁ kvacit ॥

(The mountain roads) should be twice or thrice as broad (as the roads in plains). Streams could have small or large bridges.

पक्षयोस्सलिलस्रावो घनकल्पनमेदुरः । महाजलगतिस्स्यादप्यादुरे दूरतरेऽपि वा ॥ नदीमेलनकल्पा वा चाब्धिमेलनकल्पनम् । मध्योन्नतिः पार्श्वनिम्नं घनकल्पनसंयुतम् ॥	Pakṣayossalilasrāvo ghanakalpanameduraḥ । Mahājalagatissyādapyādure dūratare'pi vā ॥ Nadīmelanakalpā vā cābdhimelanakalpanam । Madhyonnatiḥ pārśvanimnaṁ ghanakalpana saṁyutam ॥

The draining of (rain) water from the sides of the culvert (should be) to a fast flowing river nearby or farther away. Or to a river or reservoir. The culvert should be high in the middle and low in the sides.

शिलाखण्डैः कुम्भिखण्डैर्घनमेंदूरकल्पनम् । गजपादैरश्वपादैर्मर्दितं च दृढीकृतम् ॥	Śilākhaṇḍaiḥ kumbhikhaṇḍair-ghanamedūrakalpanam ॥ Gajapādairaśvapādairmarditaṁ ca dṛḍhīkṛtam ॥

The road on the culvert must be made hard by compressing stones and brickbats under the legs of elephants and horses.

Source

Vāstu-śāstram, Adhyāyaḥ 68, Mārga-lakṣaṇam, Ślokaḥ 4-7, Viśvakarmā (6th century AD)

Western Reference

John Loudon McAdam (born September 21, 1756 in Ayr, Scotland; died November 26, 1836 in Moffat, Scotland) was a Scottish engineer and road-builder. In 1823 AD, he invented a new process, "macadamization", for building roads with a smooth hard surface that would be more durable and less muddy than dirt-based tracks.

9.3.3 Town Planning - Bund Constructions

चतुर्दण्डावकृष्टपरिखायाः षड्दण्डोच्छ्रितमवरुद्धं तद्विगुणविष्कम्भं खाताद्वप्रं कारयेत् ऊर्ध्वचयं मञ्चपृष्ठं कुम्भकुक्षिकं वा हस्तिभिर्गोभिश्च क्षुण्णं कण्टकिगुल्मविषवल्लीप्रतानवन्तं पांसुशेषेण वास्तुच्छिद्रं वा पूरयेत् ।

Caturdaṇḍāvakṛṣṭaparikhāyāḥ ṣaḍdaṇḍocchritamavaruddhaṁ taddviguṇaviṣkambhaṁ khātādvapraṁ kārayet ūrdhvacayaṁ mañcapṛṣṭhaṁ kumbhakukṣikaṁ vā hastibhirgobhiśca kṣuṇṇaṁ kaṇṭakigulmaviṣavallīpratānavantaṁ pāṁsuśeṣeṇa vāstucchidraṁ vā pūrayet ।

For a moat[1] of 4 danda depth, from the moat a rampart[2] of 6 dandas height should be built. The support beam (of the rampart) should be twice (the height). It (the rampart) could be

- Urdhvacaya a trapezoidal[3] section, having small topwidth, increasing towards bottom
- Mancapṛṣṭha one of constant width or
- Kumbhakukṣika one having more width at mid-height.

By elephants and bullocks (the earth) should be compacted.

Thorny bush, poisonous low spreading creepers (should be planted). With the remaining earth, fill the cracks in the construction.

[1] Moat - A deep trench around a castle or fortified place.

[2] Rampart - A flat topped defensive mound.

[3] Trapezoidal - Four legged.

Source

Arthaśāstram, Adhikaraṇam 2, Prakaraṇam 19, Adhyāyaḥ 3, Ślokaḥ 1 Kauṭilyaḥ (4th century BCE)

Etymology

Ūrdhvacayam	=	Ūrdhva + Cayam = lump in the top.
	=	Trapezodial section having small top width.
Mañcapṛṣṭham	=	Mañca + Pṛṣṭham = Back of a throne
	=	Straight and of even width.
Kumbhakukṣikam	=	Kumbha + Kukṣi
	=	Like the interior of a pot, burgeoning in the middle.

The Dam

The Grand Anicut, Kallanai, located on Cauvery River in Tamil Nadu, is the oldest dam in the world that is still in use today. This masonry dam was built in the 2nd century AD by Chola king Karikalan. It was remodelled and fitted with sluice gates in 1899 - 1902.

9.3.4 Town Planning - Svastika Plan

स्वस्तिकमुदितं ग्रामे यथा तथा स्वस्तिकं विद्यात् ।
प्रागुत्तरमुखमार्गाः षट्षडभीष्टास्तु तद्बाह्ये ॥

Svastikamuditaṁ grāme yathā tathā svastikaṁ vidyāt ।
Prāguttaramukhamārgāḥ ṣaṭṣaḍabhīṣṭāstu tadbāhye ॥

A village known as swastikam shall have a svastika road formation (meeting of four roads). Six streets go east and north. The roads reaching these six are in the outside.

प्रागिव मार्गोपेतं वीथिपदं स्वस्तिकं चैव ।
प्राचीनोदीचीनाश्चत्वारश्चैव मार्गाः स्युः ॥

Prāgiva mārgopetaṁ vīthipadaṁ svastikaṁ caiva ।
Prācīnodīcīnāścatvāraścaiva mārgāḥ syuḥ ॥

(In the periphery) As mentioned earlier, the street layout would be a road junction. The east and north roads shall be only 4.

Source

Mayamatam, Kalā-mūla-śāstram, Kapila-vātsyāyanaḥ, Ślokaḥ 60, 61 (6th Century AD)

Notes:

Svastika is a scheme of parallel roads of cities, the layout of principal roads forming a Svastika. The features of the svastika format are:

- The central districts would have 6 roads running North to South and 6 roads East to West.
- In the periphery, there would be only 4 roads in each direction.
- In the periphery, all roads would turn in the clockwise direction.

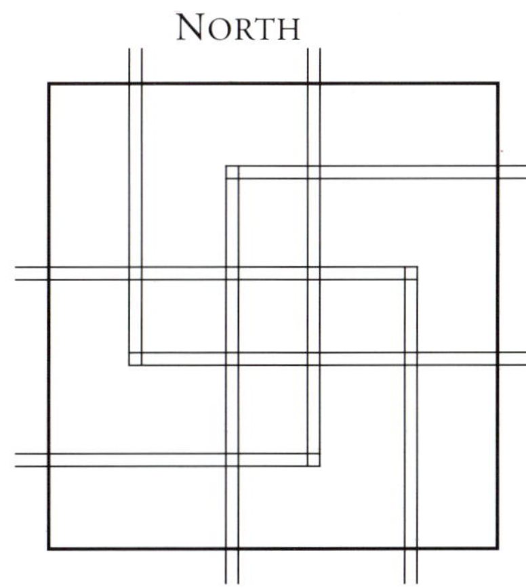

The obvious benefits of such an arrangement are:

- The plan provides higher road density in the central part of the town compared to the periphery, which would correspond with the traffic density in any city.
- The roads permit one-way traffic in each direction.
- The arrangement discourages traffic skirting the city from going through the central part of the city.

9.3.5 Town Planning - Law for housing given by Kauṭilya

सर्ववास्तुकयोः प्रक्षिप्तयोर्वा शालयोः किष्कुरन्तरिका त्रिपदी वा । तयोश्चतुरङ्गुलं नीप्रान्तरं समारूढकं वा । किष्कुमात्रमणिद्वारमन्तरिकायां खण्डफुल्लार्थमसम्पातं कारयेत् । प्रकाशार्थमल्पमूर्ध्ववातायनं कारयेत् । सम्भूय वा गृहस्वामिनो यथेष्टं कारयेयुरनिष्टं वारयेयुः ।

Sarvavāstukayoḥ prakṣiptayorvā śālayoḥ kiṣkurantarikā tripadī vā । Tayoścaturaṅgulaṁ nīprāntaraṁ samārūḍhakaṁ vā । Kiṣkumātra-maṇidwāramantarikāyāṁ khaṇḍaphullārthama-sampātaṁ kārayet । Prakāśārthamalpamūrdhvavātāyanaṁ kārayet । Sambhūya vā gṛha-swāmino yatheṣṭaṁ kārayeyuraniṣṭaṁ vārayeyuḥ ।

Generally, distance between two houses should be of 3 steps, the rule is applicable to the houses having Chajjās or Varandas. The distance between roofs of two adjacent houses should be four 'Aṅgulas' or may touch each other. Towards the lane, there should be a window of one 'Kiṣku' dimension, which could be closeable. For light, window should be made at higher level. The house owners should come together and do whatever is good and avoid bad.

Source

Arthaśāstram, Adhikaraṇam 3, Prakaraṇam 8, Adhyāyaḥ 19, Kauṭilyaḥ (4th century BCE)

Notes

While Kautilya lays down the rules, in the last sentence, he places the onus of doing good and avoiding the undesirable on the community of house-owners.

Functioning Municipality (Sorry, long ago)

The houses had bathrooms, the design of which shows that the Harappan, like the modern Indian, preferred to take his bath standing, by pouring pitchers of water over his head. The bathrooms were provided with drains, which flowed to sewers under the main streets, leading to soak-pits. The sewers were covered throughout their length by large brick slabs. The unique sewerage system of the Indus people must have been maintained by some municipal organization, and is one of the most impressive of their achievements. No other ancient civilization until that of the Romans had so efficient a system of drains.

Dr. A.L. Basham, The Wonder that was India, 3rd edition (2003), P. 16.

MECHANICAL ENGINEERING

Machines

Introduction

There are several references to machines and mechanical devices in Samskrit literature, from the ancient Vedas to modern plays and secular publications like the Yantrarnava and Yantra-sarvasva. Let us peep into this range.

- The Vedas talk of wheels and apparatus for churning milk and producing fire and shuttle of handloom.
- In the Mahabharata, the continuously circulating fish that Arjuna shot down to win the hand of Draupadi in marriage is, of course, well known.

- The Bhagavata-purana refers to an oil-expelling device, with description of a gear arrangement.
- Kautilya's Arthashastra, the 4th Century BCE masterpiece on statecraft, describes 32 machines including one for throwing stones and a weighing balance of unequal beam, indicating theoretical development of mechanics and sophistication of technology to sustain it.
- Aryabhata (5h Century AD) describes a perpetual motion machine.
- In Uttara-rama-charita, a drama written by Bhavabhuti, a king requests the royal tutor to teach the prince the art of making machines driven by fire, air, water etc., which is indicative of the importance that royalty placed on physical and mechanical sciences.

10.1 Machine - Definition & Attributes

दण्डैश्चक्रैश्च दन्तैश्च सरणिभ्रमणादिभिः ।	Daṇḍaiścakraiśca dantaiśca saraṇibhramaṇādibhiḥ I
शक्तेरुत्पादनं किं वा चालनं यन्त्रमुच्यते ॥	Śakterutpādanaṁ kiṁ vā cālanaṁ yantramucyate II

The generation of energy or motion, through the continuous movement or rotation of shafts, wheels or wedges is called a machine.

यथावद्बीजसंयोगः सौश्लिष्ट्यं श्लक्ष्णतापि च ।	Yathāvadbījasaṁyogaḥ sauśliṣṭyaṁ ślakṣṇtāpi ca I
अलक्ष्यतानिर्वहणं लघुत्वं शब्दहीनता ॥	Alakṣyatānirvahaṇaṁ laghutvaṁ śabdahīnatā II
शब्दे साध्ये तदाधिक्यमशैथिल्यमगाढता ।	Śabde sādhye tadādhikyamaśaithilyamagādhatā I
वहनीषु समस्तासु सौश्लिष्ट्यं चासलद्गतिः ॥	Vahanīṣu samastāsu sauśliṣṭyaṁ cāsaladgatiḥ II
यथेष्टार्थकारित्वं लयतालानुगामिता: ॥	Yatheṣṭārthakāritvaṁ layatālānugāmitā I
इष्टकालेऽर्थदर्शित्वं पुनः सम्यक्त्वसंवृतिः ॥	Iṣṭakālerthadarśitvaṁ punaḥ samyaktvasaṁvṛtiḥ II
अनुल्बणत्वं ताद्रूप्यं दार्ढ्यमसृणता तथा ।	Anulbaṇatvaṁ tādrupyaṁ dārḍhyamasṛṇatā tathā II
चिरकालसहत्वञ्च यन्त्रस्यैते महागुणाः ॥	Cirakālasahatvañca yantrasyaite mahāguṇāḥ II

These are the great attributes of machine - proper union of effort and result, good contact, smoothness, requiring no attention, sustaining, lightness, and noiselessness, when sound is required its predominance, not loosening or clogging, good contact in all moving parts, no break in action, attainment of results as desired, adherence to rhythm and timing, showing results at the moment desired, returning to normalcy at other times, not bulging and staying in shape, strength, softness and durability.

Source

Yantrārṇavaḥ (14th Century AD)

Samarāngaṇa-sūtradhāraḥ, Chapter 31, Rājā Bhojaḥ (11th Century AD)

Notes

1. Yantra + arnava = the ocean of machines. This is a collection of materials dealing with machines of various kinds.
2. We find these attributes echoed in today's brochures of a variety of products-air-conditioners (no noise), car-stereo (enhanced sound output), scooters requiring (no attention).

10.2 Machine - Physical Balance

पञ्चविंशतिपललोहां द्विसप्तत्यङ्गुलयामां समवृत्तां कारयेत् । तस्याः पञ्चपालिकं मण्डलं बध्वा समकरणं कारयेत् । ततः कर्षोत्तरपलं फलोत्तरदशपलं द्वादश पञ्चदश विंशतिरिति पदानि कारयेत् । तत आशताद् दशोत्तरं कारयेत् । अक्षेषु नद्ध्रीपिनद्धं कारयेत् ।

Pañcaviṁśatipalalohāṁ dvisaptatyaṅgulayāmāṁ samavṛttāṁ kārayet ।
Tasyāḥ pañcapālikaṁ maṇḍalaṁ badhvā samakaraṇaṁ kārayet ।
Tataḥ karṣottarapalaṁ phalottaradaśapalaṁ dvādaśa pañcadaśa viṁśatiriti padāni kārayet ।
Tata āśatād daśottaraṁ kārayet ।
Akṣeṣu naddhrīpinaddhaṁ kārayet ।

Make (the beams) balance at 72 finger-width for an iron piece of 25 pala weight; on it bind a 5-pala ring and make it balance. Then on the opposite side, make gradation of eleven, twelve, fifteen and twenty (palas). From there, make steps of ten (palas) up to hundred (palas).

Source

Arthaśāstram, Adhyāyaḥ 2, Section 35, Ślokaḥ 16, Kauṭilyaḥ (4th Century BCE)

Notes

Wedge = A shaft that is thick at one end and sloping to a thin edge at the other.

Units of measure

3 Tolas = 1 Pala
40 Palas = 1 Veesa
1 Veesa = 1.400 kg.
These measures were in day-to-day usage till the metric system was adopted in the 1950s.

Tula

10.3 Machine - Earth Model

काष्ठमयं समवृत्तं समन्ततः समगुरुं लघुं गोलम् ।
पारद-तैल-जलैस्तं भ्रमयेत् स्वधिया च
कालसमम् ॥

Kāṣṭhamayaṁ samavṛttaṁ samantataḥ
samaguruṁ laghuṁ golam ।
Pārada-taila-jalaistaṁ bhramayet svadhiyā ca
kālasamam ॥

A small wooden sphere with its weight distributed uniformly on all sections fixed on its axis should be rotated by mercury, oil and water (for one revolution per day).

Source

Āryabhaṭīyam, Golapādaḥ, Ślokaḥ 22, Āryabhaṭaḥ (499 AD)

Etymology

Kāla + samam = In equal time = in a day = uniformity

Notes

This sphere is a model of the earth. It is kept on its axis passing through north and south poles and is free to rotate on bearings. Assuming that the first zodiac Aries on eastern horizon, a nail is inserted on western side on its equator. Bhaskara describes this point as the centre of Virgo and Libra. One end of the thread is hooked to this nail, the thread is wound anti-clockwise and a pumpkin is suspended at the other end. A pot having circular cross-section and deep bottom (Sama vrtta & Dirgha Tala) is placed between North and South towards east. It is filled with water having volume equivalent to six "Ghatikas". Ghatika is a unit of time. Here it means that the volume of water should be such that it empties from the pot through a small hole made at the bottom in a period of six "Ghatikas". The water is filled and float is placed on the water surface at sun set. Then as the water comes out through the hole its level should fall and the float should descend making the sphere to rotate one revolution per day automatically.

Table of linear measures

8 paramanus	=	1 trasarenus
8 trasarenus	=	1 ratharenus
8 ratharenus	=	1 kosas
8 kosas	=	1 tilabijas
8 tilabijas	=	1 sarsapas
8 sarsapas	=	1 yavas
8 yavas	=	1 angulas
12 angulas	=	1 vitasti
2 vitasti	=	1 hasta
4 hastas	=	1 danda
2000 dandas	=	1 krosa
4 krosas	=	1 yojana

Aryabhatiya, Aryabhata, Ed. by Kripa Shankar Shukla, p. x1iii

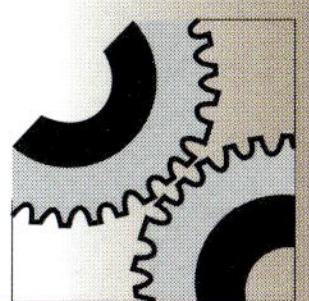

10.4 Machine - Carts

द्विचक्रबाह्ये विस्तारं षट् सप्ताष्टवितस्तियुगम् । चक्रनाभिच्छायामोक्षान्तरस्य च ॥	Dvicakrabāhye vistāraṁ ṣaṭ saptāṣṭavitastiyugam । Cakranābhicchāyāmokṣāntarasya ca ॥

The outside length of the line between hubs of the two wheels may be six, seven or eight sets of extended palms.

मध्यभारोपरि तुला मध्यनिर्गमनाग्रतः । अक्षमोक्षान्तरं चक्रमद्भारोपयानकम् ॥ पोतिकाकारसंयुक्तम् अयःपट्टैर्दृढीकृतम् ।	Madhyabhāropari tulā madhyanirgamanāgrataḥ । Akṣamokṣāntaraṁ cakramadbhāropayānakam ॥ Potitākārasaṁyuktaṁ ayaḥpaṭṭairḍhīkṛtam ।

Weight should be balanced in the middle. The center (of the laden weight) may be stretched forward. The laden weight (may be placed) between the two axis.

Source

Vāstuśāstram, Ratha-lakṣaṇam, Viśvakarmā (6th Century AD)

Notes

While the ideal is to keep the weight in the centre of the cart, the direction for error is to move the weight to the front. This is essential for any animal / human-drawn vehicle, since the locomotion is in the front. If the weight were to be towards the rear, then there would be the risk of the vehicle tilting. This format answers the norm of prescribing the ideal and also suggesting the direction for error.

Unit of Measure

Vitasti = Palm length

Vitasti + yuga = Set of palm lengths = two palm lengths.

METALLURGY

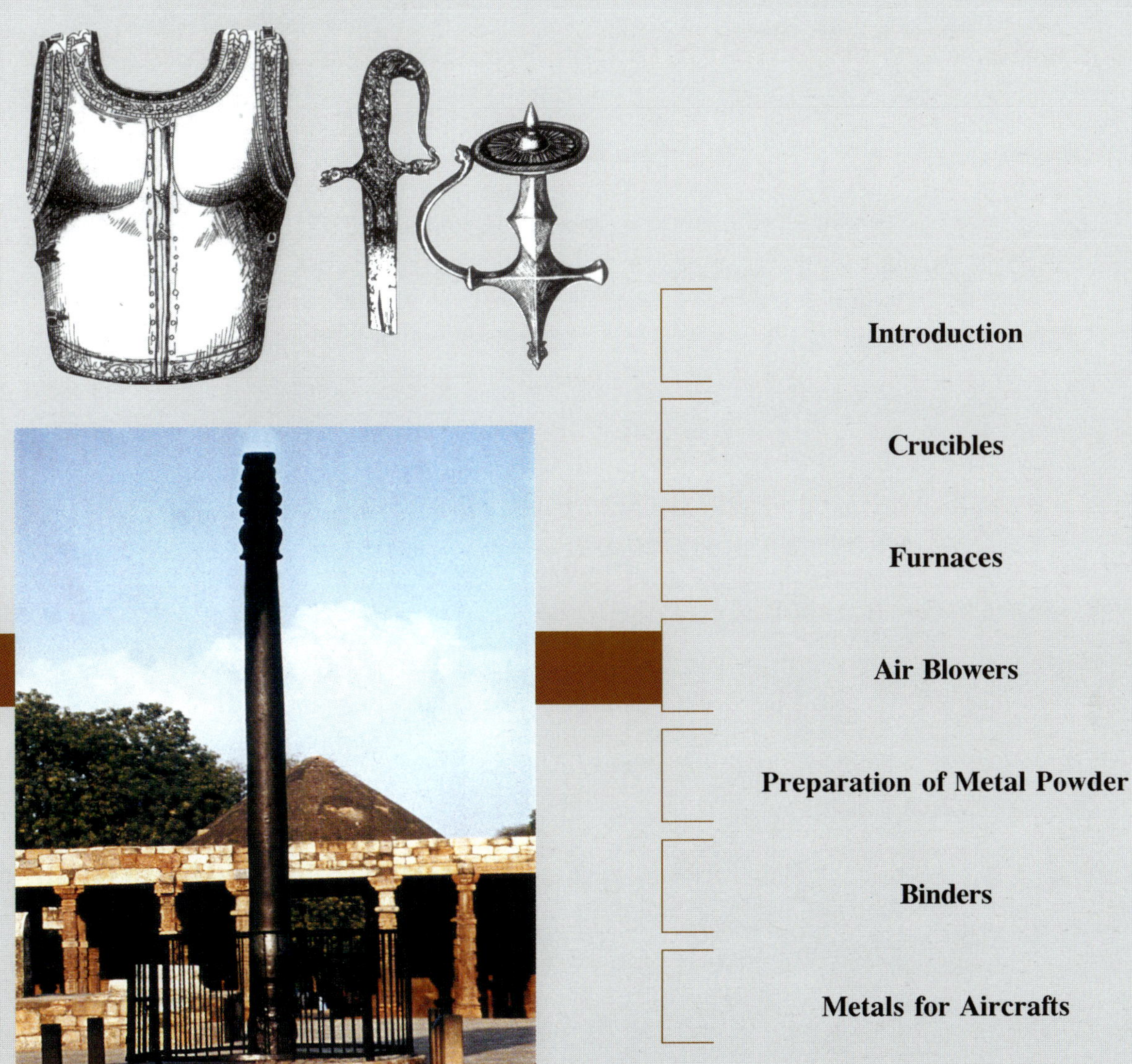

Introduction

Indian heritage in Gold, Silver, Bronze, Copper, Zinc and Iron and Steel is a celebrated one. Smelting of metals and derivation of alloys was done since 3000 BCE in ancient India. In the exchanges of goods between India, Egypt and Rome, metal trade from India was significant. Indian tools made from iron and steel were in great demand for war as well as agriculture.

Records show that the first supplies of the weapons that figure in the earliest recorded history of the people of Mediterranean came from India. As did Wootz steel, from which the famous Damascus blades were made. In fact, 'Wootz' derived its name from the Kannada word 'ukku' meaning crucible steel. Literary accounts suggest that steel from southern part of Indian subcontinent was exported to Europe, China, and countries of the Middle East.

The most outstanding examples of the capability and workmanship of Indian artisans include the famous iron pillar at Delhi that stands rust-free even after some 1500 years, and the 1 ton, 2.1metre high, 4th century copper statue of Buddha that was found in Bihar and is now housed in a British museum. Yet another contribution of ancient India to metallurgy is the technology to produce pure zinc and high zinc content copper alloys.

These, along with hundreds of other beautiful sculptures and icons in bronze and copper, belonging to periods earlier than 2000 BCE, bear testimony to the technological excellence and consummate skill of early Indians in producing and shaping metals.

British records of the 18th century show that the country had 20,000 furnaces operating across the country indicating the geographical spread of this knowledge.

11.1 Crucibles

पूर्वोक्त-बीजलोहानामेतस्यामेव वर्णितम् ।
उत्तमाधममध्यापभ्रंशानां गालनविधौ ।
मूषास्सप्तोत्तरचतुश्शतभेदा इतीरिताः ॥

Pūrvokta-bījalohānāmetasyāmeva varṇitam ।
Uttamādhamamadhyāpabhraṁśānāṁ gālanavidhau ।
Mūṣāssaptottaracatuśśatabhedā itīritāḥ ॥

(The melting) of the aforesaid base metals is described here only.

In the melting methodology, of good, coarse, average and pig metals, 407 varieties of crucibles are mentioned.

तासां द्वादशवर्गाः स्युर्जातिनिर्णयः क्रमात् ।

Tāsāṁ dvādaśavargāḥ syurjātinirṇayaḥ kramāt ।

In the order of origin, there are 12 groups in them.

लोहेषु ये बीजलोहास्तेषां गालनकर्मणि ॥
द्वितीयवर्गोक्तमूषा एव श्रेष्ठा इतीरिताः ।

Loheṣu ye bījalohāsteṣāṁ gālanakarmaṇi ॥
Dvitīyavargoktamūṣā eva śreṣṭhā itīritāḥ ।

In the melting of base metals, it is said, that the second group of crucibles is the best.

एतेषां गालने मूषाः प्रत्येकं वर्गतस्स्मृताः ।
तेषु द्वितीयवर्गस्थमूषाभेदा महर्षिभिः ॥
चत्वारिंशदिति प्रोक्ता मूषाकल्पा यथाक्रमम् ।
तासु या पञ्चमीत्युक्ता मूषान्तर्मुखनामिका ॥
गालने बीजलोहानां सुप्रशस्ता इतीरिताः ॥

Eteṣāṁ gālane mūṣāḥ pratyekaṁ vargatassmṛtāḥ ।
Teṣu dvitīyavargasthamūṣābhedā maharṣibhiḥ ॥
Catvāriṁśaditi proktā mūṣākalpā yathākramam ।
Tāsu yā pañcamītyuktā mūṣāntarmukhanāmikā ॥
Gālane bījalohānāṁ supraśastā itīritāḥ ॥

In the melting of these (base metals), crucibles are remembered from each class of these. The crucible varieties in the second category is mentioned as forty, in order, by the great sages, in (the work) Musha-kalpa.

Amongst these, the one that is mentioned as the fifth named Antar-mukhä (inward reflecting) is said to be the best in the melting of base metals.

Source

Bṛhad-vimāna-śāstram, Mūṣādhikaraṇam, Ślokaḥ 54-56, 58-60, Maharṣiḥ Bharadvājaḥ. Date- See box below.

Dating of Brihad Vimana Sastra
Nineteenth Century?
Bharadvaja-pranitha-vimana-shastra (BVS) came into being in the modern times as a revealed text, the revelation having occurred through one Mr. Anekal Subharaya Sastry (born in 1866). An (unpublished) enquiry with the descendents of the family shows that Mr. Sastry had found the manuscript and attempted glory for himself by delivering it as a *revelation.* Swami Dayananda Saraswati (1824:1888) in his "A treatise on Rig-veda" (1875) refers to Bharadwaja's Vimana-shastra. In the same year, a manuscript of the text had been discovered in a temple in India. Thus in the 19th century, this work was certainly known.

Post Vedic?
Bharadwaja's Vimana-shastra is considered a part of Yantra-sarwaswam - "All about machines". This is one of the 40 sections that Yantra Sarwaswam is made of. One school of thought places Bharadwaja in 4th century BCE. There are others who believe that Bharadwaja belonged to the Puranic period or earlier.

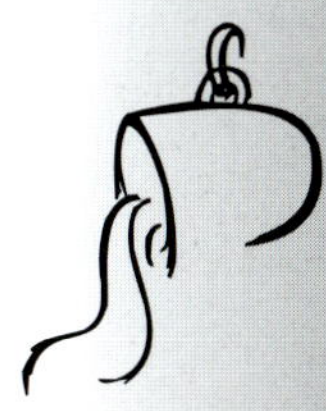

11.2 Tortoise Furnace

कूर्मव्यासटिकामेवमुक्त्वा शास्त्रानुसारतः । तत्स्वरूपपरिज्ञानार्थमाकारं सम्प्रचक्षते ॥	Kūrmavyāsaṭikāmevamuktvā śāstrānusārataḥ । Tatsvarūpaparijñānārthamākāraṁ sampracakṣate ॥

Having stated the Tortoise furnace, as per the scientific treatise, now let us study the shape and size, for further study.

चतुरस्रं वर्तुलं वा कूर्माकारं यथाविधि । वितस्तिदशकं कुण्डं कारयेत् भुवि शोभनम् ॥	Caturasraṁ vartulaṁ vā kūrmākāraṁ yathāvidhi । Vitastidaśakaṁ kuṇḍaṁ kārayet bhuvi śobhanam ॥

A square, circular or tortoise shaped pit of ten palms may be prepared nicely in the earth.

भस्त्रिकास्थापनाय तु तत्पुरोभागतस्स्फुटम् । कूर्माङ्गवत् पञ्चमुखं पीठमेकं प्रकल्पयेत् ॥	Bhastrikāsthāpanāya tu tatpurobhāgatassphuṭam । Kūrmāṅgavat pañcamukhaṁ pīṭhamekaṁ prakalpayet ॥

For the installation of the air-blower, clear space may be marked on the front side. A tortoise like five-corned structure may be constructed.

तत्कुण्डस्यान्तराले तु मूषाकुण्डं च वर्तुलम् । कल्पयित्वा बहिर्भागे कुण्डस्यावरणद्वयम् ॥	Tatkuṇḍasyāntarāle tu mūṣākuṇḍaṁ ca vartulam । Kalpayitvā bahirbhāge kuṇḍasyāvaraṇadvayam ॥

Inside may be finished circular to take up crucible and outside the furnace two coats of plaster shall be provided.

इङ्गालपूरणार्थाय यथाशास्त्रं प्रकारयेत् । पाश्र्वयोरुभयोस्तस्य यन्त्रस्थापनं कल्पयेत् ॥	Iṅgālapūraṇārthāya yathāśāstraṁ prakārayet । Pārśvayorubhayostasya yantrasthāpanaṁ kalpayet ॥

For charging coal, two parts on each side may be provided and on the rear, metal pouring mechanism may be erected.

सम्यग्गालितलोहानां रससम्पूरणे सुधीः । रचना कूर्मकुण्डस्य उक्तमेव महर्षिभिः ॥	Samyaggālitalohānāṁ rasasampūraṇe sudhīḥ । Racanā kūrmakuṇḍasya uktameva maharṣibhiḥ ॥

Perfectly molten metals, in fully molten state are viscous, the furnace described by the saints here is to handle this in proper manner.

Source

Bṛhad-vimāna-śāstram, Ślokaḥ 77-83. Vyāsaṭikādhikaraṇam, Maharṣiḥ Bharadvājaḥ. For dating see box in page no 113.

Etymology

Kūrma-kuṇḍa = tortoise-furnace.

11.3 Air Blowers (Bellows)

सर्वेषां लोहवर्गाणां गालनार्थं विशेषतः ।
द्वात्रिंशदुत्तरपञ्चशतं भस्त्रा इतीरिताः ॥

Sarveṣāṁ lohavargāṇāṁ gālanārthaṁ viśeṣataḥ ।
Dvātriṁśaduttarapañcaśataṁ bhastrā itīritāḥ ॥

For melting all types of metals, there are five hundred and thirty two types of air blowers.

तासां वर्गभेदस्तु अष्टधा सम्प्रकीर्तितः ।
वर्गेष्वष्टमवर्गीयो भस्त्रिकासु यथाक्रमम् ॥
निर्णिता कूर्मकुण्डस्य षोडशी कूर्मभस्त्रिका ।
सर्वेषां भस्त्रिकानां तु रचनाक्रमनिर्णयः ॥

Tāsāṁ vargabhedastu aṣṭadhā samprakīrtitaḥ ।
Vargeṣvaṣṭamavargīyo bhastrikāsu yathākramam ॥
Nirṇitā kūrmakuṇḍasya ṣoḍaśī kūrmabhast rikā ।
Sarveṣāṁ bhastrikānāṁ tu racanākramanirṇayaḥ ॥

They are divided into eight classes.

Sixteenth in the eighth class is called Kurma-bhastrika (Tortoise air–blower) which is associated with Kurma-vyasatika (Tortoise furnace).

भस्त्रिकानिबन्धनाख्यग्रन्थे सम्यङ्निरूपितः ।

Bhastrikānibandhanākhyagranthe
samyaṅnirūpitaḥ ।

Construction details of all air-blowers are provided in the book, Bhastrika-nibandhana.

Source

Bṛhad-vimāna-śāstram, Ślokaḥ 91, 92, 93. Bhastrikādhikaraṇam, Maharṣiḥ Bharadvājaḥ. For dating see box in page no 113.

Zinc Distillation in Rajasthan

Europe learnt to produce zinc in 1746.
In late 17th century, zinc was imported in small quantities from the East and used in the production of brass. Before the advent of present-day high-pressure technology, zinc had to be produced as a vapour because of the vast difficulties in its distillation process.
But it was distilled in India more than 2,000 years earlier through the use of a highly sophisticated pyro-technology. Distillation of this metal in India was brought to light through a series of nearly intact structural remains of ancient Indian zinc distillation furnaces at Zawar near Udaipur in Rajasthan.

Md.Vazeeruddin, Who remembers ancient India's scientific wealth?
World Institute for Asian Studies, Vol.5 No.361 (19/04/2006).

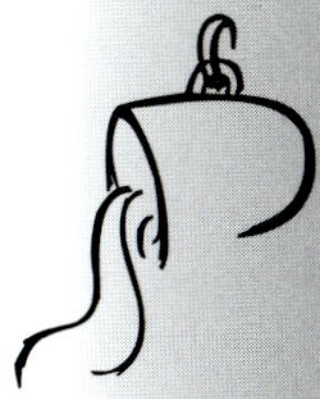

11.4 Preparation of Metal Powder

रेतितं घृतसंयुक्तं क्षिप्त्वायः खर्परे पचेत् ।	Retitaṁ ghṛtasaṁyuktaṁ kṣiptvāyaḥ kharpare pacet ।
लौहे दृषदि लौहञ्च मुद्गरेण हतं मुहुः ।	Lauhe dṛṣadi lauhañca mudgareṇa hataṁ muhuḥ ।

Throw flowing iron mixed with water in a broken pot and melt it.

Iron is beaten repeatedly in an iron mortar with a pestle.

अथ स्वर्णं पेषणार्थं पत्रीकृत्य यथामृदु ॥	Atha svarṇaṁ peṣaṇārthaṁ patrīkṛtya yathāmṛdu ॥
तत्पत्रं शकलीकृत्य सूक्ष्मात्सूक्ष्मतरं पुनः ।	Tatpatraṁ śakalīkṛtya sūkṣmātsūkṣmataraṁ punaḥ ।
किञ्चित्सिकतासम्मिश्रं शुद्धतोयविमिश्रितम् ॥	Kiñcitsikatāsaṁmiśraṁ śuddhatoyavimiśritam ।
पेषयेत्पेषणीश्वभ्रे सुश्लक्ष्णदृषदा सुधीः ।	Peṣayet peṣaṇīśvabhre suślakṣṇadṛṣadā sudhīḥ ।

A wise person, for grinding, after making the gold into soft leaves, after making the leaves into finer than finer fragments, mixing it with sand and clean water, grinds the ground gold, in a grinder with a very soft pestle.

जाते सुपिष्टे तत्पिष्टे काचपात्रे जलैः सह ।	Jāte supiṣṭe tatpiṣṭe kācapātre jalaiḥ saha ।
आलोड्योर्ध्वगतं पङ्कं सिकतां च पुनः पुनः ।	Āloḍyordhvagataṁ paṅkaṁ sikatāṁ ca punaḥ punaḥ ।
सन्त्यज्य जातं स्वर्णस्य पङ्कमत्युज्ज्वलं बुधाः ॥	Santyajya jātaṁ svarṇasya paṅkamatyujjvalaṁ budhāḥ ॥

When the mixture is ground finely, knowledgeable people, stirring the mixture with water in a glass vessel, filtering and discarding repeatedly the slurry of sand that comes up, get the highly shining slurry of gold.

Source

Rasa-ratna-samuccayaḥ, Chapter 5, Ślokaḥ 106, Vāgbhaṭaḥ (12th Century AD)

Rasendra-sāra-saṅgrahaḥ (9th century AD)

Śilpa-ratnam, Chapter 46, Ślokaḥ 124-128 (11th century AD).

Notes

Grind the ground gold would mean to grind repeatedly.

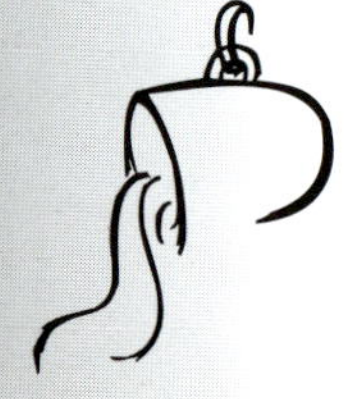

11.5 Binders and Glues-1

आमं तिन्दुकमामं कपित्थकं पुष्पमपि शाल्मल्याः ।
बीजानि शल्लकीनां धन्वनवल्को वचा चेति ॥

Āmaṁ tindukamāmaṁ kapitthakaṁ
puṣpamapi ca śālmalyāḥ ।
Bījāni śallakīnām dhanvanavalko vacā ceti ॥

Take unripe tinduka, unripe woodapple, flower of silk cotton, seeds of sallaki, bark of dhanvana and the vaca root.

एतैः सलिलद्रोणः क्वाथयितव्योऽष्टभागशेषश्च ।
अवतार्योऽस्य च कल्को द्रव्यैरेतैः समनुयोज्यः ॥

Etaiḥ saliladroṇaḥ
kvāthayitavyoऽṣṭabhāgaśeṣaśca ।
Avatāryoऽsya ca kalko dravyairetaiḥ
samanuyojyaḥ ॥

These materials mixed in a bucketful of water should be boiled till it (the mixture) is reduced to one eighth in volume. This residue should be mixed with the following materials.

श्रीवासकरसगुग्गुलुभल्लातककुन्दुरुकसर्जरसैः ।
अतसीबिल्वैश्च युतः कल्कोऽयं वज्रलेपाख्यः ॥

Śrīvāsakarasaguggulubhallātakakunduru-
kasarjarasaiḥ ।
Atasībilvaiśca yutaḥ kalkoऽyam vajralepākhyaḥ ॥

Turpentine, guggula resin, resin of bhallataka, jasmine, sarja, linseed and vilvam. This mixture is called Vajra-lepa.

Source

Bṛhat-saṁhitā, Varāhamihiraḥ (6th century AD)

Notes

Varahamihira's Brihat-samhita describes Vajra-lepa and Vajra-sanghata. The Ashoka Pillar is basically a sand-stone pillar coated with Vajra-Sanghata to look like a metal pillar. Mauryan caves in Bihar also have a coating that gives the surface the look of glass.

S.No	Samskrit name	Common name	Botanical name
1	Tinduka		Diospyros paniculata
2	Kapitthaka	Wood apple	Feronia elephantum
3	Shālmalī	Silk cotton	Morus acedosa
4	Śallakī		Bosewellia serrata
5	Dhanvana		Dhanvana
6	Vacā	Orris root	Vaca
7	Shrīvasaka	Turpentine	Myrrh
8	Guggula		Commiphora roxburghu
9	Bhallāṭaka		Semecarpus anacardium
10	Kunduruka	Jasmine	Cunduru
11	Sarja		Resin
12	Atasī	Linseed	Linum usikatissimum
13	Bilva	Vilva	Aegle marmelos

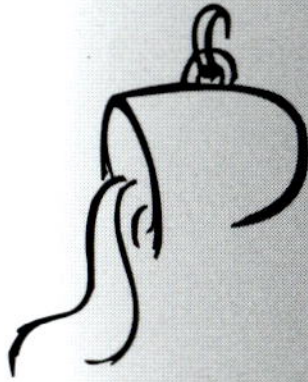

11.6 Binders and Glues-2

गोमहिषाजविषाणैः खुररोम्णा महिषचर्मगव्यैश्च । निम्बकपित्थरसैः सह वज्रतलो नाम कल्कोऽन्यः ।।	Gomahiṣājaviṣāṇaiḥ khuraromṇā mahiṣacarmagavyaiśca । Nimbakapittharasaiḥ saha vajratalo nāma kalko nyaḥ ।।

With the horn, hoof and mane of cow, buffaloes and goat and with the hide of buffaloes and cow along with the juice of neem and wood apple another paste called Vajra-tala (is produced).

प्रासादहर्म्यवलभीलिङ्गप्रतिमासु कुड्यकूपेषु । सन्तप्तो दातव्यो वर्षसहस्रायुतस्थायी ।।	Prāsādaharmyavalabhīliṅgapratimāsu kuḍyakūpeṣu । Santapto dātavyo varṣasahasrāyutasthāyī ।।

The ten thousand year enduring heated (paste) should be given in (the construction of) palaces, mansions, roofs, lingas, idols, walls and wells.

अष्टौ सीसकभागाः कांसस्य द्वौ तु रीतिकाभागः । मयकथितो योगोऽयं विज्ञेयो वज्रसङ्घातः ।।	Aṣṭau sīsakabhāgāḥ kāṁsasya dvau tu rītikābhāgaḥ । Mayakathito yogoऽyaṁ vijñeyo vajrasaṅghātaḥ ।।

Taking 8 parts of lead, 2 parts of bell metal, and 2 parts of the calx of brass, this mixture is called Vajra-sanghata by Maya.

Source

Bṛhat-saṁhitā, Varāhamihiraḥ (6th century AD)

Notes

Maya is a reference to Maya-matam authored by Kapila-Vatsyayana (6th Century AD), who had named his work after the celestial Architect Maya.

You seem to have put on a little weight

What is the secret behind Delhi's famous Iron Pillar that stands rust-free even after more than 1600 years? Metallurgists at the Indian Institute of Technology, Kanpur, have discovered that a thin layer of 'misawite', a compound of iron, oxygen and hydrogen, has protected the cast iron pillar from rust.

In a millennium and a half, it is calculated that this layer has grown to a thickness of 50 micron. The protective film was formed catalytically by the presence of high amounts of phosphorous in the iron –1% as against less than 0.05% in today's iron. The high phosphorous content is the result of the unique iron-making process practised by ancient Indians, who reduced iron ore into steel in one step by mixing it with charcoal.

The pillar—over 7 metres high and weighing more than 6 tonnes – was originally erected outside a Vishnu temple during the Gupta dynasty's rule in AD 320 – 540.

The Hindu (29/8/2002), Iron pillar and nano powder, B.G.Prakash.

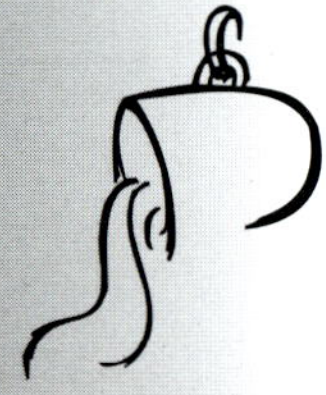

11.7 Metallurgy - Metals for Aircraft

अथ वैमानिकान् लोहाननुक्रमिष्यामः सौमक-
सौण्डालिक-मौर्त्विकाश्चैतत् सम्मेलनादूष्मपाः
षोडशधा भवन्तीति ते वैमानिकाः ॥

Atha vaimānikān lohānanukramiṣyāmaḥ saumaka-
sauṇḍālika-maurtvikāścaitat sammelanādūṣmapāḥ
ṣoḍaśadhā bhavantīti te
vaimānikāḥ ॥

Now we sequence the metals for aircrafts - Thermal (Saumaka), Acidic (Soundalika) and relating to shape (Maurtvika). The aircraft technologists say that by alloying these (three metal categories) 16 varieties of heat-conducting metals come into being.

उष्णम्भरोष्णपोष्णहनराजाम्लतृड्वीरहा
पञ्चघ्नोऽग्नितृड् भारहनश्शीतहनो गरलघ्नाम्लहनो
विषम्भर-विशल्यकृद् द्विजमित्रश्च
वातमित्रश्चेतीत्यादिः ॥

Uṣṇambharoṣṇapoṣṇahanarājāmlatṛḍvīrahā
pañcaghnognitṛḍ bhārahanaśśītahano
garalaghnāmlahano viṣambhara-viśalyakṛd
dvijamitraśca vātamitraścetītyādiḥ ॥

These are heat bearing, heat conducting (thermal), heat proof, shining, acid-proof, toxic (weapon grade) non-malleable, fire-proof, weight-proof, cold-proof, poison-proof (anti toxic), acid proof (alkaline), toxic (weapon grade), surgical grade, wrought metal and wind-proof.

Source

Bṛhad-vimāna-śāstram, Lohādhikaraṇam, Maharṣiḥ Bharadvājaḥ. For dating see box in page no 113.

Etymology

Saumaka = Of the moon = Cool = Relating to temperature = Thermal

Sauṇḍālika = Relating to juices/acids

Maurtvika = Concerned with shape/form.

Pañca+ghna = Non-malleable

Garala+ghna = Poison-proof = Anti-toxin

Uṣṇa+hana = Heat-proof

Bhāra+hana = Weight-proof

Śīta+hana = Cold-proof

Amla+hana = Acid-proof = Alkaline

Amla+tṛd = Acid-proof

Agni+tṛd = Fire-proof

Ghna, han, tṛd mean to kill, quench.

The rest are based on positive attributes.

Uṣṇa+hana = Heat + bearing

Viṣam+bhara = Poison + bearing = Toxic (weapon-grade)

Usṇam+pā = Heat + protecting = Heat conducting

Rāja = Shining = White

Vi+śalya+kṛt = Special + Cut + Do = Surgical grade

Dvija+mitra = Twice born = Wrought metal

Vāta+mitra =Wind + friend (wind-proof)

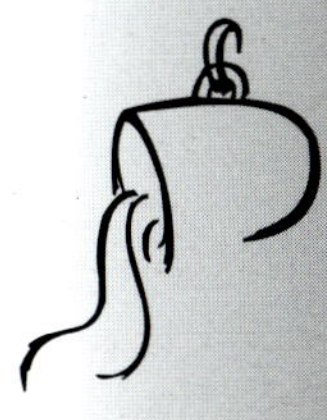

CHEMISTRY

Laboratory

Distillation Vessel

Caustic Alkali

Generation of electricity in a cell

Explosives

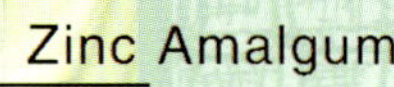

Introduction

In India, chemistry was practised as an art to manufacture mercury, zinc, copper and their alloys as early as around 3000 BCE. Production of medicines and plant extracts to cure diseases was very well developed as aids to Ayurveda and other forms of Healthcare.

Similar to that of Paracelsus in Europe, the chief aim of chemistry in India was to provide relief to humans from ailments. There are treatises like those of Charaka and Sushruta dealing with chemistry, medicine and surgery in ancient times. Great attention was paid to carry out minute details of the formulae for the preparation of drugs such as extract of plants by leaching, decoction or distillation. Manufacture of various metal powders under specific conditions of temperatures and pressures. This systematic development of chemistry, coupled with some accidental discoveries, ultimately led to the development of 'Kimaya', the term used for alchemy (the infant stage of chemistry) in India.

Ancient Indian chemists were using more than 32 types of apparatus for chemical and pharmaceutical investigations in their laboratories and they are called "Yantras". The Rasa-ratna-samuccaya talks of a variety of furnaces for melting and distillation. Of these 3 types of furnaces are dealt with here:

- The Koshti-yantra
- The Deki-yantra and
- The Tiryak-patana-yantra.

12.1 Chemical Laboratory - Location and Layout

रसशालां प्रकुर्वीत सर्वबाधाविवर्जिताम् । सर्वौषधिमये देशे रम्ये कूपसमन्विते ॥	Rasaśālāṁ prakurvīta sarvabādhāvivarjitām । Sarvauṣadhimaye deśe ramye kūpasamanvite ॥

Build a laboratory in a beautiful place that abounds in medicinal plants, devoid of any disturbance and has a well.

यक्ष-त्र्यक्ष-सहस्राक्ष-दिग्विभागे सुशोभने । नानोपकरणोपेतां प्राकारेण सुशोभिताम् ॥	Yakṣa-tryakṣa-sahasrākṣa-digvibhāge suśobhane । Nānopakaraṇopetāṁ prākāreṇa suśobhitām ॥

Build a laboratory bound by corridors, furnished with a variety of equipment facing north, northeast, or the eastern direction.

शालायाः पूर्वदिग्भागे स्थापयेद्रसभैरवम् । वह्निकर्माणि चाग्नेये याम्ये पाषाणकर्म च ॥ नैर्ऋत्ये शस्त्रकर्माणि वारुणे क्षालनादिकम् । शोषणं वायुकोणे च वेधकर्मोत्तरे तथा ॥	Śālāyāḥ pūrvadigbhāge sthāpayedrasabhairavam । Vahnikarmāṇi cāgneye yāmye pāṣāṇakarma ca ॥ Nairṛtye śastrakarmāṇi vāruṇe kṣālanādikam । Śoṣaṇaṁ vāyukoṇe ca vedhakarmottare tathā ॥

Establish mercury in the eastern side of the laboratory, melting in the southeast and stone instruments in the southern direction. Cutting tasks in southwest, cleaning etc., in west, drying in northwest and piercing in north.

स्थापनं सिद्धवस्तूनां प्रकुर्यादीशकोणके । पदार्थसङ्ग्रहः कार्यो रससाधनहेतुकः ॥	Sthāpanaṁ siddhavastūnāṁ prakuryādīśakoṇake । Padārthasaṅgrahaḥ kāryo rasasādhanahetukaḥ ॥

Ready to use goods should be kept in the northeast. Materials useful in the production of metal should be gathered.

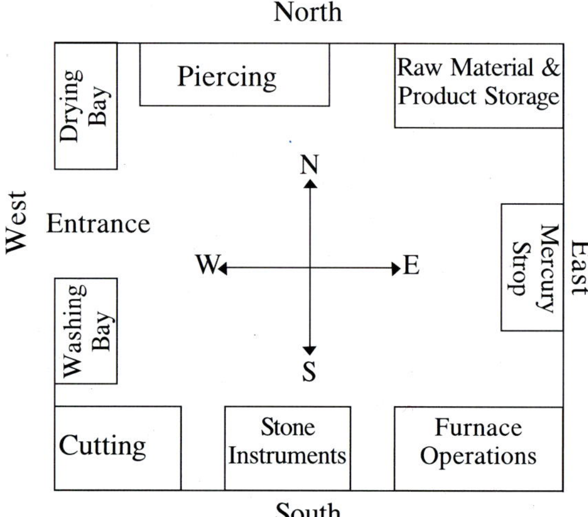

Source

Rasa-ratna-samuccayaḥ, Adhyāyaḥ 7, Ślokaḥ 11-14 Vāgbhaṭaḥ (12th Century AD)

Etymology

Vahni-karmāṇi	=	Fire related activities	=	Melting
Rasa-bhairavaḥ	=	King amongst chemicals	=	Mercury
Sulba-ariḥ	=	The enemy of metals	=	Sulphur

Notes

1. Chemistry was a hand-maid of medicine. Hence the need to locate a laboratory where medicinal plants are available.

2. The poetic style used to indicate the 3 directions is quite interesting, full of alliteration. Yaksha (a particular class of divine-beings), Traksha (the 3-eyed-Shiva) and Sahasraksha (the 1000-eyed-Indra).

3. The recommended layout for laboratories is in consonance with the Hindu thought on gods and their domain. Northwest is the direction of the god of wind and therefore drying should be located in the northwest. The recommended layout is tabulated below:

S.No	Direction (in Samskrit)	Direction (in English)	Presiding deity	Domain of the lord	Recommended activity
1	Uttara	North	Kubera	Wealth	Piercing
2	Uttara-poorva	Northeast	Shiva	Ownership	Storage of ready to use goods.
3	Poorva	East	Indra	Chief of the Devas	Storage of the king of chemicals.
4	Dakshina-poorva	Southeast	Agni	Fire	Heating / burning
5	Dakshina	South	Yama	Death	Work with stone
6	Dakshina-pashchima	Southwest	Nirriti	Destruction	Cutting
7	Pashchima	West	Varuna	Ocean	Cleaning
8	Uttara-pashchima	Northwest	Vayu	Wind	Drying

12.2 Chemical Laboratory - Equipments

सत्त्वपातनकोष्ठींश्च सुराकोष्ठीं सुशोभनाम् । भूमिकोष्ठीं चलत्कोष्ठीं जलद्रोण्योऽप्यनेकशः ॥	Sattvapātanakoṣṭhīñca surākoṣṭhīṁ suśobhanām । Bhūmikoṣṭhīm calatkoṣṭīm jaladroṇyoऽpyanekaśaḥ ॥

Chamber for pouring molten metal, good chamber for alcohol (distillation), earthen chamber, movable chamber and many water buckets (should be arranged).

भस्त्रिकायुगलं तद्वन्नलिके वंशलोहयोः । स्वर्णायोघोषशुल्बाश्मकुण्ड्यश्चर्मकृतां तथा ॥	Bhastrikāyugalaṁ tadvannalike vaṁśalohayoḥ । Svarṇāyoghoṣaśulbāśmakuṇḍyaścarmakṛtāṁ tathā ॥

A pair of bellows, similarly, tubes of bamboo and iron and vessels made of gold, iron, bellmetal, copper, stone and leather (should be there).

करणानि विचित्राणि द्रव्याण्यपि समाहरेत् ॥ कण्डणी पेषणी खल्वा द्रोणीरूपाश्च वर्तुलाः ।	Karaṇāni vicitrāṇi dravyāṇyapi samāharet ॥ Kaṇḍaṇī peṣaṇī khalvā droṇīrūpāśca vartulāḥ ।

A variety of materials and instruments should be gathered. Mortar (wooden) for cutting, grinders and oval and circular pestles (should be gathered).

आयसास्तप्तखल्वाश्च मर्दकाश्च तथा विधाः ॥ सूक्ष्मच्छिद्रसहस्राढ्या द्रव्यगालनहेतवे ।	Āyasāstaptakhalvāśca mardakāśca tathā vidhāḥ ॥ Sūkṣmacchidrasahasrāḍhyā dravyagālanahetave ।

Heat-treated iron pestles, similar (heat-treated) pounding instruments, fine sieves (are required) for fusing materials.

चालनी च कटत्राणि शलाका हि च कुण्डली ॥ मूषामृत्तुपकार्पासवनोपलकपिष्टकम् ।	Cālanī ca kaṭatrāṇi śalākā hi ca kuṇḍalī ॥ Mūṣāmṛttupakārpāsavanopalakapiṣṭakam ।

Sieves, wooden vessels, sticks, mortar, circular rings and frames, earth suitable for making crucible, husk, cotton, cakes of forest dung (are required).

Source

Rasa-ratna-samuccayaḥ, Adhyāyaḥ 7, Ślokaḥ 15-19 Vāgbhaṭaḥ (12 Century AD)

Etymology

Bhastrikā-yugalam	=	Two leather bags	=	Bellows.
Ayasa-tapta-khalvāḥ	=	Of iron - burnt - pestles	=	Heat treated iron pestles.
Sūkṣma-cchidra-sahasrāḍyaḥ	=	Subtle - holes - abounding in thousands	=	Fine sieves.

12.3 Distillation Vessel - The Koṣṭhī-yantram & The Dhekī-yantram

षोडशाङ्गुलविस्तीर्णं हस्तमात्रायतं समम् ।	Ṣoḍaśāṅgulavistīrṇaṁ hastamātrāyataṁ samam ।
धातुसत्त्वनिपातार्थं कोष्ठीयन्त्रमिति स्मृतम् ॥	Dhātusattvanipātārthaṁ koṣṭhīyantramiti smṛtam ॥

The Koshti equipment (furnace) is 16 inches in breadth and is of equal height and length of 1 palm length (6 inches). It enhances the strength of ores.

भाण्डकण्ठादधश्छिद्रे वेणुनालं विनिक्षिपेत् ।	Bhāṇḍakaṇṭhādadhaśchidre veṇunālaṁ vinikṣipet ।
कांस्यपात्रद्वयं कृत्वा सम्पुटं जलगर्भितम् ॥	Kāṁsyapātradvayaṁ kṛtvā sampuṭaṁ jalagarbhitam ॥

In the opening under the neck of the vessel fit the bamboo tube. Taking two (hemispherical) brass vessels, fill them with water and close them and place the mouth of the tube appropriately and firmly there.

नलिकास्यं तत्र योग्यं दृढं तच्चापि कारयेत् ।	Nalikāsyam tatra yogyaṁ dṛḍhaṁ taccāpi kārayet ।
युक्तद्रव्यैर्विनिक्षिप्तः पूर्वं तत्र घटे रसः ॥	Yuktadravyairvinikṣiptaḥ pūrvaṁ tatra ghaṭe rasaḥ ॥
अग्निना तापितो नालात्तोये तस्मिन् पतत्यधः ।	Agninā tāpito nālāttoye tasmin patatyadhaḥ ।
यावदुष्णं भवेत्सर्वभाजनं तावदेव हि ।	Yāvaduṣṇaṁ bhavetsarvabhājanaṁ tāvadeva hi ।
जायते रससन्धानं ढेकीयन्त्रमितीरितम् ॥	Jāyate rasasandhānaṁ ḍhekīyantramitīritam ॥

Mercury mixed with proper ingredients (is) previously poured in the vessel. The mixture heated with fire, falls down on the water (through the tube). As long as the whole vessel is hot, distillation takes place. This is called Deki yantra.

Source

Rasa-ratna-samuccayaḥ, Adhyāyaḥ 9, Ślokaḥ 43, 11-14, Vāgbhaṭaḥ (12th Century AD)

Etymology

Koṣhṭa + yantram = Enclosed + device = Closed furnace

Koshti-yantra

Deki-yantra

12.4 Slant Distillation Vessel - The Tiryak-pātana-yantram

क्षिपेद्रसं घटे दीर्घे नताधोनालसंयुते ।	Kṣipedrasaṁ ghaṭe dīrghe natādhonālasaṁyute I
तन्नालं निक्षिपेदन्यघटकुक्ष्यन्तरे खलु ॥	Tannālaṁ nikṣipedanyaghaṭakukṣyantare khalu II

In a long vessel with a tube going downward pour the chemical. Place that tube in the belly of another vessel.

तत्र रुद्ध्वा मृदा सम्यग्वदने घटयोरधः ।	Tatra ruddhvā mṛdā samyagvadane ghaṭayoradhaḥ I
अधस्ताद्रसकुम्भस्य ज्वालयेत्तीव्रपावकम् ॥	Adhastādrasakumbhasya jvālayettīvrapāvakam II

Closing well with mud the top and the bottom of the two vessels, burn an intense fire under the vessel containing the chemical.

इतरस्मिन् घटे तोयं प्रक्षिपेत्स्वादु शीतलम् ।	Itarasmin ghaṭe toyaṁ prakṣipetsvādu śītalam I
तिर्यक्पातनमेतद्धि वार्तिकैरभिधीयते ॥	Tiryakpātanametaddhi vārtikairabhidhīyate II

On the other pot, pour sweet cold water. This is the slanting distillation vessel.

Source

Rasa-ratna-samuccayaḥ, Adhyāyaḥ 9, Ślokaḥ 47-49, Vāgbhaṭaḥ (12th Century AD)

Etymology

Tiryak + pātana + yantram = Slanting + causing to fall + device
= The slanting distillation vessel.

Tiryak-patana-yantra

12.5 Generation of Electricity in a Cell

संस्थाप्य मृण्मयं पात्रं ताम्रपत्रं सुसंस्कृतम् ।
छादयेत् शिखिग्रीवेन चार्द्राभिः काष्ठपांसुभिः ॥

Saṁsthāpya mṛṇmayaṁ pātraṁ tāmrapatraṁ susaṁskṛtam ।
Chādayet śikhigrīvena cārdrābhiḥ kāṣṭhapāṁsubhiḥ ॥

After placing the earthen vessel as well as the copper vessel securely, close (the vessels) with copper sulphate and sawdust.

दस्तालोष्टो निधातत्वः पारदाच्छादितस्ततः ।
उत्पादयति तन्मित्रं संयोगस्ताम्रदस्तयोः ॥

Dastāloṣṭo nidhātatvaḥ pāradācchāditastataḥ ।
Utpādayati tanmitraṁ saṁyogastāmradastayoḥ ॥

Lumps of gems generate electricity by the union of copper and zinc.

संयोगाज्जायते तेजो यन्मित्रमिति कथ्यते ।
एवं शतानां कुम्भानां संयोगः कार्यकृत्स्मृतः ।

Saṁyogājjāyate tejo yanmitramiti kathyate ।
Evaṁ śatānāṁ kumbhānāṁ saṁyogaḥ kāryakṛtsmṛtaḥ ।

By the union, energy is born which is referred to as the sun. Such a union of hundreds of cells is remembered as the doer (of generating electricity).

सुसंमृष्टा च सुभगा घृतयोनिः पयोधरा ।
मृत्कुम्भी सर्वदा ग्राह्या...

Susaṁmṛṣṭā ca subhagā ghṛtayoniḥ payodharā ।
Mṛtkumbhī sarvadā grāhyā...

Earthen pot, which is well cleaned, pretty, fit for storing ghee and capable of holding water (watertight) should always be taken.

Source

Agastya-saṁhitā (14th Century AD)

Etymology

Śikhi-grīvaḥ = Peacock neck coloured = Copper.

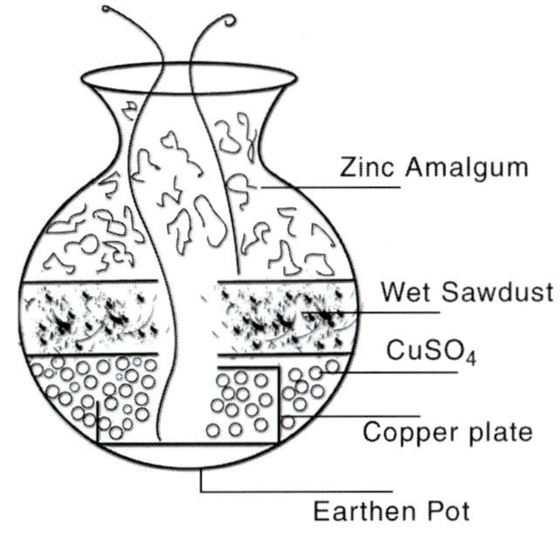

12.6 Caustic Alkali

तं चिकीर्षुः शरदि गिरिसानुजं शुचिरुपोष्य प्रशस्तेऽहनि प्रशस्तदेशजातम् अनुपहतं मध्यमवयसं महान्तम् असित-मुष्ककमधिवास्य अपरेद्युः पाटयित्वा खण्डशः प्रकल्प्य अवपात्य निर्वाते देशे निचितिं कृत्वा सुधाशर्कराश्च प्रक्षिप्य तिलनालैः आदीपयेत् ।	Taṁ cikīrṣuḥ śaradi girisānujaṁ śuciruposya praśasteऽhani praśastadeśajātam anupahataṁ madhyamavayasaṁ mahāntam asitamuṣkakamadhivāsya aparedyuḥ pāṭayitvā khaṇḍaśaḥ prakalpya avapāṭya nirvāte deśe nicitim kṛtvā sudhāśarkarāśca prakṣipya tilanālaiḥ ādīpayet ।

The one desiring that (Caustic alkali), being pure, after fasting on an auspicious autumn day, living near a tree – that is born in a table land, in a known place, that is middle aged, not mutilated, big and not pale – on the next day cleaving the tree, cutting into blocks, breaking it further, piling them in a windless place, throwing lime crystals on top ignite it with tubes of a sesame stock.

अथ उपशान्ते अग्नौ तद्भस्म पृथक् गृह्णीयात् भस्मशर्कराश्च ।	Atha upaśānte agnau tadbhasma pṛthak gṛhṇīyāt bhasmaśarkarāśca ।

On the fire subsiding, collect separately the ash of the tree and of the lime.

ततः क्षारद्रोणम् उदकद्रोणैः परिस्राव्य, महति कटाहे शनैः दर्व्या अवघट्टयन् विपचेत् ।	Tataḥ kṣāradroṇam udakadroṇaiḥ parisrāvya, mahati kaṭāhe śanaiḥ darvyā avaghaṭṭayan vipacet ।

Dissolving the ash in water, cook it in a large pan turning with a ladle.

तमादाय महति वस्त्रे परिस्राव्य इतरं विभज्य पुनः अग्नौ अधिश्रयेत् ।	Tamādāya mahati vastre parisrāvya itaraṁ vibhajya punaḥ agnau adhiśrayet ।

Taking it, filter it through a large cloth, remove the sediment and place the material again on fire.

स यथा नातिसान्द्रो नातिद्रवश्च भवति मध्यमः, एष एव अप्रतीवापः पक्वः मृदुः, स एव सप्रतीवापः पक्वः पाक्यः तीक्ष्णः ॥	Sa yathā nātisāndro nāti-dravaśca bhavati madhyamaḥ, eṣa eva apratīvāpaḥ pakvaḥ mṛduḥ, sa eva sapratīvāpaḥ pakvaḥ pākyaḥ tīkṣṇaḥ ॥

When it is neither thick nor liquid, then it is of medium consistency. That is the concentrate ripe and soft. This when processed becomes dilute, mild or caustic.

Source

Suśruta-saṁhitā, Sūtra-sthānam, Adhyāyaḥ 11, paragraph 11-13 (6th Century BCE)

12.7 Explosives

अङ्गारस्यैव गन्धस्य सुवर्चिलवणस्य च ।
शिलाया हरितालस्य तथा सीसमलस्य च ॥
हिङ्गुलस्य तथा कान्तरजसः कर्पूरस्य च ।
जतोर्णिल्याश्च सरलनिर्यास्य तथैव च ॥
समन्युनाधिकैरंशैरग्निचूर्णान्यनेकशः ।

Aṅgārasyaiva gandhasya suvarcilavaṇasya ca ।
Śilāyā haritālasya tathā sīsamalasya ca ॥
Hiṅgulasya tathā kāntarajasaḥ karpūrasya ca ।
Jatorṇilyāśca saralaniryāsya tathaiva ca ॥
Samanyunādhikairaṁśairagnicūrṇānyanekaśaḥ ।

Explosives (are prepared), in different ways by mixing in varying proportions with fire, charcoal, sulphur, potassium nitrate, red arsenic, yellow arsenic, lead oxide, vermilion, steel powder, camphor, lac, turpentine and gum.*

Source

Śukra-nītiḥ, Chapter 4, Section 7, Ślokaḥ 194-196 Śukrācāryaḥ (Post-vedic period)

Etymology

1. Agni + cūrṇam = Fire + powder = Explosive
2. Harita –> Haritalam = Yellow pigment = Arsenic
3. Suvarci + lavaṇam = Hydrated + salt = Potassium nitrate

Indigo dyes of the Kurmis

While the Europeans used woad or isatis tinctoria, the Indian plant indigofera tinctoria or Nila, has a higher indigo content and the methodology used by the dyers in India is remarkably similar and efficient. The technology in our country was handed down from fathers to sons over centuries. In a nation full of castes and communities, each specializing in one art, craft or technology, it was the kurmis of Maratha and Deccan, the Niralis of Central India, and certain groups of Muslim dyers who have been exponents of this form of medieval biotechnology.

Exports without quota

Eighth century Central Asia and Egypt knew of Indian textiles. Marco Polo, who passed through India in the 13th century, was the first to report on the preparations of Indigo dye in India.

Block printed, resist - dyed textiles from Gujarat and the Deccan adorned Europeans and their homes from the 15th to the 19th centuries. Flourishing trade in textiles and dyes existed between the Golconda kingdom of Telangana and Qutub Shahi, Persia for centuries.

The Hindu (25/4/2002), Indigo nation: Champaran to Chandigarh, D.Balasubramanian.

Vedas and Upanishads, Ramayana and Mahabharata, Bhagvad-gita and Dharma-shastras...all that's sacred to this land and enriching to mankind as a whole, is in Samskrit. Many of the most astounding and original contributions to the world of science, philosophy, arts and literature are in this ancient language.

The roots of many languages of the world are found in Samskrit, the mother of all languages, distinguished from the rest by its longevity, stability of form over the many millennia and the status of a sacred language.

Sri Aurobindo observed that Samskrit is "one of the most magnificent, the most perfect and wonderfully sufficient literary instruments developed by human mind...at once majestic and sweet and flexible, strong and clearly formed and full and vibrant and subtle..." It's a language so vast and versatile, scientific and systematic that it's capable of expressing every subtlety of human thought, every nuance of human feeling. It can also create any number of new words for a new situation, concept or thing.

It is not surprising that the 21st century scientists find Samskrit ideally suited for state-of-the-art software. Dr. Rick Briggs, a researcher for NASA, says in an article that "Samskrit grammarians had already found a way of solving what is perhaps the most important problem in computer science - natural language understanding and machine translation."[1] In fact, several concepts which are fundamental to today's theoretical computer science have their origin in the works of Panini (520 - 460 BCE) a Samskrit grammarian who gave a comprehensive and scientific theory of phonetics, phonology, and morphology. Currently, the Indian Defence Ministry is developing secret codes using Samskrit and applying 'The Panini Methodology'[2].

In Samskrit, sound and sense are inseparable; the harmonious relationship between these two is based on eternal principles. Every one of its vowels and consonants has particular and inalienable force which exists by the nature of things and not by development or human choice. Interestingly, according to a research recently completed by Dr. Fred Travis, director of the ERG / psychophysiology lab of Maharishi University of Management in Fairfield, Iowa, USA, the physiological effects of reading Samskrit are similar to those experienced during the Transcendental Meditation technique.[3]

For ages, Samskrit has been the language of documentation in our land, lauded as the longest continuing civilisation of the world. Sages and seers, poets and philosophers, scholars and scientists have preserved their wisdom, in all its purity, in Samskrit. Today, we know from worldwide research, that it will continue to command pride of place in mankind's progress, spiritual and scientific.

The testimonies to the eternal relevance of Samskrit are truly endless.

Samskrit is the soul of India, the symbol of its unity. Knowledge of Samskrit will bring us closer together as a nation; help us gain immensely beneficial insights into our rich cultural, literary and scientific heritage; and guide us to a glorious future.

1 Dr. Rick Briggs, Knowledge Representation in Sanskrit and Artificial Intelligence, AI Magazine, Vol 6, 1985, p. 32-39.

2 The Times of India (28/12/2002), Panini methodology for secret defence codes.

3 Dr. Fred Travis, International Journal of Neuroscience, 2001, vol.109, issue 1-2, p. 71, ISSN 0020-7454.

MEDICINE

Medicine

History and Philosophy

History

Atharva-veda, the youngest of the four Vedas (placed as earlier than 5000 BCE), contains hymns on diseases and their treatment. The Atharva-veda also talks of the 8 branches of Ayurveda. Shilajit (black bitumen), a material used as a drug even today in Ayurveda, was found in the Mohenjo Daro excavations (3500 BCE). These two are indicative of the scientific handling of diseases in India from a very early date.

In this country, learning and preservation of knowledge has been through an oral tradition which is built on a succession of teacher-mentors and disciple–followers. In the field of medical science, these teacher-disciple lineages are traced to three original teachers:

- Atreya (Internal medicine)
- Dhanvantari (Surgery) and
- Kashyapa (Gynaecology and Paediatrics).

Some of these teacher–students had, defying the prevailing practice, chosen to document what they had heard, seen and learnt. The teachers to whom we owe the survival of the ancient knowledge are:

- Charaka (1st Century BCE) of the Atreya school, who codified the percepts and practices in internal medicine.
- Sushruta (6th Century BCE) of the Dhanvantari school, who codified surgical practices.
- Vagbhata (6th Century AD) of the Kashyapa school, dealing with Gynaecology and Paediatrics.

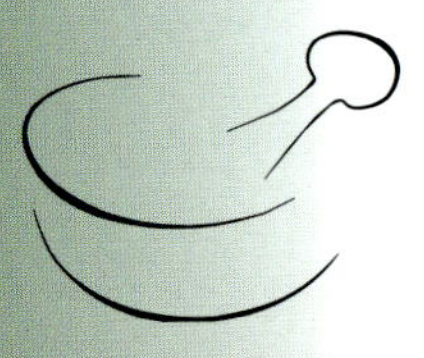

The names of the authors vouch for their being compilers: Charaka – the one who has travelled (and learnt); Sushruta - the one who has heard well (and learnt); and Vagbhata - the one who is eloquent (in communicating what he has learnt).

The three epochal works (Charaka-samhita, Sushruta-samhita and Ashtanga-hridaya), of these illustrious authors, are referred to as the Brihat-trayi - the Big Three of Ayurvedic literature. Then there is the Laghu Trayi, the Small Three made of Sarangadhara-samhita, Madhava-nidana and the Bhava-prakasha.

The periods of the authors only indicate the time of the knowledge being codified and reduced to writing, while the knowledge itself would have endured for several centuries preceding the compilation.

Philosophy

Ayurveda is a system of medicine that is holistic. It is holistic in more ways than one

- It looks at the body as a whole.
- It looks at prevention and care in addition to treatment.
- It looks at food as an essential ingredient of good health and treatment in addition to medication.
- It looks at the body and the mind.
- It considers genetic and environmental factors.

Ayurveda has a medico-social and medico-philosophical approach to health and treatment. It concerns itself as much with good health and disease-preventing lifestyle as with the treatment of illness.

14.1.1 Overview - Factors Responsible for Promotion of Strength

बलवृद्धिकरास्त्विमे भावा भवन्ति । तद्यथा बलवत्पुरुषे काले च सुखश्च कालयोगः सत्त्वसम्पच्च स्वभावसंसिद्धिश्च यौवनं च कर्म च संहर्षश्चेति ॥

Balavṛddhikarāstvime bhāvā bhavanti | Tadyathā balavatpuruṣe kāle ca sukhaśca kālayogaḥ sattvasampacca svabhāvasaṁsiddhiśca yauvanaṁ ca karma ca saṁharṣaśceti |

These factors are strength promoters. They are: birth in a place of strong men in times of strong men and in pleasant climate, healthy seed and uterus, nourishing food, good physique, good maintenance, healthy mind, natural disposition, youth, action and cheerfulness.

Source

Caraka-saṁhitā, Śārīra-sthānam, Adhyāyaḥ 6, Paragraph 13 (1st Century BCE)

Notes

The causative factors listed here include:

- Genetic and environmental
- Physiological and psychological

Besides, there is no preoccupation with disease and treatment. The science emphasises the role of factors like food.

The White House Commission

Eastern systems of medicine attach more importance to nutrition and prevention of disease than western medicine, and we should be more open minded to indigenous Asian systems of medicines like Ayurveda and Tai Chi. Certain CAM (Complementary & Alternative Medicine) practices such as acupuncture, bio-feedback, yoga, massage-therapy and Tai Chi may be useful in contributing to the achievements of the nation's health-goals and objectives. The application of CAM practices to cure chronic diseases and disabilities is a largely unexplored area. CAM principles and practices are useful not only in preventing some of these diseases but also in enhancing recovery and preventing further illness. Increased research in this area will help to determine how CAM principles and practices can best be used to meet the goals of the healthcare system.

Dr. James S. Gordon, Final report of The White House Commission, Executive order no. 13147, 22 March 02.

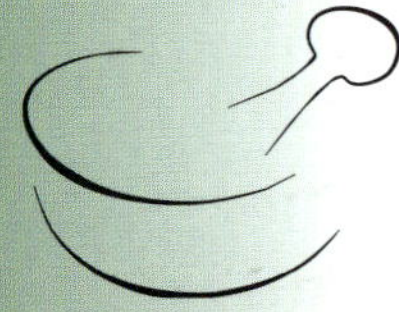

14.1.2 Overview - Test of Cure

कार्यं धातुसाम्यं तस्य लक्षणं विकारोपशमः । परीक्षा त्वस्य रुगुपशमनं स्वरवर्णयोगः शरीरोपचयः बलवृद्धिः अभ्यवहार्याभिलाषः रुचिराहारकाले अभ्यवहृतस्य चाहारस्य काले सम्यग्जरणं निद्रालाभो यथाकालं वैकरीणां च स्वप्नानामदर्शनं सुखेन च प्रतिबोधनं वातमूत्रपुरीषरेतसां मुक्तिः सर्वाकारैर्मनोबुद्धीन्द्रियाणां चाव्यापत्तिरिति ॥

Kāryaṁ dhātusāmyaṁ tasya lakṣaṇaṁ vikāropaśamaḥ । Parīkṣā tvasya rugupaśamanaṁ svaravarṇayogaḥ śarīropacayaḥ balavṛddhiḥ abhyavahāryābhilāṣaḥ rucirahārakāle abhyahṛtasya cāhārasya kāle samyagjaraṇaṁ nidrālābho yathākālaṁ vaikariṇāṁ ca svapnānāmadarśanaṁ sukhena ca pratibodhanaṁ vātamūtrapurīṣaretasāṁ muktiḥ sarvākārairmanobuddhīndriyāṇāṁ cāvyāpattiriti ॥

The task is the equilibrium of the primary fluids (humours). Its characteristic feature is the pacification of aberrations. The test of the cure is the abating of the disease, normalcy of voice and colour (of the skin), non-decay of the body, increase in strength, desire for eating, interest (Ruchi)* in eating, timely digestion of the food that is eaten, getting sleep at the proper time, not having nightmare, waking up happily, the release of wind, urine, excrement and semen, non-impairment of the mind, intellect and sense organs in all aspects.

*Ruchi means both interest and taste. One test of complete cure that is mentioned here is both interest in eating and appreciation of the taste while eating.

कार्यफलं सुखावाप्तिः तस्य लक्षणम् मनोबुद्धीन्द्रियशरीरतुष्टिः ॥

Kāryaphalaṁ sukhāvāptiḥ, tasya lakṣaṇam-manobuddhīndriyaśarīratuṣṭiḥ ॥

Attainment of good health is the fruit of this effort. Its characteristic is the contentment of the mind, the intellect, the sense organs and the body.

अनुबन्धस्तु खल्वायुः, तस्य लक्षणम् - प्राणैः सह संयोगः ॥

Anubandhastu khalvāyuḥ tasya lakṣaṇam prāṇaiḥ saha saṁyogaḥ. ॥

Is not longevity the long-term result? Its feature is union with life energy (prana)*.

* Prana: The breath of life, vitality, life, vital air, principle of life. Usually plural in this sense, the pranas being five - prana, apana, samana, vyana and udana indicative of the 5-fold metabolic functions of respiration (prana), excretion (apana), digestion (samana), reversal - cough, sneeze, hiccups, vomit - (vyana), and circulation (udana).

Source

Caraka-saṁhitā, Vimāna-sthānam, Adhyāyaḥ 8, Paragraph 89-91 (1st Century BCE)

Handling the Root Cause

Here is a passage from Astanga-hrdaya of Vagbhata, a very much later author who however continues the tradition outlined by Bhela.

"Sages know man as having his root in his mind (Bhela's context here) and the branches below (i.e. the seat of the body controlled by this mind). Therefore (a physician) who strikes at the (very) root (i.e. the mind, the crucial factor, in any disease whatsoever) would conquer the diseases more quickly."

Bhela-samhita, Ed. by K.V. Krishnamoorthy and P.V. Sharma, p. xviii.

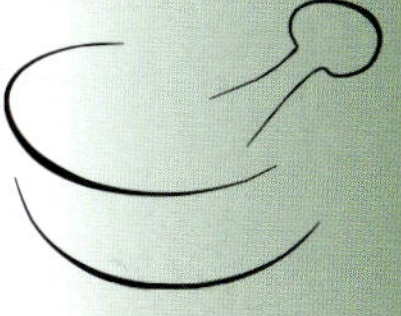

Notes

1. The three paragraphs tell the students and practitioners of medicine the test of the application of their craft in the immediate, intermediate and long terms.

2. The first quote contains an amazingly simple Process for Treatment as well as the Test for Cure.

In the antibiotic regime, initially the patient suffers from the disease and later from the debilitating effect of the antibiotic, while the patient would have been declared cured once the thermometer hits the 98.4° mark.

The Ayurveda test is simply what every single patient looks for and understands as relief from illness. The tests are health-centric and match well with the patient's understanding of well-being. The nature of the tests warrants the attending physician eliciting the status from the patient, as he can not declare the patient cured through measurable parameters like temperature or blood pressure. 2000 years ago, at least in this land, the doctors understood cure the same way as patients did. These tests for discharging a patient as cured are relevant for illness of any kind.

Western Reference

Hippocrates Aphorism (460 BCE)

"In every disease, it is a good sign when the patient's intellect is sound and he enjoys his food; the opposite is a bad sign".

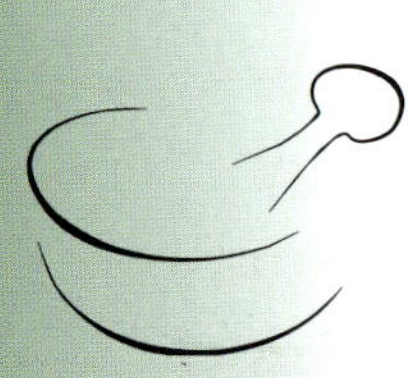

14.1.3 Overview - Eight Specialities in Āyurveda

तस्यायुर्वेदस्याङ्गान्यष्टौ तद्यथा – कायचिकित्सा शालाक्यं शल्यापहर्तृकं विषगरवैरोधिकप्रशमनं भूतविद्या कौमारभृत्यकं रसायनं वाजीकरणमिति ॥

Tasyāyurvedasyāṅgānyaṣṭau tadyathā kāyacikitsā śālākyaṁ śalyāpahartṛkaṁ viṣagaravairodhikapraśamanaṁ bhūtavidyā kaumārabhṛtyakaṁ rasāyanaṁ vājīkaraṇamiti ॥

The parts of this Ayurveda are eight, they being internal medicine, relating to the upper branches of ear, nose, throat and eye, surgery, toxicology, psychiatry, paediatrics, science of rejuvenation and the science of aphrodisiacs.

Source

Caraka-saṁhitā, Sūtra-sthānam, Adhyāyaḥ 30, Paragraph 28 (1st Century BCE)

Etymology

1. Kāya + cikitsā = Body + treatment.
   = Internal medicine.
2. Śala -> Śālākyam = Relating to the upper branches.
   = Of ear, nose and throat and the eyes.
3. Śalya + apa + hartṛkam = To be removed by thorn (knife).
   = Surgery.
4. Viṣa + gara + vairodhika + pra + śamanam = Poison + venom + resisting + pacification.
   = Toxicology.
5. Bhūta + vidyā = That which was (ghost) + knowledge
   = Psychology.
6. Kaumāra + bṛtyakam = Child + service.
   = Paediatrics.
7. Rasāyanam = Treatment with chemicals.
   (Science of rejuvenation).
8. Vajikaranam = Stimulating amorous desires = Aphrodisiacs.

Notes

The very name for paediatrics - Kaumara-brityakam (in the service of the child) is suggestive of the attitude that physicians should bring to bear in the treatment of children.

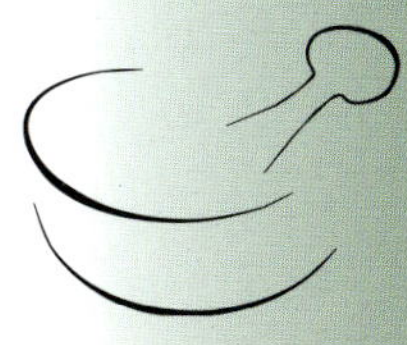

14.1.4 Overview - Classification of Diseases

तच्च दुःखं त्रिविधम् आध्यात्मिकम् आधिभौतिकम् आधिदैविकमिति ॥	Tacca duḥkhaṁ trividham ādhyātmikam ādhibhautikam ādhidaivikamiti ॥

They (the classification of diseases by origin) are of three types – exogenous, endogenous, psychic or natural

---

तत्तु सप्तविधे व्याधावुपनिपतति । ते पुनः सप्तविधा व्याधयः । तद्यथा आदिबलप्रवृत्ताः जन्मबलप्रवृत्ताः दोषबलप्रवृत्ताः सङ्घातबलप्रवृत्ताः कालबलप्रवृत्ताः दैवबलप्रवृत्ताः स्वभावबलप्रवृत्ता इति ॥	Tattu saptavidhe vyādhāvupanipatati । Te punaḥ saptavidhā vyādhayaḥ । Tadyathā ādibalapravṛttāḥ janmabalapravṛttāḥ doṣabalapravṛttāḥ saṅghātabalapravṛttāḥ kālabalapravṛttāḥ daivabalapravṛttāḥ svabhāvabalapravṛttā iti ॥

Diseases are of three types - endogenous, exogenous and cosmic. They fall under seven categories of diseases. They are:

- Those caused by pre-conception hereditary factors
- Those caused by post-conception hereditary factors
- Those caused by vitiation of humours
- Contagious
- Seasonal
- Those caused by divine forces (of unknown origin) and
- Those that are natural to the body.

व्याधिविशेषास्तु प्रागभिहिताः सर्व एवैते त्रिविधाः साध्याः याप्याः प्रत्याख्येयाश्च ।	Vyādhiviśeṣāstu prāgabhihitāḥ sarva evaite trividhāḥ sādhyāḥ yāpyāḥ pratyākhyeyāśca ।

Diseases have been mentioned earlier. All these are of three types – treatable, to be endured and to be rejected.

Source

Suśruta-saṁhitā, Sūtra-sthānam, Adhyāyaḥ 1, Paragraph 24; Adhyāyaḥ 24, Paragraph 4; Adhyāyaḥ 35 Paragraph 18 (6th Century BCE)

Notes

1. While quotes 1 and 2 above deal with the origin of diseases, quote 3 above concerns itself with the response to diseases.

2. Even though it does not emerge from this quote alone, the 7 disease types are classified under three main groups:

i. Endogenic	=	Pre-conception and post- conception hereditary diseases and those caused by vitiation of humours.
ii. Exogenic	=	Contagious and seasonal
iii. Cosmic	=	Of unknown origin and those natural to the body.

14.2.1 Anatomy - Parts of the Body

त्वश्च सप्त कलाः सप्त आशयाः सप्त धातवः सप्त सप्त सिराशतानि पञ्च पेशीशतानि नव स्नायुशतानि त्रीण्यस्थिशतानि द्वे दशोत्तरे संधिशते सप्तोत्तरं मर्मशतं चतुर्विंशतिर्धमन्यः त्रयो दोषाः त्रयो मलाः नव स्रोतांसि षोडश कण्डराः षोडश जालानि षट् कूर्चाः चतस्रो रज्जवः सप्त सेवन्यः चतुर्दश संघाताः चतुर्दश सीमन्ताः द्वाविंशतिर्योगवहानि स्रोतांसि द्विकान्यन्त्राणि चेति समासः ॥

Tvañcaḥ sapta kalāḥ sapta āśayāḥ sapta dhātavaḥ sapta sapta sirāśatāni pañca peśīśatāni nava snāyuśatāni trīṇyasthiśatāni dve daśottare sandhiśate saptottaraṁ marmaśataṁ catur-viṁśatirdhamanyaḥ trayo doṣāḥ trayo malāḥ nava srotāṁsi ṣoḍaśa kaṇḍarāḥ ṣoḍaśa jālāni ṣaṭ kūrcāḥ catasro rajjavaḥ sapta sevanyaḥ caturdaśa saṅghātāḥ caturdaśa sīmantāḥ dvāviṁśatiryogavahāni srotāṁsi dvikānyantrāṇi ceti samāsaḥ ॥

(The human body) is a collection of 7 layers of skin, 7 tissues, 7 receptacles, 7 elements, 700 tubular vessels, 500 muscles, 900 sinews, 300 bones, 210 joints, 107 vital parts, 24 (blood) vessels, 3 humors, 3 impurities, 9 sense organs, 16 tendons*, 16 plexuses#, 6 bunches (of muscles), 4 (muscular) chords, 7 (fibrous) sutures, 14 bony complexes, 14 terminal formations, 22 capillaries and 2 intestines.

* Tendons - a band of fibrous tissues attaching a muscle to a bone or other structure

\# Plexuses - a network.

Source

Suśruta-saṁhitā, Śārīra-sthānam, Adhyāyaḥ 5, Paragraph 6 (6th Century BCE)

Etymology

1. Kalāḥ	=	Parts or divisions
	=	Tissue which is an aggregation of many parts
2. Dhamanī	=	Reed / tube
	=	Blood vessel
3. Srotaḥ	=	That through which (the mind) pours out
	=	Sense organs
4. Jālam	=	Web (of muscles, veins, ligaments and bones)
	=	Plexus
5. Yoga + vāhini	=	Body fluid flows
+ srotaḥ	=	Vehicle through which blood flows
	=	Capillary.

Notes

With the exception of tendons, the numbers indicated here for the various body components are remarkably close to the modern knowledge.

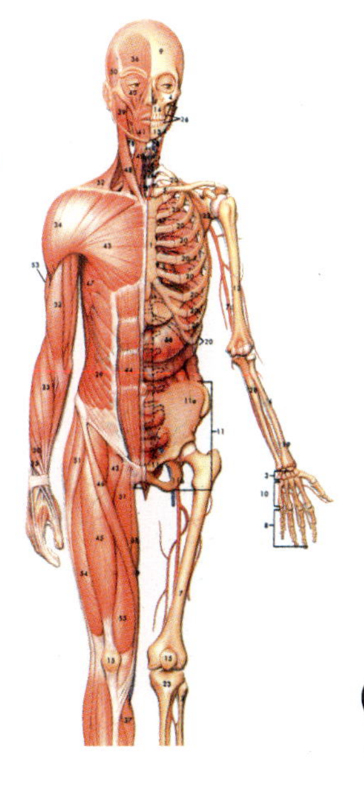

14.2.2 Anatomy - Vulnerable Spots (Marma)

तत्रैकादश मांसमर्माणि एकचत्वारिंशत् सिरामर्माणि सप्तविंशतिः स्नायुमर्माणि अष्टावस्थिमर्माणि विंशतिः सन्धिमर्माणि चेति । तदेतत् सप्तोत्तरं मर्मशतम् ॥

Tatraikādaśa māṁsamarmāṇi ekacatvāriṁśat sirāmarmāṇi saptaviṁśatiḥ snāyumarmāṇi aṣṭāvasthimarmāṇi viṁśatiḥ sandhimarmāṇi ceti । Tadetat saptottaraṁ marmaśatam ॥

There (are)

Muscle related vulnerable spots are 11
Blood vessel related vulnerable spots are 41
Sinew related vulnerable spots are 27
Bone related vulnerable spots are 8
Joints related vulnerable spots are 20
These are the 107 vulnerable spots.

तेषामेकादशैकस्मिन् सक्थि भवन्ति एतेनेतरसक्थिबाहू च व्याख्यातौ उदरोरसोर्द्वादश चतुर्दश पृष्ठे ग्रीवां प्रत्यूर्ध्वं सप्तत्रिंशत् ॥

Teṣāmekādaśaikasmin sakthi bhavanti etenetarasakthibāhū ca vyākhyātau udarorasordvādasa caturdaśa pṛṣṭhe grīvāṁpratyūrdhvaṁ saptatriṁśaṭ ॥

These vulnerable spots are in

The thighs	11 each
The two arms	11 each
Stomach/Chest	12
Back	14
Neck and above	37.

सप्तोत्तरं मर्मशतम् । तानि मर्माणि पञ्चात्मकानि भवन्ति तद्यथा मांसमर्माणि सिरामर्माणि स्नायुमर्माणि अस्थिमर्माणि सन्धिमर्माणि चेति । न खलु मांससिरास्नाय्वस्थिसन्धिव्यतिरेकेणान्यानि मर्माणि भवन्ति यस्मान्नोपलभ्यन्ते ॥

Saptottaraṁ marmaśatam । Tāni marmāṇi pañcātmakāni bhavanti tadyathā māṁsamarmāṇi sirāmarmāṇi snāyumarmāṇi asthimarmāṇi sandhimarmāṇi ceti । Na khalu māṁsasirā-snāyvasthisandhivyatirekeṇānyāni marmāṇi bhavanti yasmānnopalabhyante ॥

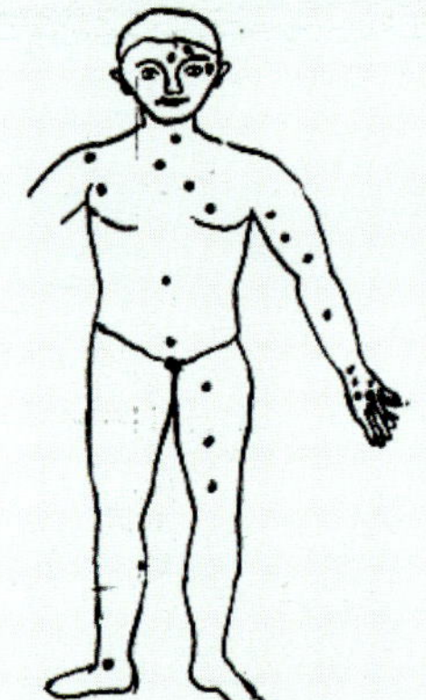

Vulnerable spots (are) 107. These vulnerable spots are five-fold, they being:

- Muscle-related vulnerable spots
- Blood vessel-related vulnerable spots
- Sinew-related vulnerable spots
- Bone-related vulnerable spots and
- Joints-related vulnerable spots.

Surely, there are no vulnerable spots other than these - muscle, blood vessel, sinew*, bone and joint-related vulnerable spots; because none else is found.

* Sinew - That which joins a muscle to a bone

तान्येतानि पञ्च विकल्पानि मर्माणि भवन्ति । तद्यथा – सद्यःप्राणहराणि कालान्तरप्राणहराणि विशल्यघ्नानि वैकल्यकराणि रुजाकराणि चेति ।

Tānyetāni pañca vikalpāni marmāṇi bhavanti । Tadyathā ~ sadyaḥprāṇaharāṇi kālāntaraprāṇa-harāṇi viśalyaghnāni vaikalyakarāṇi rujākarāṇi ceti ।

These vulnerable spots are of five kinds, they being:

- Those immediately fatal
- Those belatedly fatal
- Those which would be fatal when touched by instruments
- Those that are debilitating
- Those that are painful.

तत्र सद्यःप्राणहराण्येकोनविंशतिः कालान्तरप्राणहराणि त्रयस्त्रिंशत् त्रीणि विशल्यघ्नानि चतुश्चत्वारिंशद्वैकल्यकराणि अष्टौ रुजाकराणीति ॥

Tatra sadyaḥprāṇaharāṇyekonaviṁśatiḥ kālāntaraprāṇaharāṇi trayastriṁśatat trīṇi viśalyaghnāni catuścatvāriṁśadvaikalyakarāṇi aṣṭau rujākarāṇīti ॥

There

- Those immediately fatal = 19
- Those belatedly fatal = 33
- Those which would be fatal when touched by instruments = 3
- Those that are debilitating = 44
- Those that are painful = 8

Source

Suśruta-saṁhitā, Śārīra-sthānam, Adhyāyaḥ 6, Paragraph 3-5 & 8 (6th Century BCE)

Notes

The word 'marma' in Samskrit connotes the following:

• Vital • Vulnerable • Hidden.

Wherever the word "vulnerable" has been used in this translation, the word should be understood as enveloping all these attributes.

Current Relevance

1. The text presents the vulnerable spots from three different windows

- The system (sinew or skeleton) they form part of
- The part of the body they are present in and
- The extent of their vulnerability.

These vulnerable spots match with those contained in the martial art literature underscoring a certain commonality in the Indian system of knowledge.

An understanding and validation of this insight could help minimise the risks incidental to allopathic surgical procedures.

2. An application of this principle of "Vulnerable Points" is found in the martial art form "Varmam" which is still found in practice fairly widely in the state of Kerala and to a lesser degree in Tamilnadu. One of the offshoots of this science is Acupuncture, which, ironically, is more commonly known and is seeing a revival. This science and its art form are finding application in Sports medicine.

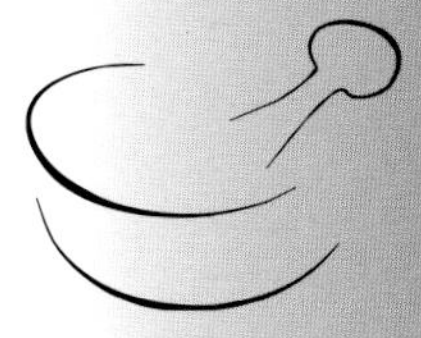

Embryology & Obstetrics

Introduction

One of the three streams of medical education in ancient India was Obstetrics (The science of mid-wifery) and Paediatrics, which had as its original teachers Kashyapa, Vasishta, Atri and Bhrigu. The codification of the practices of this school was made by Vagbhata (6th century AD), who in addition to capturing the knowledge of Obstetrics and Paediatrics, documented facets of the other six segments of Ayurveda also, in his Ashtanga-sangraha.

The Ashtanga-sangraha was updated by Vagbhata II in the seventh century AD. The updated version is known as Ashtanga-hridaya.

In addition to these specialised secular texts, the Atharva-veda and the associated Garbhopanishad (800 BCE) are repositories of knowledge in this field of medicine

The knowledge found in this ancient Samskrit literature is presented in two sections:

- Embryology
- Obstetrics

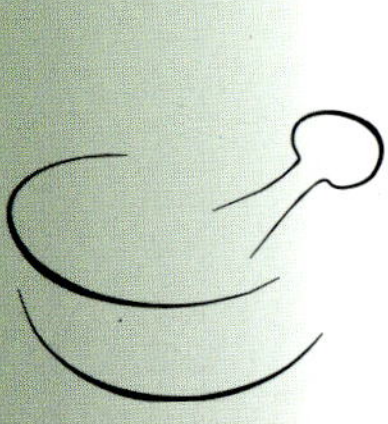

14.3.1 Embryology - Blood Circulation in the Foetus

किन्तु गर्भो मातुरुदरस्थोऽश्नाति न वेति । अत्रोच्यते नाश्नाति । यदि ह्यश्नीयात् स्यादस्य पुरीषमतीतकालं न चेदमस्ति । कथं तर्हि ? नाभ्यां नाडी प्रतिष्ठिता । तस्यामपरा मातुर्हृदयमाश्रिता मातुरन्नरसमभिवहन् गर्भं प्रीणयत्यभिवर्द्धयति तद्यथा कुल्याः केदारमभिसंश्रयन्त्यो भावयन्ति तद्वत् ॥

Kintu garbho māturudarasthoऽśnāti na veti । Atrocyate nāśnāti । Yadi hāśnīyāt syādasya purīṣamatītakālaṁ na cedamasti । Kathaṁ tarhi ? Nābhyāṁ nāḍī pratiṣṭhitā । Tasyāmaparā māturhṛdayamāśritā māturannarasamabhivahan garbhaṁ prīṇayatyabhivarddhayati tadyathā kulyāḥ kedāramabhisaṁśrayantyo bhāvayanti tadvat ॥

Does the foetus in the mother's womb eat or not? It is said here that it does not eat. If it were to eat, later (there would be) fecal matter. That does not exist. Then how? In the navel (of the child) a tubular vessel is fixed. In that (vessel) another (vessel) sheltering in mother's heart, carrying the digested food of the mother the tubular vessel satisfies and grows the foetus just as canals pervading the fields nourish them.

Source

Bhela-saṁhitā, Śārīra-sthānam, Adhyāyaḥ 4, Paragraph 31 (8th Century AD)

Etymology

Nāḍī = Tubular vessel

Western Reference

In the year 1604, an Italian physician Heironymus Fabricius published a book 'Defornata foetu' (On the formation of the foetus). It is the first important study of embryology in the West and describes blood circulation in the umbilical cord.

14.3.2 Embryology - Foetal Growth and Development

चतुर्थे सर्वाङ्गप्रत्यङ्गविभागः प्रव्यक्तो भवति गर्भहृदयप्रव्यक्तिभावाच्चेतनाधातुरभिव्यक्तो भवति, कस्मात् ? तत्स्थानत्वात् । तस्माद् गर्भचतुर्थे मास्यभिप्रायामिन्द्रियार्थेषु करोति । द्विहृदयां च नारीं दौहृदिनीमाचक्षते दौहृदविमाननात् कुब्जं कुणिं खञ्जं जडं वामनं विकृताक्षमनक्षं वा नारी सुतं जनयति, तस्मात् सा यद्यदिच्छेत्तत्तत्तस्यै दापयेत् । लब्धदौहृदा हि वीर्यवन्तं चिरायुषं च पुत्रं जनयति ॥

Caturthe sarvāṅgapratyaṅgavibhāgaḥ pravyakto bhavati, garbhahṛdaya-pravyaktibhāvāccetanādhāturabhivyakto bhavati, kasmāt ? Tatsthānatvāt I Tasmād garbhacaturthe māsyabhiprāyāmindriyārtheṣu karoti I Dvihṛdayāṁ ca nārīṁ dauhṛdinīm ācakṣate, dauhṛdavimānanāt kubjaṁ kuṇiṁ khañjaṁ jaḍaṁ vāmanaṁ vikṛtākṣam anakṣaṁ vā nārī sutaṁ janayati, tasmāt sā yadyadicchettattattasyai dāpayet I Labdhadauhṛdā hi vīryavantaṁ cirāyuṣaṁ ca putraṁ janayati II

In the fourth month, the division of all the major and minor organs manifests. Because of the manifestation of the heart, the gaining of consciousness (also) becomes evident. How? Because of its position. Therefore, in the fourth month of pregnancy, (the foetus) seeks sense objects. (The foetus) communicates its desire to the pregnant woman. By the dishonouring of such desires, the woman generates hunchbacked, crippled, lame, paralytic, dwarfed, cross-eyed or blind child. Therefore, whatever she desires, have them given to her. The pregnant woman who gets what she desires generates energetic and long-living child.

Source

Suśruta-saṁhitā, Śārīra-sthānam, Adhyāyaḥ 3, Paragraph 18 (6th Century BCE)

Notes

The Puranas (Hindu mythology) have at least two stories of learning by children in the womb

- Prahlada about Vishnu from sage Narada, which preempted the post birth teachings of his rakshasa father Hiranyakashipu and
- Abimanyu of warfare from his father Arjuna.

It is today accepted that the happiness of the child in the womb (by implication of the mother) determines all aspects of a person's growth.

The threat of begetting a defective child is held out possibly to ensure that the pregnant woman is kept happy all the time.

Western Reference

1. Limb buds appear late in the 4th week or early 5th week. In the 7th week, embryo, the three parts characteristic of the adult extremities can be recognised and muscular development of arm reaches almost complete organisation by 7 weeks. (Lewis, 1901 - 1902 AD).
2. Histological differentiation of gonads - the male or female organs - occurs in the 7th week of development (14-16 mm stage). Gillmanpro, 1948 AD
3. Foetal heart tones can often be detected as early as the 16th week (Reid, 1962 AD).

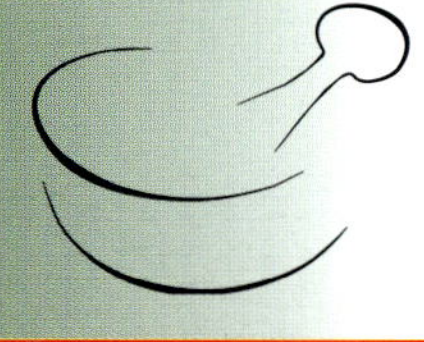

14.3.3 Embryology - Deformity in the new born child

यदा ह्यस्याः,शोणिते गर्भाशयबीजभागः प्रदोषमापद्यते, तदा वन्ध्यां जनयति, यदा पुनरस्याः शोणिते गर्भाशयबीजभागावयवः प्रदोषमापद्यते, तदा पूतिप्रजां जनयति, यदा त्वस्याः.शोणिते गर्भाशयबीजभागावयवः स्त्रीकराणां च शरीरबीजभागानामेकदेशः प्रदोषमापद्यते, तदा स्त्र्याकृतिभूयिष्ठामस्त्रियं वार्तां नाम जनयति, तं स्त्रीव्यापदमाचक्षते ॥

Yadā hyasyāḥ śoṇite garbhāśayabījabhāgaḥ pradoṣamāpadyate, tadā vandhyāṁ janayati, yadā punarasyāḥ śoṇite garbhāśayabīja-bhāgāvayavaḥ pradoṣamāpadyate, tadā pūtiprajāṁ janayati, yadā tvasya śoṇite garbāśayabījabhāgāvayavaḥ strīkarāṇāṁ ca śarīrabījabhāgānāmekadeśaḥ pradoṣam āpadyate, tadā styākṛtibhūyiṣṭhāmastriyaṁ vārtāṁ nāma janayati, tāṁ strīvyāpadamācajṣateı ॥

When in her blood, a part of the seed that has reached the uterus is vitiated, then she produces a sterile girl child.

When again, in her blood, a portion of a part of the seed that has reached the uterus is vitiated, then she gives birth to a stillborn child.

When in her blood, a portion of a part of the seed that has reached the uterus or a part of the seed that causes female organs (in the child) is vitiated then, (she) germinates a non-female, with female characteristics called "*Varta*".

Source

Caraka-saṁhitā, Śārīra-sthānam, Adhyāyaḥ 4, Paragraph 30 (1st Century BCE)

Notes

This paragraph deals with the adverse effects of humours on the ovum as well as the seed (of the male) that has reached the uterus. The damage to the seed itself is seen in three levels, affecting:

- the seed
- a part of the seed
- a portion of a part of the seed,

possibly corresponding with the modern understanding of :

- the semen or the ovum
- the chromosome of the semen or the ovum and
- the gene.

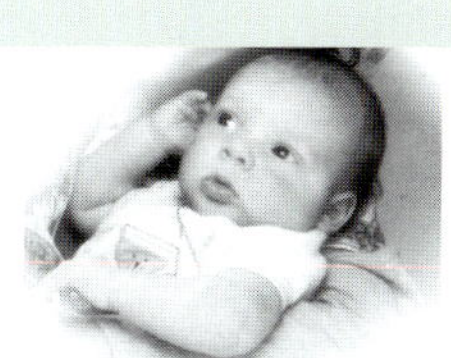

It is heartening to note that 3000 years ago, congenital deformity was traced to the genes of the parent and not attributed to supernatural factors.

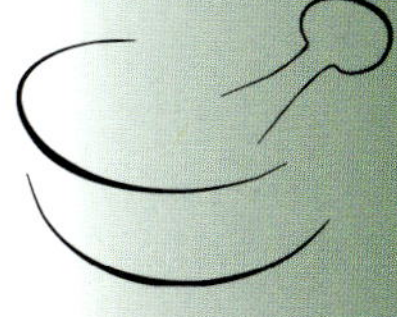

14.3.4 Obstetrics - Regimen for Pregnant Women

परमतो निर्विकारमाप्याय्यमानस्य गर्भस्य मासे मासे कर्मोपदेक्ष्यामः।	Paramato nirvikāramāpyāyyamānasya garbhasya māse māse karmopadekṣyāmaḥ ।

Now (we) shall advise the measures, month by month of the foetus growing without malady.

प्रथमे मासे शङ्किता चेद्गर्भमापन्ना क्षीरमनुपस्कृतं मात्रावच्छीतं काले काले पिबेत् साम्त्यमेव च भोजनं सायं प्रातश्च भुञ्जीत;	Prathame māse śaṅkitā cedgarbhamāpannā kṣīramanupaskṛtaṁ mātrāvacchītaṁ kāle kāle pibet, sāmtyameva ca bhojanaṁ sāyaṁ prātaśca bhuñjīta ।

In the first month if (she is) suspected to have attained pregnancy, should drink milk unboiled and a little cold, regularly, and should eat only wholesome food in evening and morning.

द्वितीये मासे क्षीरमेव च मधुरौषधसिद्धं;	Dvitīye māse kṣīrameva ca madhurauṣadhasiddham;

In the second month, only milk boiled with sweet medicines,

तृतीये मासे क्षीरं मधुसर्पिर्भ्यामुपसंसृज्य;	Tṛtīye māse kṣīraṁ madhusarpibhyamupasamsṛjya;

In the third month, milk after mixing with honey and ghee,

चतुर्थे मासे क्षीरनवनीतमक्षमात्रमश्नीयात्;	Caturthe māse kṣīranavanītamakṣamātramaśnīyāt;

In the fourth month, should consume milk with butter of 1 aksa (12 gms),

---

पञ्चमे मासे क्षीरसर्पिः;	Pancame māse kṣīrasarpiḥ;

In the fifth month, ghee directly obtained from milk,

षष्ठे मासे क्षीरसर्पिर्मधुरौषधसिद्धं; तदेव सप्तमे मासे।	Śaṣṭhe māse kṣīrasarpirmadhurauṣadha-kṣīrauṣdhasiddham; Tadeva saptame māse

In the sixth month, ghee directly obtained from milk boiled with sweet medicines, in the seventh month, the same.

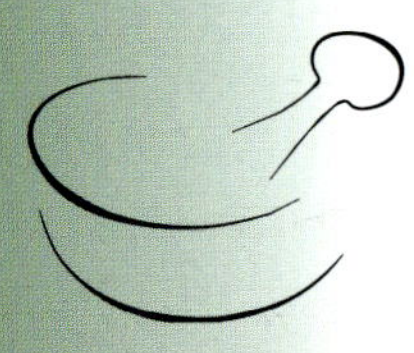

अतश्चैवास्यास्तैलात् पिचुं योनौ
प्रणयेद्गर्भस्थानमार्गस्नेहनार्थम्।
यदिदं कर्म प्रथमं मासं समुपादायोपदिष्टमानवमान्मासात्तेन
गर्भिण्या गर्भसमये गर्भधारिणीकुक्षिकटीपार्श्वपृष्ठं मृदूभवति,
वातश्चानुलोमः संपद्यते, मूत्रपुरीषे च प्रकृतिभूते सुखेन
मार्गमनुपद्येते, चर्मनखानि च मार्दवमुपयान्ति, बलवर्णौ
चोपचीयेते; पुत्रं चेष्टं संपदुपेतं सुखिनं सुखेनैषा काले
प्रजायत इति॥

Ataścaivāsyāstailāt picum yonau
praṇayedgarbhasthānamārgasnehanārtham ।
Yadidaṁ karma prathamaṁ māsaṁ
samupādāyopadiṣṭmānmāsāttena garbhiṇyā
garbhasamaye garbhadhāriṇīkukṣi-
kaṭīpārṣvapṛṣṭhaṁ mṛdūbhavati, vātascānulomaḥ
sampadyate, mūtrapurīṣe ca prakṛtibhūte;
putraṁ ceṣṭaṁ sampadupetaṁ sukhinaṁ
sukhenaiṣā kāle prajāyata iti ॥

If this action advised from first to the ninth month (be followed) by that pregnant woman, her placenta, pelvis, hip, sides and back become soft, the flatus attains downward movement, urine and stool become normal, come out with ease, the skin and nails attain softness, strength and (good) complexion increases, and thus she generates a desired son with excellence and health, easily on time.

Source

Caraka-saṁhitā, Śārīra-sthānam, Adhyāyaḥ 8, Paragraph 32 (1st Century BCE)

Notes

This prescription looks at good progeny and normal delivery as the objectives of the care of pregnant women. Food is seen as an integral and important part of care.

In the first three months, calcium is needed for the formation of bones. Hence the prescription of generous quantity of milk. Milk, an organic substance is readily absorbed and therefore superior to other kinds of calcium ingestion.

The regimen looks at the prevention of post-delivery birth mark instead of looking at it as an issue to be handled after the delivery.

Milk, milk, milk! is today's prescription also.

Current Relevance

Both milk consumption and vitamin D intake were significant predictors of birth weight, said Kristine G. Koski, Ph.D., Director of the School of Dietetics and Human Nutrition at McGill University in Canada. "For every 215 millilitres of milk that you drink ...it correlates with an extra 41 grams of birth weight," medical expert Dr. Marla Shapiro said. Medical experts say smaller babies have higher rates of hypertension, obesity and diabetes as they age. According to Scotsman, the report, whose authors included Dr Kristine Koski said: "Our study showed that restricting milk or vitamin D intake during pregnancy lowered infant birth weight in otherwise healthy, non-smoking, well-educated mothers."*

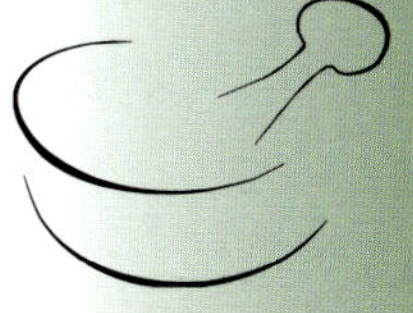

* Canada Medical Association Journal (25/4/04), Research on association of low intake of milk and vitamin D during pregnancy with decreased birth weight.

Introduction

The surgical stream is traced to Dhanvantari, one of whose students Sushruta (6th century BCE) carved a name for himself in the history of science by codifying the knowledge of the school he belonged to.

Sushruta's work - the Sushruta-samhita was revised and updated (for current knowledge) by the great Mahayana Buddhist scholar Nagarjuna in the 5th century AD and by Chandradutta in the 10th century AD. In the Buddhist period (the nearly 1000 years from the 5th century BCE to the 4th century AD), along with Buddhism, the science of Ayurveda also spread to countries like China and Tibet.

Later authors of Sushruta-samhita also added to the contents, apart from surgery, which are found in the Appendix to the book (Uttara-tantra).

Surgery

1. Intestinal Surgery
2. Absorbable Ligatures
3. Bladder Stone Removal
4. Plastic Surgery of the Nose
5. Suturing

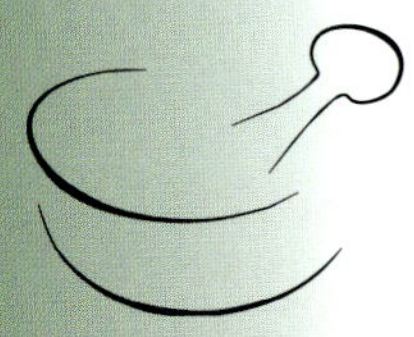

14.4.1 Surgery - Intestinal Surgery

बद्धगुदे परिस्राविणि च स्निग्धस्विन्नस्याभ्यक्तस्याधो नाभेर्वामतश्चतुरङ्गुलमपहाय रोमराज्या उदरं पाटयित्वा चतुरङ्गुल-प्रमाणमन्त्राणि निष्कृत्य निरीक्ष्य बद्धगुदस्यान्त्रप्रतिरोधकरमश्मानं वालं वाऽपोह्य मलजातं वा ततो मधुसर्पिर्भ्यामभ्यज्यान्त्राणि यथास्थानं स्थापयित्वा बाह्यं व्रणमुदरस्य सीव्येत् ।

Baddhagude parisrāviṇi ca snigdhasvinnasyābhyaktasyādho nābhervāmataścaturaṅgulamapa-hāya romarājyā udaraṁ pāṭayitvā caturaṅgulapramāṇamantrāṇi niṣkṛtya nirīkṣya baddha-gudasyāntrapratirodhakaramaśmānaṁ vālaṁ vāऽpohya malajātaṁ vā tato madhusarpirbhyāmabhyajyāntrāṇi yathāsthānaṁ sthāpayitvā bāhyaṁ vraṇamudarasya sīvyet ।

In blocked large intestine and intestinal perforation

- put the patient through fomentation, oleating and massaging
- make a 4 finger-width incision below the navel 4 finger-width left of the hair (that stretches downward from the navel),
- extracting the intestine and checking it,
- remove stone, hair or fecal matter blocking the intestine of the patient,
- smear the intestine with honey and clarified butter,
- place the stitched intestine in its original position
- stitch the external wound of the abdomen.

Source

Suśruta-saṁhitā, Cikitsā-sthānam, Adhyāyaḥ 14, Paragraph 17 (6th Century BCE)

They said it

"Surgery is the first and the highest division of the healing art, pure in itself, perpetual in its applicability, a working product of heaven and sure of fame on earth" - Sushruta (600 BCE).

N. Kothare & Sanjay A. Pai, An introduction to the history of Medicine.

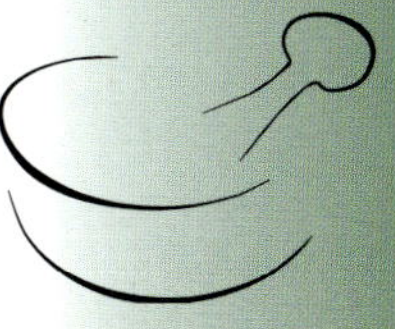

14.4.2 Surgery - Absorbable Ligatures (Pipilika Sivanam)

परिस्राविण्येवमेव शल्यमुद्धृत्यान्त्रस्रावान् संशोध्य तच्छिद्रमान्त्रं समाधाय कालपिपीलिकाभिर्दंशयेत् दष्टे च तासां कायानपहरेन्न शिरांसि, ततः पूर्ववत् सीव्येत्, सन्धानं च यथोक्तं कारयेत् यष्टीमधुकमिश्रया च कृष्णमृदाऽवलिप्य बन्धेनोपचरेत् ततो निवातमागारं प्रवेश्याचारिकमुपदिशेत् वासयेच्चैनं तैलद्रोण्यां सर्पिर्द्रोण्यां वा पयोवृत्तिमिति ॥

Parisrāviṇyapyevameva śalyamuddhṛtyāntrasrāvān saṁśodhya tacchidramāntraṁ samādhāya kālapipīlikābhi-rdaṁśayet daṣṭe ca tāsāṁ kāyānapaharenna śirāṁsi, tataḥ pūrvavat sīvyet, sandhānaṁ ca yathoktaṁ kārayet yaṣṭīmadhukamiśrayā ca kṛṣṇamrudāऽvalipya bandhenopacaret tato nivātamāgāraṁ praveśyācārikamupadiśet vāsayeccainaṁ tailadroṇyāṁ sarpirdroṇyāṁ vā payovṛttimiti ॥

In intestinal perforated tract also, similarly, after lifting the block and cleaning the intestinal fluids, bringing together the torn intestine, have black ants bite it. On biting, remove their bodies, but not their heads. Then stitch as before (the stomach); cause the union as told. Pasting a mixture of liquorice* and black earth secure with a bandage. Then entering (the patient) in an airless room advise the procedure. Make him sit in a bath of oil or bath of clarified butter. (Advise) diet of milk.

*Liquorice - A Papilionaceous (butterfly like) plant of Asia

Source

Suśruta-saṁhitā, Cikitsā-sthānam, Adhyāyaḥ 14, Paragraph 17 (6th Century BCE)

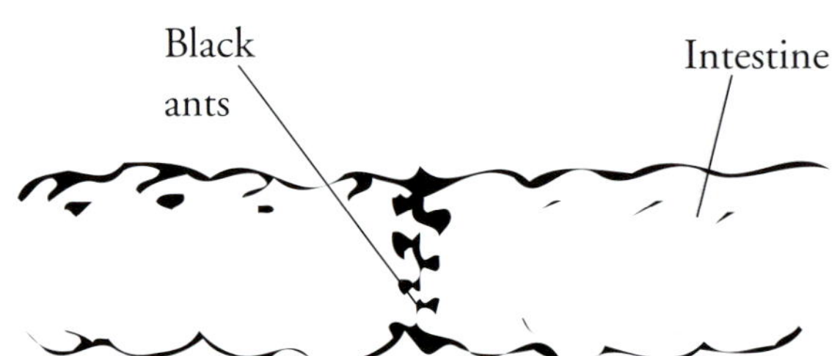

Notes

The pincers remained *in situ* due to rigor mortis retaining the cut ends of the intestine in position for some time. The heads and the pincers of the ants, being organic matter, get digested in due course of time, not unlike the catgut of present-day surgery.

Surgeon Jivaka

The oldest operation we know of is trepaning - making a hole in the skull.

It is said that Jivaka (the royal physician of King Bimbisara) once opened a man's skull and removed a centipede from inside the man's head. The man recovered. Pathologists say he might have removed a dog tapeworm which sometimes lodges in the human brain.

The Hindu (24/07/2004), Stone Age Surgeons.

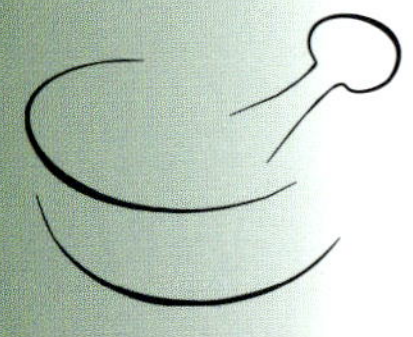

14.4.3 Surgery - Bladder Stone Removal

ततः सव्ये पार्श्वे सेवनीं यवमात्रेण मुक्त्वाऽवचारयेच्छस्त्रमश्मरीप्रमाणं दक्षिणतो वा क्रियासौकर्यहेतोरित्येके, यथा सा न भिद्यते चूर्ण्यते वा तथा प्रयतेत, चूर्णमल्पमप्यवस्थितं हि पुनः परिवृद्धिमेति तस्मात् समस्तामग्रवक्त्रेणाददीत ॥

Tataḥ savye pārśve sevanīṁ yavamātreṇa muktvāsvacārayecchastramaśmarīpramāṇaṁ dakṣiṇato vā kriyāsaukaryahetorityeke, yathā sā na bhidyate cūrṇyate vā tathā prayateta, cūrṇamalpamapyavasthitaṁ hi punaḥ parivṛddhimeti tasmāt samastāmagravaktreṇādadīta ॥

Then employ the needle on the left side leaving out only a grain of space. Some say, for the convenience of operation, employ the knife on the right side leaving out bladder-stone size space. Attempt such that it (the bladder stone) is not broken or powdered. Even if a small quantity of particle remains, it would again grow. Therefore, remove entirely with a curved forceps.

स्त्रीणां तु बस्तिपार्श्वगतो गर्भाशयः सन्निकृष्टः । तस्मात्तासामुत्सङ्गवच्छस्त्रं पातयेत् अतोऽन्यथा खल्वासां मूत्रस्रावी व्रणो भवेत्, पुरुषस्य वा मूत्रप्रसेक क्षणनान्मूत्रक्षरणम्; अश्मरीव्रणादृते भिन्नबस्तिरेकधाऽपि न भवति द्विधा भिन्नबस्तिराश्मरिको न सिध्यति ॥

Strīṇāṁ tu bastipārśvagato garbhāśayaḥ sannikṛṣṭaḥ । Tasmāttāsāmutsaṅgavacchastraṁ pātayet atosnyathā khalvāsāṁ mūtrasrāvī vraṇo bhavet, puruṣasya vā mutraprasekа kṣaṇanānmūtra-kṣaraṇam; aśmarīvraṇādṛte bhinnabastirekadhāspi na bhavati dvidhā bhinnabastirāśmariko na sidhyati ॥

For women, the womb is near, below the bladder. Therefore for them, drop the knife (only) on the surface (of the bladder). Otherwise the bladder would be injured for them. Is it not? For men because of injury to the ureter abnormal flow of urine (occurs). With the exception of the injury by bladder stone surgery, there should not be any injury even once. With two incisions to the uterus, freedom from stone would never be achieved.

Source

Suśruta-saṁhitā, Cikitsā-sthānam, Adhyāyaḥ 7, Paragraph 33 (6th Century BCE)

Etymology

1. Aśma -> Aśmari = Stone -> Bladder stone
2. Agra + vaktram = Front + mouth = Forceps
3. Mūtra+srāvi = Urine + oozer = Bladder.

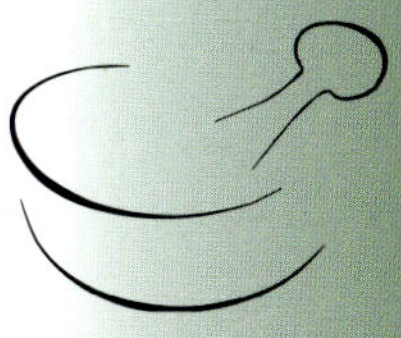

14.4.4 Surgery - Plastic Surgery of the Nose (Rhinoplasty)

विश्लेषितायास्त्वथ नासिकाया वक्ष्यामि सन्धानविधिं यथावत् ।	Viśleṣitāyāstvatha nāsikāyā vakṣyāmi sandhānavidhiṁ yathāvat ।

I will tell (you) exactly, the method of joining of disjointed nose.

नासाप्रमाणं पृथिवीरुहाणां पत्रं गृहीत्वा त्ववलम्बितस्य ॥ तेन प्रमाणेन हि गण्डपार्श्वादुत्कृत्य बद्धं त्वथ नासिकाग्रम् । विलिख्य चाशु प्रतिसन्दधीत तत् साधुबन्धैर्भिषगप्रमत्तः ॥	Nāsāpramāṇaṁ pṛthivīruhāṇāṁ patraṁ gṛhītvā tvavalambitasya ॥ Tena pramāṇena hi gaṇḍapārśvādutkṛtya baddhaṁ tvatha nāsikāgram । Vilikhya cāśu pratisandadhīta tat sādhubandhairbhiṣagapramattaḥ ॥

The doctor should

- take a nose sized leaf of a tree supported (on the forehead)
- cut the skin from the forehead in the size of the leaf
- trace on the leaf the profile of the nose and immediately
- join that (the skin) carefully with appropriate bandage.

सुसंहितं सभ्यगतो यथावन्नाडीद्वयेनाभिसमीक्ष्य बद्ध्वा । प्रोन्नम्य चैनामवचूर्णयेत्तु पतङ्गयष्टीमधुकाञ्जनैश्च ॥	Susaṁhitaṁ sabhyagato yathāvannāḍīdvayenābhisamīkṣya baddhvā । Pronnamya caināmavacūrṇayettu pataṅgayaṣṭīmadhukāñjanaiśca ॥

With two stalks, after checking on all sides and after tying such that (the nostrils) are well joined and refined, lift the nostrils; sprinkle the nose with Pathanga, liquorice and Anjana.

सञ्छाद्य सम्यक् पिचुना सितेन तैलेन सिञ्चेदसकृत्तिलानाम् । घृतञ्च पाय्यः स नरः सुजीर्णे स्निग्धो विरेच्यः स यथोपदेशम् ॥	Sañchādya samyak picunā sitena tailena siñcedasakṛttilānām । Ghṛtañca pāyyaḥ sa naraḥ sujīrṇe snigdho virecyaḥ sa yathopadeśam ॥

Covering (the operated spot) well with white cotton, sprinkle oil. The person should be fed repeatedly with the ghee of sesame seeds. On complete digestion, the person thus lubricated should be evacuated as advised.

रूढश्च सन्धानमुपागतं स्यात् तदर्द्धशेषन्तु पुनर्निकृन्तेत् ।
हीनां पुनर्वर्द्धयितुं यतेत समाञ्च कुर्यादतिवृद्धमांसाम् ॥

Rūḍhañca sandhānamupāgataṁ syāt tadarddhaśeṣantu punarnikṛntet ।
Hīnāṁ punarvarddhayituṁ yateta samāñca kuryādativṛddhamāṁsām ॥

The joint would have grown strong and come closer. Cut the remaining half again. Try to grow that which is deficient, make uniform excess growth of flesh (if any).

Source

Suśruta-saṁhitā, Sūtra-sthānam, Adhyāyaḥ 16, Paragraph 27-31 (6th Century BCE)

Notes

During one of his battles with the British, Tipu Sultan (1793 AD), the ruler of Srirangapatna (in the present Karnataka state in South India) had, as punishment, cut the nose off of 4 Indians - Kawasajee a Maratha and 3 other soldiers - who served in the British Army. The commanding officer of the British contingent in India chanced upon an Indian merchant who had his nose fixed after being cut as a punishment for adultery. The commanding officer traced the vaidya (doctor) from Maratha (the present Maharashtra) and had him fix the noses of his Indian soldiers.

This was reported in the Madras Gazzette of 1793.

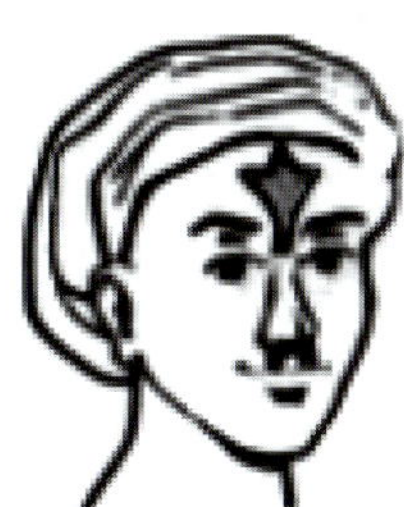

The plan of the plastic repair of a severed human nose, Indian Rhinoplasty, as per Sushruta.

An operation performed by a Maratha Vaidya (1793)

A detailed account of the reconstruction procedure was published in the October 1794 issue of the Gentleman's magazine published from London. Inspired by this account, an English surgeon J.C. Carpue performed two "Indian nose" surgeries successfully and published his experience. A German surgeon Graefe followed Carpue's example. Rhinoplasty thus moved from Maratha to Europe and has come back 200 years later as Plastic Surgery.

This ancient type of Plastic Surgery of the nose is still popular as 'Indian Rhinoplasty'.

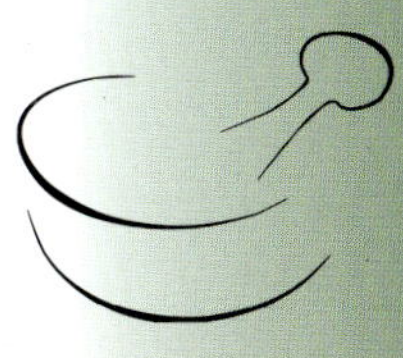

14.4.5 Surgery - Suturing

ततो व्रणं समुन्नम्य स्थापयित्वा यथास्थितम् ।
सीव्येत् सूक्ष्मेण सूत्रेण वल्केनाश्मन्तकस्य वा ॥

Tato vraṇaṁ samunnamya sthāpayitvā yathāsthitam ।
Sīvyet sūkṣmeṇa sūtreṇa valkenāśmantakasya vā ॥

Then lifting the (borders of the) wound and placing it firmly, stitch with a fine thread or the fibre of the Ashmantaka grass.

शणजक्षौमसूत्राभ्यां स्नाय्वा वालेन वा पुनः ।
मूर्वागुडूचीतानैर्वा सीव्येद्वेल्लितकं शनैः ॥

Śaṇajakṣaumasūtrābhyāṁ snāyvā vālena vā punaḥ ।
Mūrvāguḍūcītānairvā sīvyedvellitakam śanaiḥ ॥

Again slowly do a winding stitch with

- hemp
- linen or silk
- sinew
- hair
- fibre of *murva* creeper
- fibre of the medicinal plant coccvlus cordifolius or
- thread.

सीव्येद्गोफणिकां वाऽपि सीव्येद्वा तुन्नसेवनीम् ।
ऋजुग्रन्थिमथो वाऽपि यथायोगमथापि वा ॥

Sīvyedgophaṇikāṁ vāऽpi sīvyedvā tunnasevanīm ।
Ṛjugranthimatho vāऽpi yathāyogamathāpi vā ॥

Make cow horn shaped stitches or wound suture or straight knot; or stitch as appropriate.

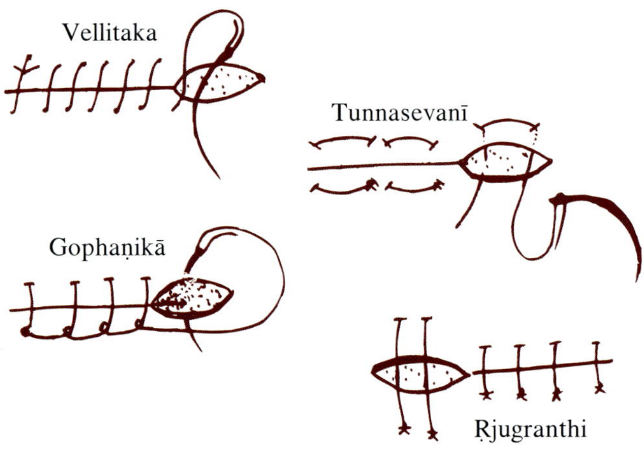

Source

Suśruta-saṁhitā, Sūtra-sthānam, Adhyāyaḥ 25, Ślokaḥ 20-22 (6th Century BCE)

Notes

Murva – the fibres drawn from this creeper are used for making bowstrings. This is indicative of the strength of this fibre used as a stitching material.

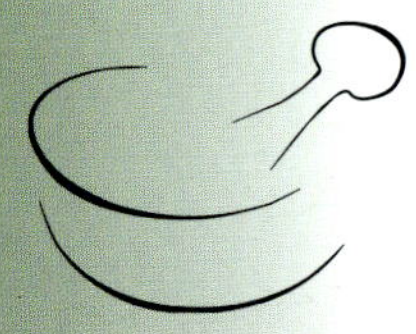

14.4.6 Surgical Instruments - Blunt Surgical Instruments (Yantra)

यन्त्राणि षट्प्रकाराणि तद्यथा स्वस्तिकयन्त्राणि सन्दंशयन्त्राणि तालयन्त्राणि नाडीयन्त्राणि शलाकायन्त्राणि उपयन्त्राणि चेति ॥	Yantrāṇi ṣaṭprakārāṇi tadyathā svastikayantrāṇi, sandaṁśayantrāṇi tālayantrāṇi nāḍī-yantrāṇi śalākāyantrāṇi upayantrāṇi ceti ॥

Controlling (blunt) instruments are of six types. They are swastikas, forceps, scoops, tubulars, probes and minor instruments.

तत्र चतुर्विंशतिः स्वस्तिकयन्त्राणि द्वे सन्दंशयन्त्रे द्वे एव तालयन्त्रे विंशतिर्नाड्यः अष्टाविंशतिः शलाकाः पञ्चविंशतिरुपयन्त्राणि ॥	Tatra caturviṁśatiḥ svastikayantrāṇi dve sandaṁśayantre dve eva tālayantre viṁśatirnāḍyaḥ aṣṭāviṁśatiḥ śalākāḥ pañcaviṁśatirupayantrāṇi ॥

There are 24 swastikas, 2 forceps, only 2 scoops, 20 tubular instruments, 28 probes and 25 minor instruments.

Source

Suśruta-saṁhitā, Sūtra-sthānam, Adhyāyaḥ 7, Paragraphs 5&6 (6th Century BCE)

Etymology

1.	Yam	=	To control
	Yantram	=	A controlling instrument
2.	Svastikam	=	Cross shaped
3.	Sam + daṁśaḥ	=	One that bites well = Forceps
4.	Tālaḥ	=	Palm leaf = Scoop
5.	Nadī	=	Tubular
6.	Salākā	=	To stir = Probe

Reiki: India ---> Japan ----> India

The concept of Reiki originated in India, but it was rediscovered by Dr. Mikao Usui in Japan in the late 19th century. Dr. Usui was a Shingon Buddhist priest and a physician. He read about an ancient healing art in an 1100 year old Buddhist Manuscript and made a brief synthesis of the essence of this seven level Tantric teaching as Reiki.

http://www.indiaparenting.com/alternativehealing/reiki/001.shtml

---

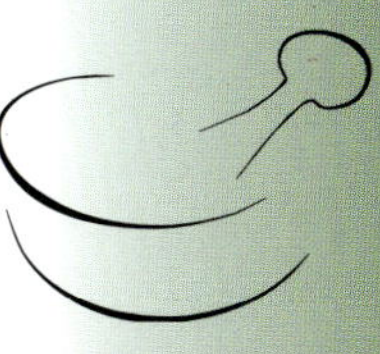

14.4.7 Surgical Instruments - Forceps

स्वस्तिकयन्त्राणि – अष्टादशाङ्गुलप्रमाणानि,
सिंहव्याघ्रवृकतरक्ष्वृक्षद्वीपिमार्जारशृगालमृगैर्वारुककाककङ्ककुरर-
चाषभासशशघात्युलूकचिल्लिश्येनगृध्रक्रौञ्चभृङ्गराजाञ्जालि-
कर्णावभञ्जाननन्दिमुखमुखानि, मसूराकृतिभिः कीलैरवबद्धानि,
मूलेऽङ्कुशवदावृत्तवारङ्गाणि, अस्थिविदष्टशल्योद्धरणार्थमुपदिश्यन्ते ॥

Svastikayantrāṇi ~ aṣṭādaśāṅgulapramāṇāni,
siṁhavyāghravṛkatarakṣvṛkṣadvīpimārjāraśṛgāla-
mṛgairvārukakākakaṅkakuraracāṣabhāsaśaśaghāt-
yulūkacilliśyenagṛdhrakrauñcabhṛṅgarājā-
ñjalikarṇāvabhañjananandimukhamukhāni,
masūrākṛtibhiḥ kīlairavabhaddhāni,
mūleऽṅkuśa-vadāvṛttavāraṅgāṇi,
asthividaṣṭaśalyoddharaṇārthamupadiśyante ॥

Swastika instruments are of 12 finger-width length.

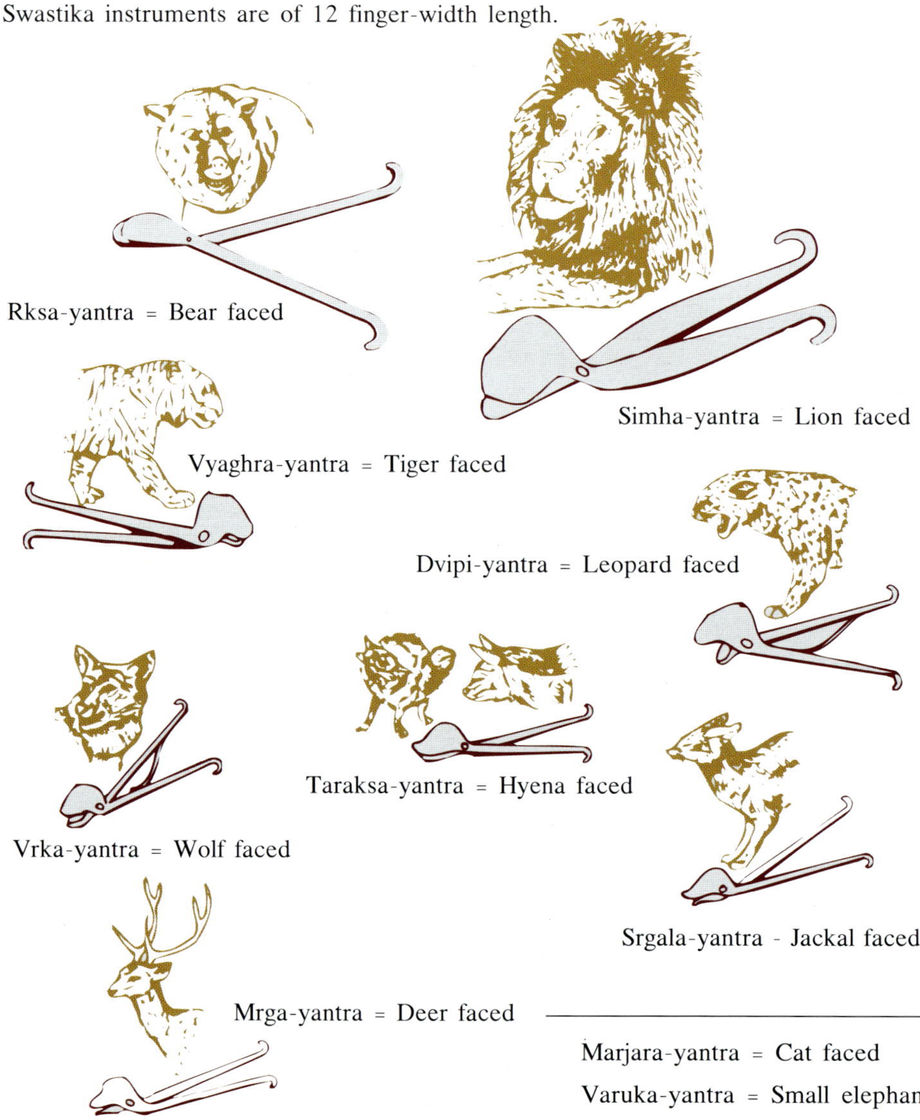

Rksa-yantra = Bear faced

Simha-yantra = Lion faced

Vyaghra-yantra = Tiger faced

Dvipi-yantra = Leopard faced

Vrka-yantra = Wolf faced

Taraksa-yantra = Hyena faced

Srgala-yantra - Jackal faced

Mrga-yantra = Deer faced

Marjara-yantra = Cat faced
Varuka-yantra = Small elephant.

Sasaghata-yantra = Eagle faced

Masa-yantra = Cock faced

Kraunca-yantra = Curlew** faced

Uluka - yantra = Owl faced

Grdhra-yantra = Vulture faced

Kaka-yantra = Crow faced

Kanka-yantra = Heron faced

Kurara-yantra = Osprey* faced

Casa-yantra = Blue jay faced

Chilli -yantra = Bengal kite faced

Syena-yantra = Hawk faced

Briga raja-yantra = Large bee faced

Anjalikarna-yantra = Horned owl faced

Avabajananandimuka-yantra = Broken bull faced.

(Instruments) bound by lentil sized nails, like the elephants held at the base by the goad (ankusha), are advised for biting and lifting thorns (foreign bodies).

Source

Suśruta-saṁhitā, Sūtra-sthānam, Adhyāyaḥ 7, Paragraph 10 (6th Century BCE)

* Osprey = Large fish-eating bird with a dark back and whitish head.

** Curlew = Water bird with a long thin beak that curves downwards.

Western Reference

Some analogous modern instruments are lion forceps, dental hawk, bill forceps, mouse teeth forceps, crocodile forceps, bulldog, volsella or tweezer, bone forceps and dental forceps.

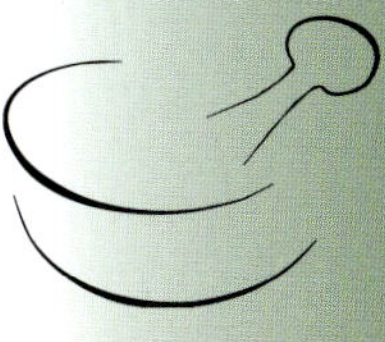

14.4.8 Surgical Instruments - Surgical Probes

शलाकायन्त्राणि अपि नानाप्रकाराणि नानाप्रयोजनानि, यथायोगपरिणाहदीर्घाणि च ।

Śalākāyantrāṇi api nānāprakārāṇi nānāprayojanāni yathāyogapariṇāhadīrghāṇi ca ।

Probes are also of different types and are of different applications. (They) are joined, circular or lengthy.

तेषां गण्डूपदसर्पफणशरपुङ्ख-बडिशमुखे द्वे द्वे एषणव्यूहनचालनाहरणार्थमुपदिश्येते ।

Teṣāṁ gaṇḍūpadasarpaphaṇaśarapuṅkha-baḍiśamukhe dve dve eṣaṇavyūhanacālanāharaṇārthamupa-diśyete ।

Of these (probes) with face like earthworm, head of the snake, the base of the arrow and a hook – each of these – are of two shapes. These are advised for probing, arranging, moving, and extracting.

मसूरदलमात्रमुखे द्वे किञ्चिदानताग्रे स्रोतोगतशल्योद्धरणार्थम्; षट् कार्पासकृतोष्णीषाणि प्रमार्जनक्रियासु ।

Masūradalamātramukhe dve kiñcidānatāgre srotogataśalyoddharaṇārtham ṣaṭ kārpāsakṛtoṣṇīṣaṇi pramārjanakriyāsu ।

(Probes) with face just the size of grains, with a little forward bend are two. (These are advised) for lifting of thorn (foreign body) gone into the alimentary canal.

त्रीणि दर्व्याकृतीनि खल्लमुखानि, क्षारौषधप्रणिधानार्थम् ।

Trīṇi darvyākṛtīni khallamukhāni, kṣārauṣadhapraṇi-dhānārtham ।

There are 6 cotton headed probes, for cleaning tasks.

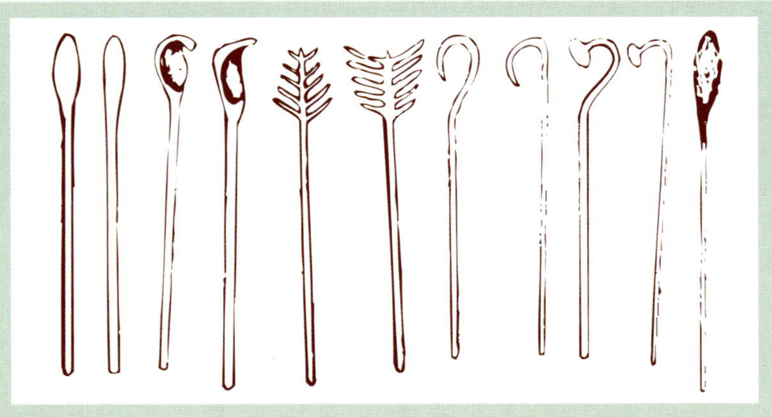

त्रीण्यन्यानि जाम्बववदनानि त्रीण्यङ्कुशवदनानि षडेवाग्निकर्मस्वभिप्रेतानि ।

Trīṇyanyāni jāmbavavadanāni trīṇyaṅkuśavadanāni ṣaḍevāgnikarmasvabhipre-tāni ।

For the application of alkaline and medicines, there are three ladle-shaped and mortar-faced probes.

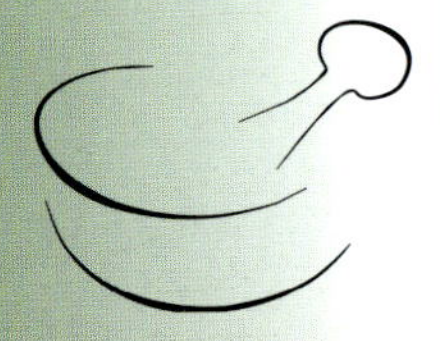

नासाऽर्बुदहरणार्थमेकं कोलास्थिदलमात्रमुखं खल्लतीक्ष्णौष्ठम् ।	Nāsāऽrbudaharaṇārthamekam kolāsthidalamātramukhaṁ khallatīkṣṇauṣṭham ।

There are three other rose-apple-faced probes; three spear-faced. These 6 are opined in cauterization.

अञ्जनार्थमेकं कलायपरिमण्डलमुभयतो मुकुलाग्रम् ।	Añjanārthamekaṁ kalāyaparimaṇḍala-mubhayato mukulāgram ।

For the removal of tumour from the nose, one (a probe) with face like a split hip bone and with sharpened lip (is advised).

मूत्रमार्गविशोधनार्थमेकं मालतीपुष्पवृन्ताग्रप्रमाण-परिमण्डलमिति ।	Mūtramārgaviśodhanārthamekaṁ mālatīpuṣpavṛntāgrapramāṇaparimaṇḍalamiti ।

For applying medicine, one that has the circumference of a seed and has bud like face on either side (is advised).

For cleaning the urinary tract, a probe with circumference of the size of the tip of the jasmine stalk (is advised).

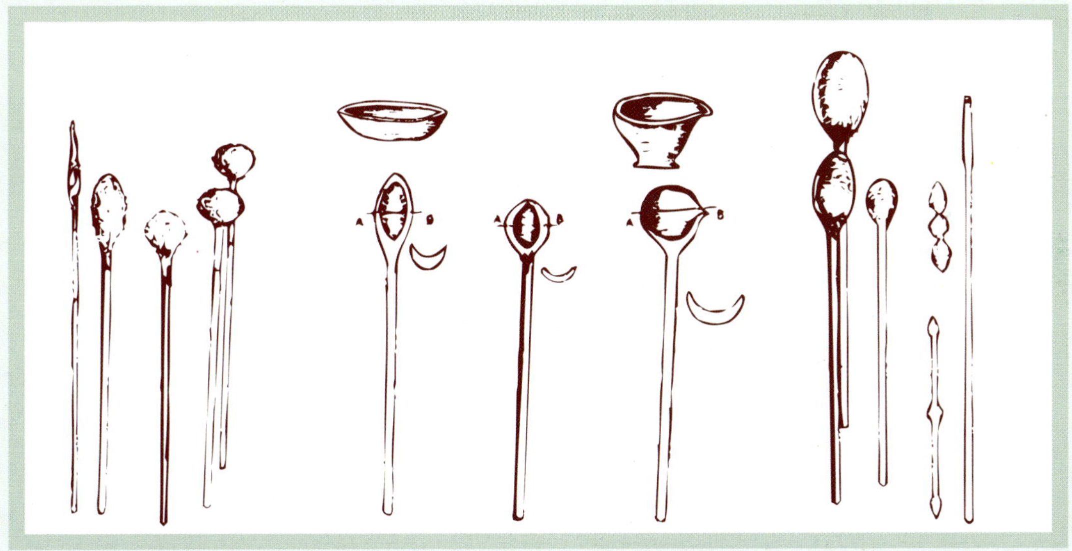

Source

Suśruta-saṁhitā, Sūtra-sthānam, Adhyāyaḥ 7, Paragraph 14 (6th Century BCE)

Etymology

Kṣāra = corrosive, caustic, alkaline.

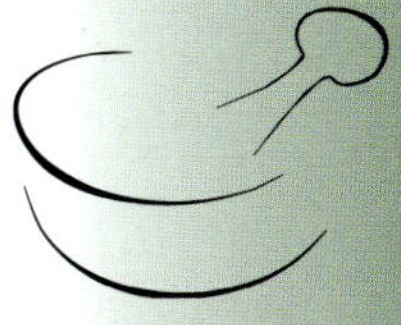

14.4.9 Surgical Instruments - Surgical Cutting Instruments

विंशतिः शस्त्राणि तद्यथा – मण्डलाग्रकरपत्र-वृद्धिपत्र-नखशस्त्र-मुद्रिकोत्पलपत्रकार्द्धधारसूची-कुशपत्राटीमुख-शरारिमुखान्तर्मुख-त्रिकूर्चक-कुठारिका-व्रीहिमुखारावेतसपत्रक-बडिश-दन्तशङ्क्वेषण्य इति ॥

Viṁśatiḥ śastrāṇi tadyathā - maṇḍalāgrakarapatra-vṛddhipatra-nakhaśastra-mudrikotpalapatrakārddha-dhārasūcī-kuśapatrāṭīmukha-śarārimukhāntarmukhatrikūrcaka-kuṭhārikā-vrīhimukhārāvetasapatraka-baḍiśa dantaśaṅkveṣaṇya iti ॥

(There are) twenty sharp instruments like this:

1. Mandala-agra = Circular fronted
2. Kara-patra = Hand–leaf
3. Vriddhi-patra = Razor
4. Nakha-shastra = Nail like
5. Mudrika = Ring like
6. Utpala-patraka = Lotus leaf
7. Ardha-dhara = Single edged
8. Suci = Needle
9. Kusha-patra = Grass leaf

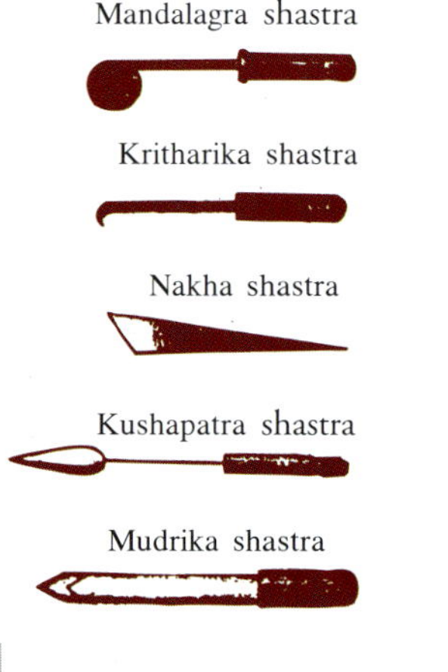
Mandalagra shastra

Kritharika shastra

Nakha shastra

Kushapatra shastra

Mudrika shastra

Eshani shastra

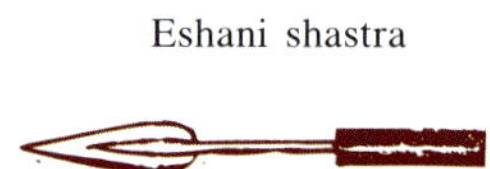
Vetaspatra shastra

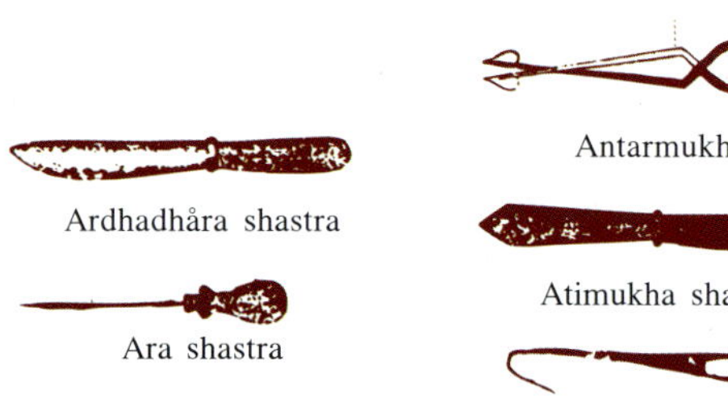
Antarmukha

Ardhadhåra shastra

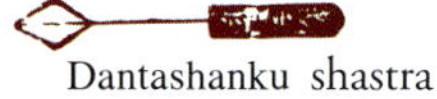
Ara shastra

Dantashanku shastra

Karapatra shastra

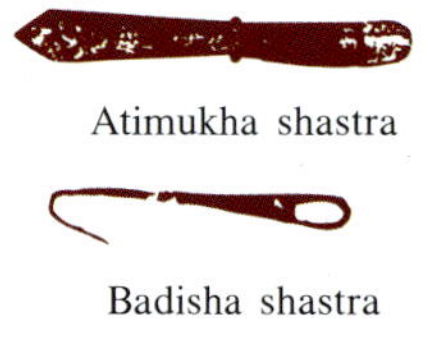
Atimukha shastra

Badisha shastra

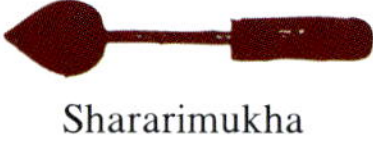
Shararimukha

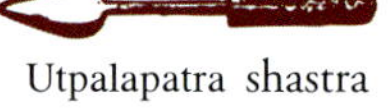
Utpalapatra shastra

Trikurchaka

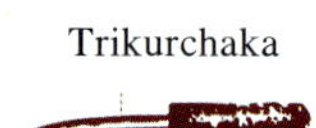
Vridhipatra shastra

10. Ati-mukha = Ati beak like
11. Sharari-mukha = Sharari beak like
12. Antar-mukha = Curved in
13. Tri-kurcaka = Three bristled
14. Kutharika = Axe
15. Vrihi-mukha = Rice faced
16. Ara = Spokes
17. Vetasa-patraka = Rattan* like
18. Badisa = Hook
19. Danta-sanku = Tooth cone
20. Eshani = Probes

* Rattan = A climbing palm with very long thin stem.

Source

Suśruta-saṁhitā, Sūtra-sthānam, Adhyāyaḥ 8, Paragraph 3 (6th Century BCE)

14.4.10 Surgical Instruments - Needles

देशेऽल्पमांसे सन्धौ च सूची वृत्ताऽङ्गुलद्वयम् ।
आयता त्र्यङ्गुला त्र्यस्रा मांसले चापि पूजिता ॥
धनुर्वक्रा हिता मर्मफलकोशोदरोपरि ।
इत्येतास्त्रिविधाः सूचीस्तीक्ष्णाग्राः सुसमाहिताः ॥

Deśeऽlpamāṁse sandhau ca sūcī vṛttāऽṅguladvayam ।
Āyatā tryaṅgulā tryasrā māṁsale cāpi pūjitā ॥
Dhanurvakrā hitā marmaphalakośodaropari ।
Ityetāstrividhāḥ sūcīstīkṣṇāgrāḥ susamāhitāḥ ॥

In areas of minimal flesh and joints, needles that are round and of two finger-width length and in fleshy parts three-cornered needles of three finger-width length are honoured.

In the vital parts, scrotum and abdomen, needle curved like a bow is appropriate. Thus these three types of sharp pointed needles are brought together.

Source

Suśruta-saṁhitā, Sūtra-sthānam, Adhyāyaḥ 25, Ślokaḥ 23, 24 (6th Century BCE)

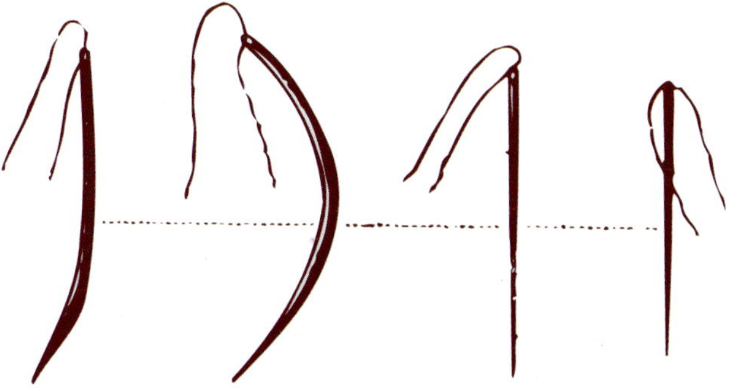

Suchi shastra (Needles)

Thai Massage: India -----> Thailand ---> India

"With Thai massage the effects are immediate, you feel significantly rejuvenated and energised after the very first session," says Anne Perry, a Thai bodywork expert. "Repeated sessions have actually cured chronic back pain, but most importantly, they seem to inspire people to do more work, live healthier lives and take up what they really love to do."

"Thai massage is a little bit like dance, it involves a lot of postures like yoga. It's not strenuous as long as you do it right," she says.

"There's evidence, in some form, of it being practised 2,500 years ago in India. And I am honoured to be able to bring the tradition back to India, the country of its origin. "Thai massage finds similarities with marma chikitsa, and probably travelled to Southeast Asia with Monastic Buddhism before being integrated with their medical and herbal systems. "In Thailand, they honour the fact that it came from India."

The Hindu (30/1/2006), In an interview with Ms. Anne Perry, The Thai Touch.

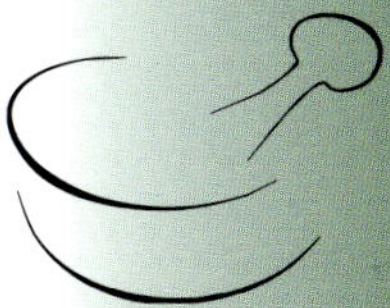

Elimination Therapy

Panchakarma

Introduction

Pancha + karma = 5 procedures of treatment used in Ayurveda, especially for detoxification or elimination of aggravated and vitiated doshas.

1.	Vamana	=	Induced Emesis
2.	Virechana	=	Medicinal Purgation
3.	Nasya	=	Nasal Administration
4.	Basti (Anuvasan)	=	Medicinal Enema (oil base)
	Basti (Niruha)	=	Medicinal Enema (decoction base)
5.	Raktamokshana	=	Blood Letting.

This therapy works on the premise of eliminating the undesirable from the body, thereby purifying the body resulting in the rejuvenation of the subject. Thus the alternate use of the words elimination therapy, purification therapy and rejuvenation therapy for this branch of medicine.

14.5.1 Blood Letting - Use of Leech

अथ जलौकोऽवसेकसाध्यव्याधितमुपवेश्य संवेश्य वा विरुक्ष्य चास्य तमवकाशं मृद्गोमयचूर्णैर्यद्यरुजः स्यात् । गृहीताश्च ताः सर्षपरजनीकल्कोदकप्रदिग्धगात्रीः सलिलसरकमध्ये मुहूर्त्तस्थिता विगतक्लमा ज्ञात्वा ताभी रोगं ग्राहयेत् । श्लक्ष्णशुक्लार्द्रपिचुप्रोतावच्छन्नां कृत्वा मुखमपावृणुयात् । अगृह्णन्त्यै क्षीरबिन्दुं शोणितबिन्दुं वा दद्याच्छस्त्रपदानि वा कुर्वीत । यद्येवमपि न गृह्णीयात्तदाऽन्यां ग्राहयेत् ॥

Atha jalaukoऽvasekasādhyavyādhitamupaveśya saṁveśya vā viruksya cāsya tamavakāśam mṛdgomayacūrṇairyadyarujaḥ syāt ।
Gṛhītāśca tāḥ sarṣaparajanīkalkodakapradigdhagātrīḥ salilasarakamadhye muhūrttasthitā vigataklamā jñātvā tābhī rogaṁ grāhayet ।
Ślakṣṇaśuklārdrapicuprotāvacchannāṁkṛtvā mukhamapāvṛṇuyāt ।
Agṛhṇantyai kṣīrabinduṁ śoṇitabinduṁvā dadyācchastrapadāni vā kurvīta ।
Yadyevamapi na gṛhṇīyāttadāऽnyāṁgrāhayet ।

Then, making the patient treatable with leeches sit or lie down; if he does not have a wound, roughen an opening, with the powder of mud and cow dung.

- Paste the selected ones (leeches) with the water of mustard, turmeric and incense
- let them soak in a pot full of water for 48 minutes
- confirm that they are rid of their tiredness and
- then have the wound gripped by them.

Covering (the leech) with smooth wet white cotton, leave the mouth alone uncovered.

If she does not bite, give her a drop of milk or blood or cut (the wound).

Even then if she does not bite, then, pick another.

Source

Suśruta-saṁhitā, Sūtra-sthānam, Adhyāyaḥ 13, Paragraph 19 (6th Century BCE)

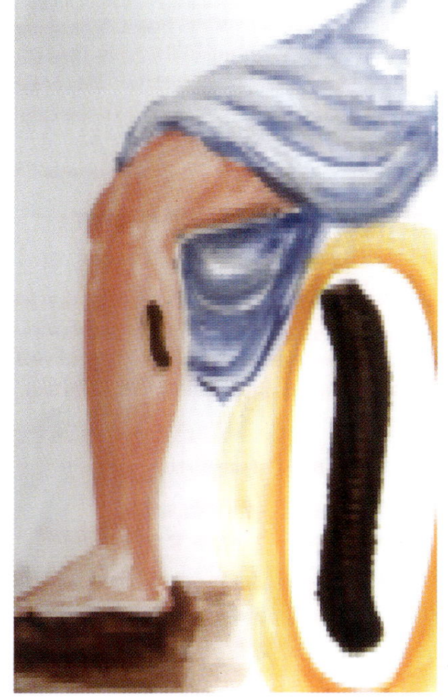

Western Reference

Therapeutic use of leech finds mention in Greek and Egyptian medical literature also in addition to Ayurveda.

Current Relevance

In 2003, in a paper by Dr. Andreas Michalsen and colleagues from Essen, Germany, titled "Effectiveness of Leech Therapy in Osteoarthritis, of the Knee", published in a recent issue of Annals of Internal Medicine, 24 patients with osteoarthritis, caused by wear and tear of the ageing knee, were given a one-shot leech therapy. Four to six leeches were allowed to attach themselves to each knee and drink blood for about an hour. 27 others with the same ailment were given twice daily

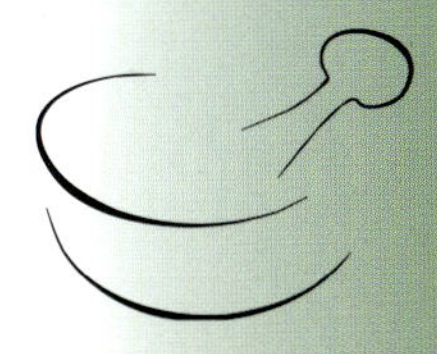

doses of the painkiller Diclofenac for a month. Conclusion: leech therapy was better than drug therapy.

While the ancient Hindus, Greeks and Egyptians knew what to do, today's scientists have identified why the leech therapy works. Nature has endowed the leech saliva with some purpose-specific chemicals:

- Vasodilator, a histamine that increases the diameter of the blood vessel
- An enzyme called hyaluronidase, which breaks down hyaluronic, the material that bonds connective tissues and
- Hirudin (named after the specie of leech that is commonly used for blood letting), which inhibits blood-clotting

The combined result of these chemicals is increased blood flow. In addition, the bite instantaneously anesthetises the bitten spot giving the leech the time to take its fill.

This combination of action is precisely what provides the patient relief from arthritic pain.

To combine all the above attributes in a chemical substance or a combination is challenge enough. The delivery is in fact considered a bigger challenge. There are doctors who believe that modern chemistry and gadgetry cannot improve upon what the leech can do. The leech, tiny as it is, absorbs blood at an extremely slow pace. The leech would also let go as soon as it has its fill. This combination virtually eliminates the risk of excessive extraction of blood. Achieving a similar result would call for delicate instruments and continuous attention from a nurse with attendant risks of human error.[*]

Leech treatment is more main stream than what is commonly understood. In 1985, a Boston surgeon who had learnt the usage of leeches in surgery in Vietnam used the procedure on a five year old boy whose ear had been bitten off by a dog. The fact that there are at least 2 companies in the United States of America - Leeches U.S.A Ltd., Long Island, New York and Biopharm of Charleston, South Carolina - whose business is supplying leeches for medical purposes, vouches for this practice gaining ground and acceptance in USA.[#]

This is a classic example of how a study of history (of medicine, in this instance) helps. The 'why' behind the solutions of yore can be figured out and alternative more convenient vehicles for delivery of the solutions can be synthesised to suit the modern times.

Note: Recently leeches are approved as 'medical equipment' by U.S.F.D.A.

* Dr. Jerry A.Rubin, Florida Hospital Celebration Health

Marillo Globe News : Health

14.5.2 Elimination Therapy - Panchakarma Benefits

एवं विशुद्धकोष्ठस्य कायाग्निरभिवर्धते ।
व्याधयश्चोपशाम्यन्ति प्रकृतिश्चानुवर्तते ॥

Evam viśuddhakoṣṭhasya kāyāgnirabhivardhate ।
Vyādhayaścopaśāmyanti prakṛtiścānuvartate ॥

For the person whose abdomen is thus cleansed, the metabolism increases, diseases subside and normalcy comes back.

इन्द्रियाणि मनोबुद्धिर्वर्णश्चास्य प्रसीदति ।
बलं पुष्टिरपत्यं च वृषता चास्य जायते ॥

Indriyāṇi manobuddhirvarṇaścāsya prasīdati ।
Balam puṣṭirapatyam ca vṛṣatā cāsya jāyate ॥

Sense faculties, mind, intellect and colour (of the skin) of the person become happy. He gets nourishment, strength, virility and offspring.

जरां कृच्छ्रेण लभते चिरं जीवत्यनामयः ।
तस्मात् संशोधनं काले युक्तियुक्तं पिबेन्नरः ॥

Jarām kṛcchreṇa labhate ciram jīvatyanāmayaḥ ।
Tasmāt saṁśodhanam kāle yuktiyuktam pibennaraḥ ॥

He does not age easily. Lives long disease-free. Therefore people should undertake cleansing when appropriate.

दोषाः कदाचित् कुप्यन्ति जिता लङ्घनपाचनैः ।
जिताः संशोधनैर्ये तु न तेषां पुनरुद्भवः ॥

Doṣāḥ kadācit kupyanti jitā laṅghanapācanaiḥ ।
Jitāḥ saṁśodhanairye tu na teṣām punarudbhavaḥ ॥

The humours (body elements) subdued by (the combination of) fasting and digestive drugs may some time aggravate. (But) when conquered by the "purification therapy", there is never their recurrence.

दोषाणां च द्रुमाणां च मूलेऽनुपहते सति ।
रोगाणां प्रसवानां च गतानामागतिर्ध्रुवा ॥

Doṣāṇām ca drumāṇām ca mūleऽnupahate sati ।
Rogāṇām prasavānām ca gatānāmāgatirdhruvā ॥

For humours (body elements) and trees, when their root is not destroyed, the reoccurrence of the disease and the flowers is a certainty.

Source

Caraka-samhitā, Sūtra-sthānam, Adhyāyaḥ 16, Paragraph 17-21 (1st Century BCE)

Etymology

1. Kāya + agniḥ = Body + fire -> Metabolism
2. Pacati -> Pachanam = Cooks -> Digestive drugs
3. Sam + śodhanam = Complete + purification = Purification therapy.

Notes

The focus on removing a problem at its root, as against quick fixes, is at the heart of the Purification stream of treatment in Ayurveda.

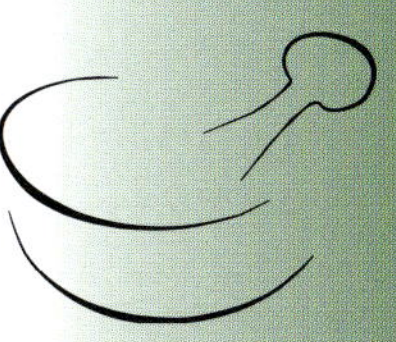

Introduction

Ayurveda → Nutraceuticals

Ayurveda is holistic; it does not try to draw a line between food and medicine, prevention and cure.

The world is waking up today to this wisdom of 3,000 years. Pharmaceutical companies all over the world are working overtime developing and bringing to the market herb-based products which blur the line between food and medicine. Herbal tea for example. The healthcare and herbal segments of the traditional pharma manufacturers are merging to bring out health and nutrition oriented products for common ailments like cough, cold, dermatological and digestive problems.

In the absence of adverse side effects, the Food and Drug Administration authorities across the world approve these formulations for use without prescription from a qualified physician, in what industry parlance is referred to as OTC (Over The Counter) drugs.

According to a World Health Organisation (WHO) report, there are about 400 families of flowering medicinal plants of which 315 families of plants occur in India. Thus India, with both the knowledge system and the material base, has the potential to assume leadership in the pharmaceutical industry in the coming years.

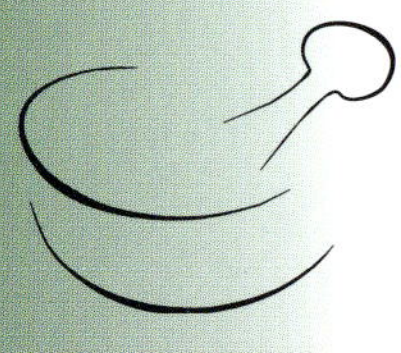

"The plant properties in the Indian tradition were discovered through a method in the Indian tradition different from that of Western science. This is described in traditional textbooks as Dravya-guna-shastra or science of the property of the materials. The challenge for Indian scientists is to develop intercultural bridges between Dravya-guna -shastra and modern Pharmacology. Such bridges can only be built when there is mutual respect and scientists feel that they own the indigenous knowledge as much as they own modern science."*

The ayurvedic pharmacology is based mostly on herbs. In ayurvedic thinking, the converse is also true. Ayurveda considers every single herb a potential medicine. In the days of yore these herbs grew naturally in forest areas and were gathered by ayurvedic students and practitioners. Since our independence in 1947, in the last nearly 60 years the forest cover of the country has come down to 21.90%[#] of the total land area, the districts of the Tamilnadu and Karnataka border presided over by the forest brigand Veerappan being the only honorable exception where the forest cover in fact has grown. Today ayurveda should be released from the handicap of inadequate availability of herbs in nature.

In olden days, an ayurvedic practitioner prepared drugs individually for each of his patients. Since independence, the population of the country has grown from 345 million to 1 billion[+]. Doctors of today do not have the time and the patience to formulate drugs individually. There is, therefore, a need for mass production of ayurvedic drugs.

In the last over 50 years, the western science has developed and fine-tuned the technology for converting medical knowledge into prescription drugs. This methodology including clinical trials is intended to ensure a high degree of safety for the user-patient in addition to product efficacy.

Could the knowledge of Charaka, Sushruta and other Ayurvedic seers be tapped and delivered to the populace using the productisation methodology currently available? This anyway is the business model that a successful pharmaceutical company The Himalaya Drug Company of India follows.

"A Weed is a Plant Whose Value has not been Discovered"

One well-known student in Takshashila (in present Pakistan) university was Jivaka who as the royal physician of King Bimbisara of Magadha (in present Bihar) acquired great fame. A story from the life of Jivaka merits quoting. After the completion of studies, Jivaka's master asked him to search for any substance within a radius of several miles, which could not be of medical use. Jivaka returned empty-handed and passed the examination proving a central belief in Ayurveda that "nothing exists in the universe which cannot be used as medicine".

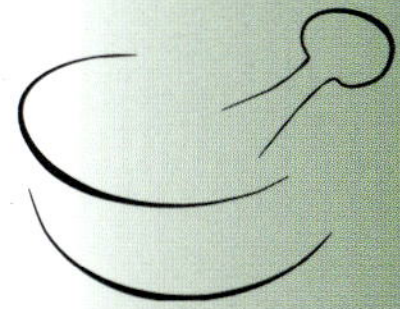

1 The Hindu (13/12/03), Garden Cure, Mr. Darshan Shankar, Director, FRLHT, Banglore.

2 http://www.overpopulation.com/discussion/read$msgnum=190

3 http://www.un.org/esa/population/pubsarchive/india/dgrow.htm

14.6.1 Pharmacology - Rejuvenation

अश्वगन्धानिलश्लेष्मश्वित्रशोथक्षयापहा ।
बल्या रसायनी तिक्ता कषायोष्णातिशुक्रला ॥

Aśvagandhānilaśleṣmaśvitraśothakṣayāpahā ।
Balyā rasāyanī tiktā kaṣāyoṣṇātiśukralā ॥

The Ashwagandha[1] - an astringent, bitter and hot (in potency) medicine removes (defects in) Vata and Kapha (humours), white leprosy, swelling and general debility. It energises and enhances sperm.

[1] Botanical name of Ashwagandha - Withania Somnifera

मेधां स्मृतिं कान्तिमनामयत्वम् आयुः प्रकर्षं बलमिन्द्रियाणाम् ।
स्त्रीषु प्रहर्षं परमग्निवृद्धिं वर्णप्रसादं पवनानुलोम्यम् ॥

Medhāṁsmṛtiṁkāntimanāmayatvam Aayuḥ prakarṣaṁbalamindriyāṇām ।
Strīṣu praharṣaṁparamagnivṛddhiṁ Varṇaprasādaṁpavanānulomyam ॥

The Rasayana promotes – intelligence, memory, lustre, immunity and longevity, strengthens sense organs and sexual excitement, stimulates (digestive) fire, gives (good) colour (to skin) and maintains favourable (state of) vata (wind humour).

रसायनस्यास्य नरः प्रयोगात् लभेत जीर्णोऽपि कुटीप्रवेशात् ।
जराकृतं रूपमपास्य सर्वं बिभर्ति रूपं नवयौवनस्य ॥

Rasāyanasyāsya naraḥ prayogāt labheta jīrṇoऽpi kuṭīpraveṣāt ।
Jarākṛtaṁ rūpamapāsya sarvam bibharti rūpaṁnavayauvanasya ॥

By taking this medicine, even an old man casts away all senility and bears the form of fresh youth.

Brahmi

Source

Bhāvaprakāśa-nighaṇṭu, Guḍuchyādigaṇah Ślokaḥ -179 (Vedic period)
Caraka-saṁhitā, Siddhi-sthānam, Adhyāyaḥ 1, Ślokaḥ 74, 75 (1st Century BCE)

Current Relevance

Scientists of the Defence Research and Development Organisation (DRDO) have developed a herbal stress buster. The drug 'Composite Indian Herbal Preparation' or CIHP-I, was prepared with 15 commonly available herbs, including 'ashwagandha', 'brahmi' and 'chyawanprash'. The Defence Institute of Physiological & Allied Sciences (DIPAS), in association with the Army Medical Corps, has completed extensive drug trials involving over 3,000 soldiers. The 'CIHP-I' was found to be beneficial for soldiers serving at high altitudes, cold areas and also in low intensity conflict situations that expose them to intense stress and high altitude sickness. It was found to be effective in improving physical and mental efficiency.*

Ashwagandha

* The Hindu (14/4/2004), A herbal stress buster for soldiers, Dr. Selvamurthy, Chief Controller (R&D), DRDO.

Relevance of Ancient Knowledge in Modern World - Malaria

Malaria is a major killer, especially in the tropics, which is home to a large number of the poor. The scientific community declared a premature victory over malaria in the 1980s, when it was thought to have been eradicated from the face of the earth. (Remember N.M.E.P the National Malaria Eradication Programme of the government of India, which did a periodical door-to-door survey to confirm that there was no occurrence of malaria.)

Malaria resurfaced with vengeance with the two principal weapons, DDT against mosquitoes which spread the disease and quinine which fights the disease, failing.

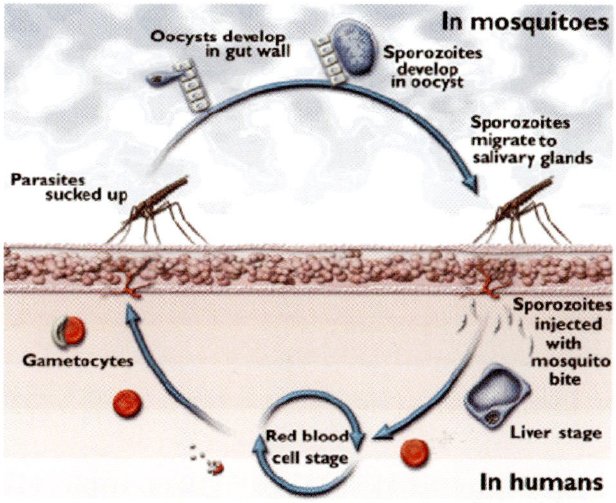

Professor Li Guoqiao from the Guangshou University of Traditional Chinese Medicine, on a trip to the mountainous Yunnan province in 1974, came across a plant called qunghao - which is mentioned as a cure for malaria in Chinese medicine books dating from 340 BCE. Prof. Li made his breakthrough in 1997 when he used artemisinin in conjunction with western synthetic drugs to create Artekin.*

Recent tests indicate that Artekin cures nearly 100 percent of patients and kills the blood parasite so quickly that it cannot build up resistance. By contrast, chloroquine - the most common anti-malarial drug available - has a success rate of less than 40 percent.

Arketin is effective not merely against the common form of malaria, which affects the liver, but also against the Falcibrum malaria, which affects the brain and is often fatal.

This drug which represents ancient Chinese wisdom delivered in modern allopathic vehicle costs only a small fraction of chloroquine and makes it possible to reach the benefit of medicine to those that need it the most - the poor.

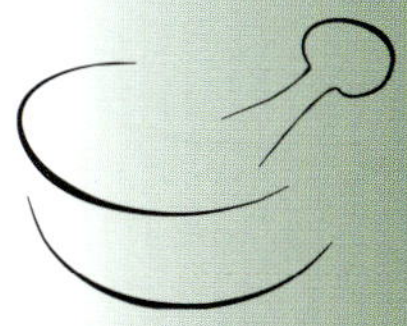

* The Hindu (30/11/2003), The end of malaria? Adam Luck. (Quoted from The Telegraph)

Other Specialities

Introduction

Charaka-samhita is a classical textbook of internal medicine. It was probably first compiled around the first century BCE. It is considered a prime work on the basic concepts of Ayurveda. Charaka represents the Atreya School of physicians. The Charaka-samhita is written in prose as well as in beautiful poetry, comparable to any Samskrit classic.

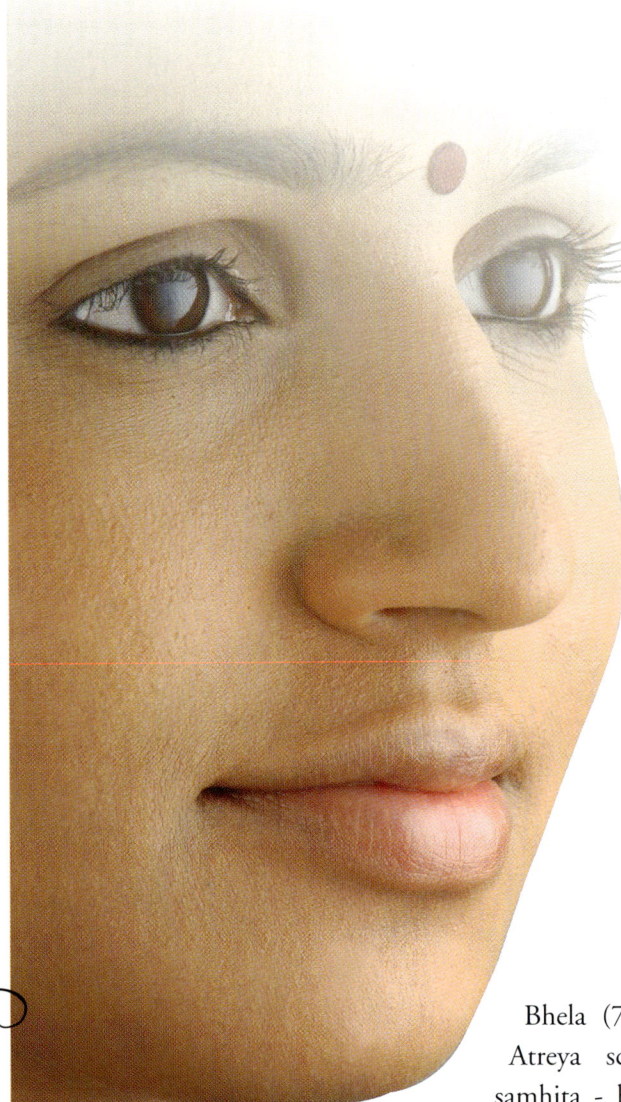

The codification of the practices of the Atreya school is believed to have taken place in 3 stages

- Agnivesha one of the original students of Atreya - 10th century BCE
- Charaka - 1st century BCE

  Updation by Drudhabala - 4th century AD.
- The dating of Charaka is derived / corroborated by the following factors:
- The language does not conform to the grammatical perceptions of the celebrated 3rd century BCE Samskrit grammarian, Panini.
- Charaka and Sushruta are quoted in each other, which should not lead us to the conclusion that these works are contemporaneous. The quoting of Sushruta in Charaka comes about because of the later "authors" of Charaka referring to the original Sushruta. Charaka is clearly ahead of Sushruta.

Bhela (7th century AD) is another scholar of the Atreya school whose compilation - the Bhela-samhita - has survived the ravages of time.

14.7.1 Cardiology - Blood Circulation

आहारस्य सम्यक् परिणतस्य यस्तेजो भूतसारः परमसूक्ष्मः स रसः इत्युच्यते । तस्य हृदयं स्थानं स हृदयात् चतुर्विंशतिर्धमनीरनुप्रवीश्य...कृत्स्नं शरीरमहरहः तर्पयति वर्धयति धारयति यापयति च अदृष्टहेतुकेन कर्मणा ॥

Āhārasya samyak pariṇatasya yastejo bhūtasāraḥ paramasūkṣmaḥ sa rasaḥ ityucyate ı Tasya hṛdayaṁ sthānaṁ sa hṛdayāt caturviṁśatirdhamanīranupravīśya...kṛtsnaṁ śarīramaharahaḥ tarpayati vardhayati dhārayati yāpayati ca adṛṣṭahetukena karmaṇā ıı

The very subtle energy that comes from the well-digested food is called 'rasa'. Its place is the heart. From the heart entering through the 24 arteries - 10 upwards, 10 downwards and 4 horizontal, it satisfies, grows, supports and maintains the entire body, day after day by unseen cause/activity.

The blood issues forth from the heart and therefrom goes everywhere; through the veins, it reaches the heart. Therefore the veins are born of the heart.

Source

Suśruta-saṁhitā, Sūtra-sthānam, Adhyāyaḥ 14, Paragraph 3 (6th Century BCE)

Etymology

1. Hṛ + da + yam = Harati + Dadati + Yati
   = Receives + Propels + Circulates
   = Heart

This is a classic example of a Samskrit noun - a word which not merely provides a "name" for the object but also defines the object.

Western Reference

In 1553 AD, Michael Servetus, a Spanish physician, published a book anonymously on Theology, postulating that blood circulated from the heart to the lungs and back. But his authorship was discovered and his unorthodox theological views resulted in his being burnt at the stake by the ruler of Geneva, John Calvin (II - Chrono.140).

It was in 1628 AD that an English physician William Harvey published a book in Netherlands concerning the motions of the heart and the blood. In it, he describes the circulation of blood as accepted now. (II - Chrono.140). Harvey is usually credited as the discoverer of blood circulation.

However, Sushruta and Bhela as well as Charaka clearly indicate not only the existence of blood circulation, but also the purpose of the blood circulation i.e. supplying nutrition. It is interesting to note that Bhela describes the blood circulation even in the foetus.

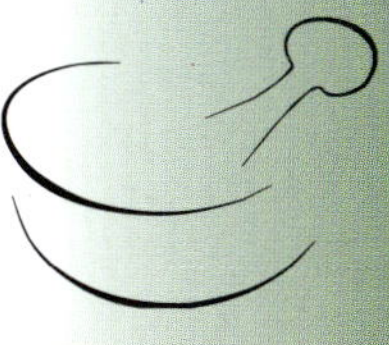

14.7.2 Cardiology - Polypill

अस्थिभङ्गास्थिसंहारे हितः कफविनाशनः । पित्तश्रम तृषादाहमेहवातविनाशकः ॥
हृद्रोगं पाण्डुरोगं च विषबाधं क्षतक्षयम् ॥

Asthibhaṅgāsthi saṁhāre hitaḥ kaphavināśanaḥ ।
Pittaśramatṛṣādāhamehavātavināśakaḥ ॥
Hṛdrogaṁ pāṇḍurogaṁ ca viṣabādhaṁ kṣatakṣayam ॥

(The Arjuna tree)[1] is good in joining disjointed bones, destroying phlegm (disorder), heart disease, jaundice, affliction due to poison and (is a) terminator of injury.

[1] Botanical name of Arjuna Tree - Terminalia Arjuna.

घृतेन दुग्धेन गुडाम्भसा वा पिबन्ति चूर्णं ककुभत्वचो ये ।
हृद्रोगजीर्णज्वरपित्तरक्तं हत्वा भवेयुश्चिरजीविनस्ते ॥

Ghṛtena dugdhena guḍāmbhasā vā pibanti cūrṇaṁ kakubhatvaco ye ।
Hṛdrogajīrṇajvarapittaraktaṁ hatvā bhaveyuścirajivinaste ॥

Those who drink with ghee, milk or molasses water, the powder of Arjuna bark, live long after (being) freed (of) heart disease, fever and profusion of blood.

Source

Nighaṇṭu-ratnākaraḥ Vṛndaḥ (Vedic period)

Current Relevance

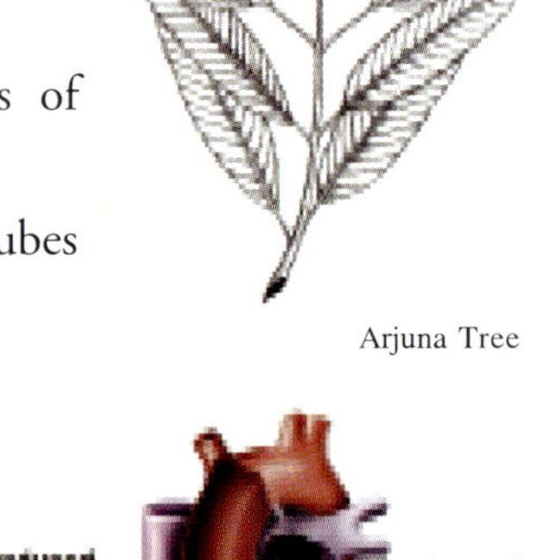
Arjuna Tree

Heart attack is caused by a multiplicity of factors like

- Abnormal levels of cholesterol and imbalance in the levels of the proteins that transport it in the body,
- Abnormal blood pressure because of blockage of the tubes that carry it,
- High levels of the harmful amino acid homocystine which damages blood vessels and
- Improper functioning of the blood cells called platelets, leading to blood clotting and vessel rupture.

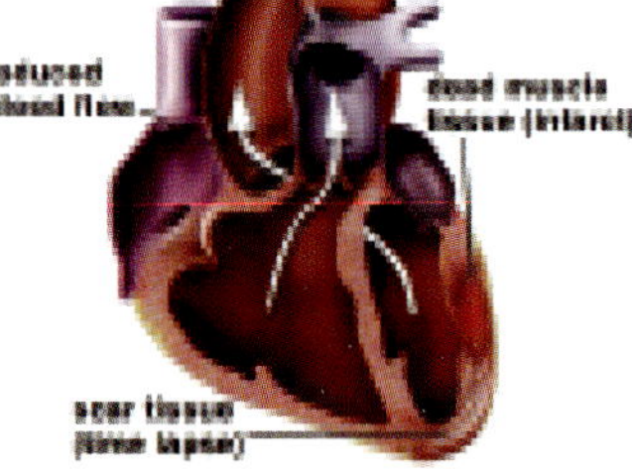
Myocardial Infarction (heart attack)

Cardiologists assess the factor that a patient is most vulnerable to and prescribe medication. Two British doctors Dr. N.J. Wald and Dr. M.R. Law of Wolfson Institute have in the 28th June 2003 edition of the British Medical Journal proposed that a tablet (a polypill) a concoction of drugs addressing all the above factors be prescribed to achieve reduction in the incidence of heart attacks and strokes.*

This idea - the polypill is still under formulation - has been welcomed in the cardiac circles as path breaking. Arjuna is halfway to being the polypill as it addresses multiple factors though not all the factors which cause a cardiac problem.

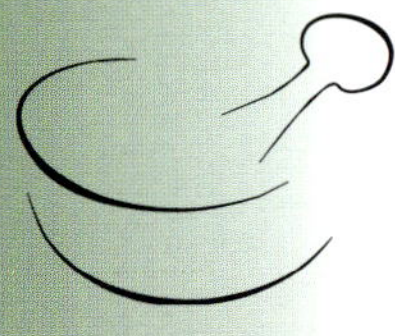

---

* Dr. Wald and Law, A strategy to reduce cardiovascular disease by more than 80% — 326 (7404): 1419 — BMJ

14.7.3 Dermatology - Skin Layers

अथ सप्त त्वग्वर्णनम् –
प्रथमाऽवभासिनी नाम या सर्वान् वर्णानवभासयति पञ्चविधां च छायां प्रकाशयति । सा व्रीहेरष्टादशभागप्रमाणा सिध्मपद्मकण्टकाधिष्ठाना ।

Atha sapta tvagvarṇanam ~
Prathamāऽvabhāsinī nāma yā sarvān varṇānavabhāsayati pañcavidhāṁ ca chāyāṁ prakāśayati । Sā vrīherasṭādaśabhāgapramāṇā sidhmapadmakaṇṭakādhiṣṭhānā ।

Then the description of the 7 (layers of) skin.

The first called Avabhasini, it exudes 5 varieties of shades. It is 1/18th a grain of rice in size. It is the abode of scab and the thorn of lotus (black head).

द्वितीया लोहिता नाम व्रीहिषोडशभागप्रमाणा, तिलकालकन्यच्छव्यङ्गाधिष्ठाना ।

Dvitīyā lohitā nāma vrīhiṣoḍaśabhāgapramāṇā, tilakālakanyacchavyaṅgādhiṣṭhānā ।

The second, Lohita, is 1/16th a grain of rice in size, the abode of mole and hollow deformation.

तृतीया श्वेता नाम व्रीहिद्वादशभागप्रमाणा, चर्मदलाजगल्लीमषकाधिष्ठाना ।

Tṛtīyā śvetā nāma vrīhidvādaśabhāga-pramāṇā, carmadalājagallīmaṣakādhiṣṭhānā ।

The third, Shveta, is 1/12th of a grain of rice in size, the abode of broken skin, wart and Mashaka, (literally mosquito, a type of skin disease).

चतुर्थी ताम्रा नाम व्रीहेरष्टभागप्रमाणा, विविधकिलासकुष्ठाधिष्ठाना ।

Caturthī tāmrā nāma vrīherasṭabhāgapramāṇā, vividhakilāsakuṣṭhādhiṣṭhānā ।

The fourth, Tamra, is 1/18th a grain of rice in size, the abode of different scabs and blotches.

पञ्चमी वेदिनी नाम व्रीहिपञ्चभागप्रमाणा, कुष्ठविसर्पाधिष्ठाना ।

Pañcamī vedinī nāma vrīhipañcabhāga-pramāṇā, kuṣṭhavisarpādhiṣṭhānā ।

The fifth, Vedini, is 1/5th a grain of rice in size, the abode of creeping leprosy.

षष्ठी रोहिणी नाम व्रीहिप्रमाणा, ग्रन्थ्यपच्यर्बुदश्लीपदगलगण्डाधिष्ठाना ।

Ṣaṣṭhī rohiṇī nāma vrīhipramāṇā, granthya-pacyarbudaślīpadagalagaṇḍādhiṣṭhānā ।

The sixth, Rohini, is equal in size to a grain of rice, the abode of swelling, gathering tumour, elephantiasis and goitre (Large swelling of the throat caused by disease of the thyroid gland.)

सप्तमी मांसधरा नाम व्रीहिद्वयप्रमाणा, भगन्दरविद्रध्यर्शोऽधिष्ठाना ।

Saptamī māṁsadharā nāma vrīhidvaya-pramāṇā, bhagandaravidradhyarśoऽdhiṣṭhānā ।

The seventh, Mamsadhara, is twice the size of a grain of rice, the abode of fistula, abscess and piles.

Source

Suśruta-saṁhitā, Śārīra-sthānam, Adhyāyaḥ 4, Paragraph 4, (6th Century BCE)

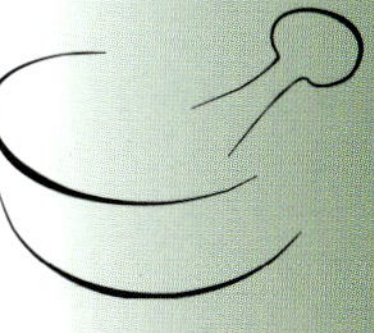

Etymology

1. Tila + kālaka	=	Black + mole	=	Mole		
2. Aja + gallī	=	The nipple hanging from goat's neck	=	Wart		
3. Kil →Kilasa	=	To become white	=	Blotch		
4. Ku + ṣṭha	=	Bad + position	=	Deformation	=	Leprosy
5. Ślī + pada	=	Swelled + foot	=	Elephantiasis		
6. Gala + gaṇḍa	=	Lump in neck				

Notes

1. The names of the seven layers of the skin are descriptive of their function or form:

   1. Avabhasini = The one that gives the shine
   2. Lohita = Copper red
   3. Shveta = White
   4. Tamra = Copper
   5. Vedini = Altar/base
   6. Rohini = Healer of wound
   7. Mamsadhara = The one that supports the flesh.

   In the above names, 2 to 4 get their name from their colour or appearance and the other four by their function.

2. The indication of the layer, in which various diseases of the skin reside, could be the starting point in the treatment of these diseases.

3. Today's dermatology talks of only five layers of skin, whereas Sushruta mentions seven. The autopsy procedure of Sushruta (next page) is a lot subtler than the allopathic method of carving with scalpel. It is conceivable that the subtler methodology has helped identify two additional layers of skin.

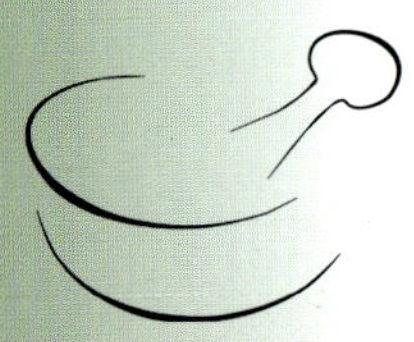

14.7.4 Autopsy

समस्तगात्रमविषोपहतमदीर्घव्याधिपीडितमवर्षशतिकं निःसृष्टान्त्रपुरीषं पुरुषमावहन्त्यामापगायां निबद्धं पारस्थं मुञ्जवल्कल-कुशशणादीनामन्यतमेनावेष्टिताङ्गमप्रकाशे देशे काथयेत्, सम्यक् प्रकुथितं चोद्धृत्य ततो देहं सप्तरात्रादुशीरबालवेणुबल्वजकूर्चानामन्यतमेन शनैः शनैरवघर्षयन्स्त्वगादीन् सर्वानेव बाह्याभ्यन्तराङ्गविशेषान् यथोक्तान् लक्षयेच्चक्षुषा ॥

Samastagātramaviṣopahatamadīrgha-vyādhipīḍitamavarṣaśatikaṁ niḥsṛṣṭāntrapurīṣaṁ puruṣa-māvahantyāmāpagāyāṁ nibaddhaṁ pañjara-sthaṁ muñjavalkalakuśaśaṇādīnāmanyatamenā-veṣṭitāṅga pratyaṅgamaprakāśe deśe kāthayet, samyak prakuthitaṁ coddhṛtya tato dehaṁ saptarātrāduśīrabālaveṇubalvajakūrcānāmanyatamena śanaiḥ śanairavagharṣayaṁstvaṅgādīn sarvāneva bāhyābhyantarāṅgaviśeṣān yathoktān lakṣayeccakṣuṣā ॥

(Select) the body of a person complete with all organs, not poisoned, not afflicted with any chronic illness and not over a hundred years of age. After evacuating his faecal matter, cover the body with munja grass, bark, dharba grass or hemp (jute); tie the body in a dark place in a river. After putrefying every organ of the body, lift the body and rubbing it very slowly for seven days with usira grass, bamboo sapling, bark or brush, observe all organs – external and internal – as told (in the text earlier) with your own eyes.

Source

Suśruta-saṁhitā, Sūtra-sthānam, Adhyāyaḥ 5, Paragraph 49 (6th Century BCE)

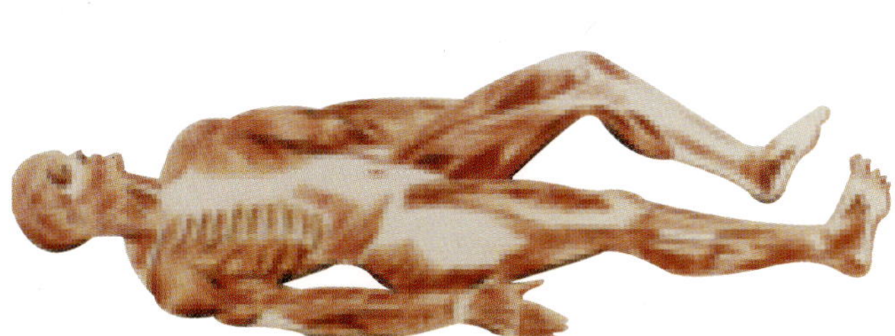

After Dissection

Notes

This is a set of instructions to students of medicine on performing autopsy. Since the intention is for the students to see and understand the internal organs of a normal person, the operating procedure starts with the selection of a body for performing autopsy. It does look as though, at this period in time (600 BCE) very many people lived for over a hundred years! Another heartening feature is that the students learn to and get to do autopsy by themselves (there appears to be no role for a teacher).

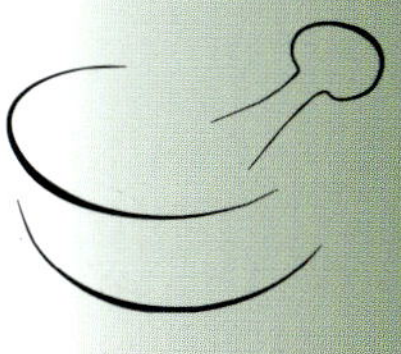

Western Reference

If Hippocrates (460 BCE Cos Island, Greece) represented the foundation of Greek Medicine, Galen (130 - 201 AD) its apex. Galen had crystallised and documented all the knowledge of all the best medical schools that preceded his own time. Galen's documentation was so exhaustive and so revered, anatomical and physiological research of no value occurred in the next 1000 years; for Galen had said everything that had to be said in these two fields of medicine.

While as the surgeon to the Emperor, Galen had gained some experience treating the wounded gladiators, bulk of his "understanding" of the human anatomy was based on dissection of animals, mainly Barbary apes.

Galen's (wrong) ideas prevailed till the 15th / 16th Century. Leonardo da Vinci (1452 - 1515 AD)* chose to ignore Galen's writings, dissected thirty corpses and made remarkable pencil drawings of his findings. Since he did not publish his work, there was no impact on the medical science. The fame of the genius stayed confined to art and engineering.

A Belgian, Andreas Vesalius (1514 - 1564 AD), like Leonardo da Vinci, ignored Galen, performed dissections and published his "De Humani Corporis Fabrica" and changed the face of anatomy. In his publication, Andreas Vesalius pointed out over 200 errors in Galen techniques.

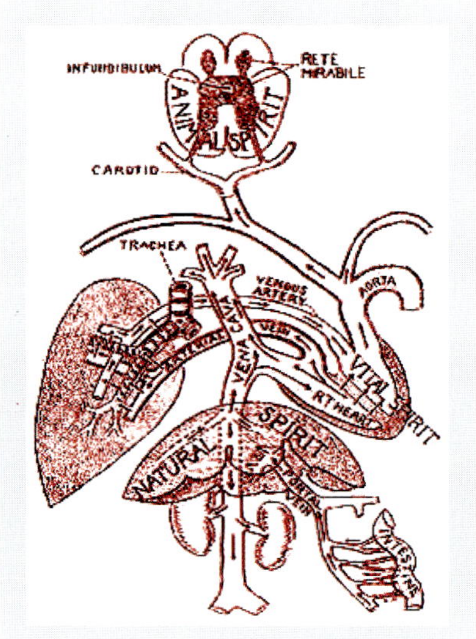

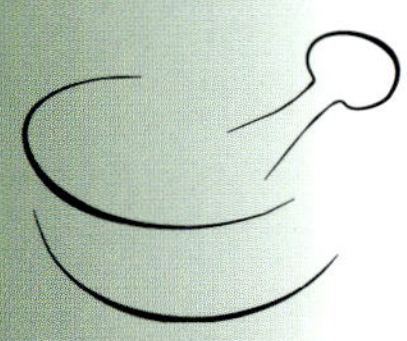

* Dr. S N Kothare & Sanjay A Pai, An introduction to the history of medicine

14.7.5 Dermatology - Parasites in Excreta

तत्र मलो बाह्यश्चाभ्यन्तरशच । तत्र बाह्यमलजान्
मलजान् संचक्ष्महे । तेषां समुत्थानम्...मृजावर्जनं स्थानं
केशश्मश्रुलोमपक्ष्मवासांसि;
संस्थानम्...अणवस्तिलाकृतयो बहुपादाश्च;
वर्णः...कृष्णः शुक्लः; नामानि...यूकाः पिपीलिकाश्च;
प्रभावः...कण्डूजननं कोठपिडकाभिनिर्वर्तनं च चिकित्सितं
तु खल्वेषामपकर्षणं मलोपघातः मूलकराणां च
भावानामनुपसेवनमिति ॥

Tatra malo bāhyaścaabhyantaraśca. Tatra bāhyamalajātān malajān samcakṣmahe. Teṣām samutthānam...mṛjāvarjanaṁ sthānam... keśaśmaśrulomapakṣmavāsāmsi; samsthānam... aṇavastilākṛtayo bahupādāśca varṇaḥ...kṛṣṇaḥ śuklaḥ; nāmāni...yūkāḥ pipīlikāśca; prabhāvaḥ ...kaṇḍūjananaṁ koṭhapiḍakābhinirvartanaṁ ca cikitsitaṁ tu khalveṣāmapakarṣaṇaṁ malopaghātaḥ mūlakarāṇāṁ ca bhāvānāmanupasevanamiti ||

Then excrements are external and internal. Then we will talk about the parasites born out of the external excrement.

Their origin	:	Lack of cleanliness.
Source	:	Hair, facial hair, body hair, eyelashes and clothing.
Their form	:	Atomic, sesame seeds sized and multi-pede.
Colour	:	Black and white.
(Common) names	:	Lice and ants.
Effect	:	Recurrence of itching, ringworm and pimples.
Treatment	:	Obviously is their (of louse / ant) dispelling.
Removal of excrement	:	Not entertaining the factors that cause the uncleanliness.

Source

Caraka-saṁhitā, Vimāna-sthānam, Adhyāyaḥ 7, Paragraph 10 (1st Century BCE)

Notes

Skin rashes have, in Allopathy, traditionally been seen as reaction to contact with plant and other allergy generating sources. Relating rashes to infection(s) in utrine area and seeing the need to address the same shows the maturity of the medical science at that point in time.

The Twain Shall Meet

The New Millineum Indian Technology Leadership Initiative (NMITLI) of the Council of Scientific and Industrial Research (CSIR), India, has launched several research programmes towards the development of usable and marketable technologies. One among these brings together traditional knowledge on plant products and native medicine practice (Ayurveda, Unani, Siddha) unique to India on one hand, and the latest chemical and biological mehtods of evaluation, improvement and drug development on the other, fusing them in a compatible manner to generate patentable and marketable products.

While these are examples in the biological and medical sciences, surely there are areas in geology, metallurgy and material sciences, mathematics and even economics and social sciences, where the twain of tradition and modern methods can meet meaningfully.

The Hindu (16/12/04), The Morning Raga and Indian Science, D.Balasubramanian.

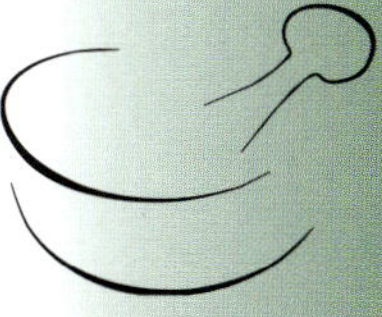

14.7.6 Orthopaedics - Fractures

काण्डभग्नमत ऊर्ध्वं वक्ष्यामः कर्कटकम् अश्वकर्णं चूर्णितं पिच्चितम् अस्थिच्छल्लितं काण्डभग्नं मज्जानुगतम् अतिपातितं वक्रं छिन्नं पाटितं स्फुटितमिति द्वादशविधम् ॥

Kāṇḍabhagnamata ūrdhvaṁ vakṣyāmaḥ karkaṭakam aśvakarṇaṁ cūrṇitaṁ piccitam asthicchallitaṁ kāṇḍabhagnaṁ majjānugatam atipātitaṁ vakraṁ chinnaṁ pāṭitaṁ sphuṭitamiti dvādaśavidham ॥

Hereafter we shall tell (you) about fractures.

1.	Karkataka	=	Crab like fracture
2.	Asvakarna	=	Horse ear like fracture
3.	Curnita	=	Powdered fracture
4.	Piccita	=	Processed / flattened fracture
5.	Asthicchallita	=	Crust of the bone fracture
6.	Kandabhagna	=	Breaking of limbs fracture
7.	Majjanugata	=	Reacting the bone narrow fracture
8.	Atipatita	=	Severely struck fracture
9.	Vakra	=	Twisted fracture
10.	Chinna	=	Broken fracture
11.	Patita	=	Pierced fracture
12.	Sphutita	=	Fissured fracture

Thus (fractures) are of 12 kinds.

प्रथमे वयसि त्वेवं मासात् सन्धिः स्थितो भवेत् ।
मध्यमे द्विगुणात् कालादुत्तरे त्रिगुणात् स्मृतः ॥

Prathame vayasi tvevaṁ māsāt sandhiḥ sthito bhavet ।
Madhyame dviguṇāt kāläduttare triguṇāt smṛtāḥ ॥

In childhood, the joint (for fractures) will become firm within a month; in middle ages in twice the time and later in thrice the time. It is thus remembered.

Source

Suśruta-saṁhitā, Cikitsā-sthānam, Adhyāyaḥ 3, Ślokaḥ 17, 19 (6th Century BCE)

The Golden Triangle

We need build a 'golden triangle' - a harmonious blend of traditional medicine modern medicine and modern science.

Dr. R.A. Mashelkar, Director, Council of Scientific and Industrial Research.
The Hindu (27/10/2003), Integrate Indian Medicine with modern science.

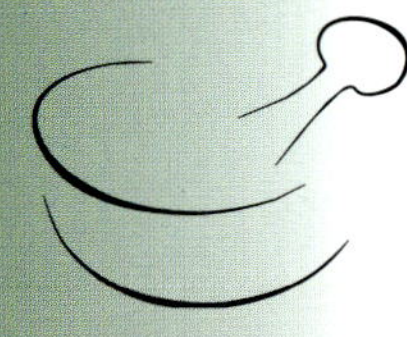

14.7.7 Orthopaedics - Dislocation (Shoulder Joint)

मुसलेनोत्क्षिपेत् कक्षामांससन्धौ विसंहते ।
स्थानस्थितं च बध्नीयात् स्वस्तिकेन विचक्षणः ॥

Musalenotkṣipet kakṣāmāṁsasandhau visaṁhate ।
Sthānasthitaṁca badhnīyāt svastikena vicakṣaṇaḥ ॥

The expert should raise the dislocated (bone of) the shoulder and the armpit with a surgical instrument, and tie with cross bandages, when properly placed.

अवनामितमुन्नह्येदुन्नतं चावपीडयेत् ।
आञ्छेदतिक्षिप्तमधो गतं चोपरि वर्तयेत् ॥
आञ्छनैः पीडनैश्चैव सङ्क्षेपैर्बन्धनैस्तथा ॥

Avanāmitamunnahyedunnataṁ cāvapīḍayet ।
Āñchedatikṣiptamadho gataṁ copari vartayet ॥
Āñchanaiḥ pīḍanaiścaiva saṅkṣepairbandhanaistathā ॥

Raise the one (the base) that is bent down; push down the one that is raised. Set the one that is severely damaged. Bring up that which has gone down. By setting, compressing, shortening and also bandaging;

सन्धीञ्छरीरे सर्वांस्तु चलानप्यचलानपि ।
एतैस्तु स्थापनोपायैः स्थापयेन्मतिमान् भिषक् ॥

Sandhīñcharīre sarvāṁstu calānapyacalānapi ।
Etaistu sthāpanopāyaiḥ sthāpayenmatimān bhiṣak ॥

The intelligent physician should set all the moving and non-moving joints in the body by these methods.

Source

Suśruta-saṁhitā, Cikitsā-sthānam, Adhyāyaḥ 3, Ślokaḥ 17-19 (6th Century BCE)

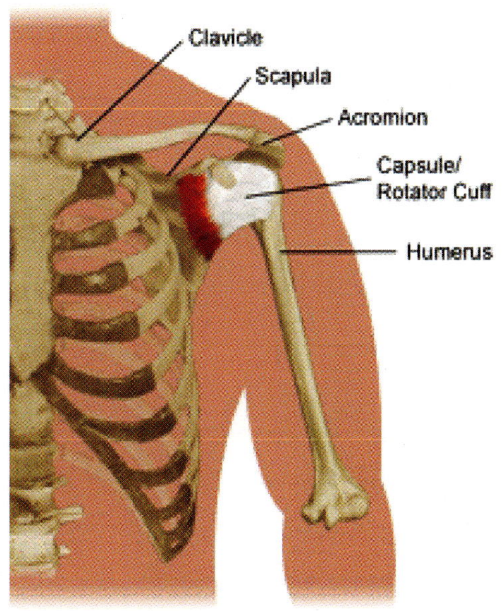

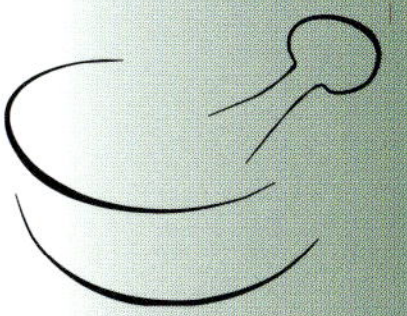

The Mahabharata can be dated in 3 different ways:

1. By linking the events of Mahabharata with the Mohenjo Daro, Harappan civilisation.
2. By working back from recorded history through a dynasty of kings.
3. Directly, independent of any other event in history, with reference to the unique astronomical events described in the epic.

This is being attempted presently.

Vs. Sindhu Sarasvati Civilisation

Unwilling to participate in the fratricidal war, Balarama goes on a pilgrimage from Dvaraka (the Somnath) to Adibidri (now in Haryana) virtually tracing Sarasvati in the reverse flow. Balarama is anguished to see the drying of the river*. The complete drying up of Sarasvati caused the abandonment of the Mohenjo Daro / Harappan cities and the south westwards migration. The Harappan excavations are carbon dated as belonging to 3500 BCE. **Therefore the Mahabharata must have taken place around 3000 BCE.**

From Modern History back to the Mahabharata

By definition, a "peak" marks the beginning of a decline. Mahabharata is one of the celebrated peaks of the Hindu society. Besides the utterance of the Gita, the Chandogya-upanishad was delivered during the Mahabharata period. Although Lord Krishna won the day and

* Vedavyasa, Mahabharata, 200 Shlokas of Shalya - parva.

helped Arjuna make up his mind and fight the war, Arjuna's worst fears as to the consequence of the war certainly turned out to be true. Kings from 56 kingdoms participated in the 18-day war and lost their armies and lives. With this sudden removal of authority, anarchy set in and the Kali-yuga came into being.

The sequence of events

- The Mahabharata war
- The destruction of kingdoms
- The decline of Vedic ritualism and
- The advent of Buddhism

The beginning of the decadence is appropriately named Kali-yuga - the Dark Ages.

Dynasty of Kings

Megasthenis (5th century BCE) who accompanied Alexander in his expedition to India, talks of 138 generations of kings between Lord Krishna (Mahabharata) and Chandragupta Maurya. We can reach alternative dates for Mahabharata from this 5th century BCE record.

Chandragupta Maurya	330 BCE
No. of generations to Mahabharata	138
• At 20 years / generation	3090 BCE
• At 25 years / generation	3780 BCE

Astronomical Evidence

It does not matter whether Ramayana and Mahabharata are historical records of actual events or imagination of prodigal minds. These epics contain accurate descriptions of astronomical events with reference to which these epics can be dated.

Duryodhana goes to his cousin on the other side - Sahadeva and requests him to fix an appropriate date for him to start the war. True to his profession, Sahadeva fixes the next new moon day for the start of the war unmindful of a victory for Duryodhana translating into a defeat for himself and his brothers. As always, Krishna steps in to save the Pandavas. A day ahead of the appropriate date fixed by Sahadeva, Lord Krishna goes to the river to perform the obsequies to the forefathers that are performed on the new-moon-day. Puzzled by this, the sun and the moon go to Lord Krishna to check how he was performing the new-moon-day rites one day too early. Krishna quips "Since you two - the sun and the moon - are here in alignment, is this not the new moon day?"

Our takehomes from this story are Duryodhana's faith in his cousin Sahadeva, Sahadeva's commitment to his profession and Krishna's smartness. What is often ignored is that the new moon had occurred in 13 days instead of the usual 14 days in that fortnight. Here is an astronomical marker that we have got on the dating of the Mahabharata war.

This astronomical event of a short duration fortnight (Kshaya-paksha) is not all that rare. It occurs once every 22 years. Fortunately, there are other events occurring close to each other which find mention in the epic.

"While Krishna tricked the sun and the moon, to get an extra new moon day, the regular new moon day also occurred the following day". That is the story. Once in a rare while the sun, moon and the earth stay aligned for over two days.

Bheeshma waited for 58 days (from the day of his fall which was on the tenth day of the 18 day war) on the bed of arrows, for the onset of Summer Solstice (Uttarayana) before breathing his last.*

The combination of these three events makes a unique dating possible.

Mahabharata and Ramayana have been in vogue for over 3000 years. At that time, it was not given to the people to work back and describe astronomical phenomenon that had occurred a millennium earlier. Therefore the description could only have been by observation.

The first astronomer to have attempted a dating of the Mahabharata war with reference to the astronomical events described in the epic is, not surprisingly, the celebrated 5th century AD mathematician, Aryabhata. He places the Mahabharata war at 3137 BCE. Another is another illustrious astronomer who followed him - Varahamihira (505 AD). In Brihad-samhita he places the great war at 2449 BCE There have been several attempts to pin a specific date to Mahabharata war based on astronomical features found in the epic. Some of the better-known datings are:

Fairly universally accepted date for the start of Kali-yuga	3102 BCE
Profs. C.V. Vaidya & Apte	3101 BCE
Mr. Kota Venkatachalam	3139 BCE
A recent study by Dr. P.V. Vartak	5561 BCE

The conclusion on sifting through this evidence is that the Mahabharata period is 3000 BCE or earlier.

*Vedavyasa, Mahabharata, Bhishmaparva, Chapter 114, Shlokas 96 & 97.

LIFE SCIENCES

Botany

Zoology

Introduction

In the Indian knowledge system, there is a clear-cut classification of creatures as living and moving. At the primary level, any being which possesses the five senses of perception – hearing, feeling (of touch), seeing, tasting and smelling – is living. The plants are living since they posses these five senses, as brought out beautifully in a conversation between the sages Bharadvaja and Bhrigu, quoted later.

Plants, while having life, are stationary; they have no locomotion and therefore they are called

Sthāvara = that which is fixed = plants (Sthā = remain in a place)

The next level of living things possess locomotion, in addition to organs of perception. The entire animal kingdom – animals, reptiles, and birds – answers this additional test. Since the distinguishing characteristic of these beings is locomotion, these are referred to as:

Jaṅgama = that which goes = animals (Gacchathi = goes)

The third in the hierarchy is the one which/who in addition to the tools of perception and action, also has the ability to think.

Manuṣyaḥ = human (Man = mind)

(It looks as though the English word "man" originated from the Samskrit word for mind.)

Another feature of the Indian knowledge system is the relevance of fundamental ideas across sciences. In Tarka (logic), Mimamsa (hermeneutics) and Vedanta (philosophy) sciences, these five senses of perception are applied in identifying and grading the elements of nature.

Elements Attributes

1. Space - sound
2. Wind - sound + touch
3. Fire - sound + touch + form
4. Water - sound + touch + form + taste
5. Earth - sound + touch + form + taste + smell

Some examples in the area of natural science are given in this section, in this same order

- Plant Kingdom (Botany) and
- Animal Kingdom (Zoology)

Human related knowledge is dealt with under Medicine.

16.1 Botany - Classification of Plants

तासां स्थावराश्चतुर्विधाः – वनस्पतयो वृक्षा वीरुधा ओषधय इति । तासु अपुष्पाः फलवन्तो वनस्पतयः । पुष्पफलवन्तो वृक्षाः । प्रतानवत्यः स्तम्बिन्यश्च वीरुधाः । फलपाकनिष्ठा ओषधय इति ॥

Tāsāṁ sthāvarāścaturvidhāḥ ~ vanaspatayo vṛkṣā vīrudhāḥ oṣadhaya iti । Tāsu apuṣpāḥ phalavanto vanaspatayaḥ । Puṣpaphalavanto vṛkṣāḥ । Pratānavatyaḥ stambhinyaśca vīrudhāḥ । Phalapākaniṣṭhā oṣadhaya iti ॥

Amongst them plants are of four kinds:

- Vanaspati - the large trees
- Vriksha - trees
- Virudha - herbs
- Oshadhi - medicinal plants

Flora are four-fold:

- Vanaspati - those that bear fruits without flowering.
- Vriksha - those that bear both flowers and fruits.
- Virudha - those that are stemless and which spread out (bushes).
- Oshadhi - those that whither away once their fruits ripen.

Source

Suśruta-saṁhitā, Sūtra-sthānam, Adhyāyaḥ 1, Paragraph 29 (6th Century BCE)

Etymology

1. Vana + pati = the lord of the forest = large tree.
2. Vṛkṣāḥ = the one that gets cut = tree.
3. Vīrudhaḥ = that which spreads/shoots = herbs.
4. Oṣadhiḥ = osho deyathe atra = the basis for digestion
   = medicinal plants.

Notes

Modern botany has 2-fold classification of plants.

Western Reference

In 1735, Carolus linnaeus, a Swedish botanist, classified plants in his book Systema Naturae.

16.2 Botany - Plants the Living

सुखदुःखयोश्च ग्रहणाच्छिन्नस्य च विरोहणात् ।
जीवं पश्यामि वृक्षाणामचैतन्यं न विद्यते ॥

Sukhaduḥkhayośca grahanācchinnasya ca virohaṇāt ।
Jīvaṁ paśyāmi vṛkṣāṇāmacaitanyam na vidyate ॥

From the grasping of happiness and unhappiness, from the healing of wounds, I see life. Plants are sentient.

तेन तज्जलमादत्तं जरयत्यग्निमरुतौ ।
आहारपरिणामाच्च स्नेहो वृद्धिश्च जायते ॥

Tena tajjalamādattaṁ jarayatyagnimarutau ।
Āhārapariṇāmācca sneho vṛddhiśca jāyate ॥

Heat and light digest the water that is drawn by it (by the plant).

From the transformation of what is brought in (the digested water) fluids comes into being; (therefore) growth occurs.

वक्त्रेणोत्पलनालेन यथोर्ध्वं जलमाददेत् ।
तथा पवनसंयुक्तः पादैः पिबति पादपः ॥

Vaktreṇotpalanālena yathordhvaṁ jalamādadet ।
Tathā pavanasaṁyuktaḥ pādaiḥ pibati pādapaḥ ॥

Just as one draws water up by the mouth and lotus stalk, plant endowed with air, drinks (water) with its feet (roots).

Source

Mahābhāratam, Śānti-parva, Chapter 184, Ślokaḥ 16-18 (3000 BCE)

Etymology

1. Pādaiḥ pibati iti = Pādapāḥ = that which drinks with its feet = plant.

Notes

1. Prof. Jagdish Chandra Bose, in the 20th century, managed to measure the reactions of plants, confirmed the faith of our sages and was honoured as a Fellow of "The Royal Society of London for the Improvement of Natural Knowledge", known simply as The Royal Society, in 1920.
2. The 16th shloka would be superfluous if it were to merely make the point that plants ingest water through their roots. The thrust of the shloka is on the Pavanasamyukta = endowed with / in the company of air - that the suction takes place because of air pressure.
3. The above quotes appear in the form of a dialogue between sages Bharadvaja and Bhrigu in the Mahabharata.

16.3 Botany - Plants have Senses

ऊष्मतो म्लायते पर्णं त्वक् फलं पुष्पमेव च । म्लायते शीर्यते चापि स्पर्शस्तेनात्र विद्यते ॥	Ūṣmato mlāyate parṇaṁ tvak phalaṁ puṣpameva ca । Mlāyate śīryate cāpi sparśastenātra vidyate ॥

Leaf, bark, fruit and flower fade from heat. Because it (plant) fades and decays, there is sense of touch.

वाय्वग्न्यशनिनिर्घोषैः फलं पुष्पं विशीर्यते । श्रोत्रेण गृह्यते शब्दस्तस्माच्छृण्वन्ति पादपाः ॥	Vāyvagnyaśaninirghoṣaiḥ phalaṁ puṣpaṁ viśīryate । Śrotreṇa gṛhyate śabdastasmācchṛṇvanti pādapāḥ ॥

By the sounds of wind, fire and lightning, fruit and flower decay rapidly. Sound is received by the ear. Therefore plants hear.

वल्ली वेष्टयते वृक्षं सर्वतश्चैव गच्छति । न ह्यदृष्टेश्च मार्गोऽस्ति तस्मात् पश्यन्ति पादपाः ॥	Vallī veṣṭayate vṛkṣaṁ sarvataścaiva gacchati । Na hyadṛṣṭeśca mārgo'sti tasmāt paśyanti pādapāḥ ॥

The creeper surrounds a tree; from all sides it moves. Unseeing, path does not exist; therefore plants see.

पुण्यापुण्यैस्तथा गन्धैर्धूपैश्च विविधैरपि । अरोगाः पुष्पिताः सन्ति तस्माज्जिघ्रन्ति पादपाः ॥	Puṇyāpuṇyaistathā gandhaiḥ dhūpaiśca vividhairapi । Arogāḥ puṣpitāḥ santi tasmājjighranti pādapāḥ ॥

Similarly, by a variety of good and bad smells and aroma (plants) blossom disease free. Therefore plants smell.

पादैः सलिलपानाच्च व्याधीनां च दर्शनात् । व्याधिप्रतिक्रियत्वाच्च विद्यते रसनं द्रुमे ॥	Pādaiḥ salilapānācca vyādhīnām cāpi darśanāt । Vyādhipratikriyatvācca vidyate rasanaṁ drume ॥

By the drinking of water with their feet, by the exhibition of diseases, by the reaction to diseases, (sense of) taste exists in trees.

Source

Mahābhāratam, Śānti-parva, Chapter 184, Ślokaḥ 11-15 (3000 BCE)

She is a nice plantain

Another research study showed how the ancient Indian Botany, as documented in works such as Amara Kosha and Vriksh Ayurveda, has clinching evidence to show how refined our knowledge of botany was. For example, the sex based classification of plant kingdom using binomial nomenclature proposed in 17th century was already practiced in ancient India. There are repeated reference to the superiority of ancient Indian works in the field of astronomy, mathematics and other materialistic sciences such as Ayurveda.

Dr. Mahadevan, Time for an Alternative perspective, International Conference on Ayurveda.

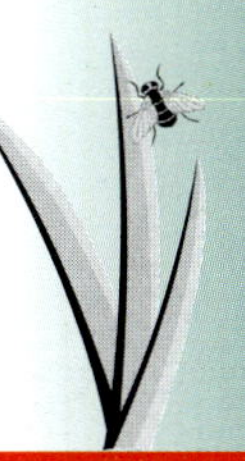

16.4 Zoology - Classification of Living Creatures

जङ्गमाः खल्वपि चतुर्विधाः
जरायुजाण्डजस्वेदजोद्भिज्जाः ।
तत्र पशु-मनुष्य-व्यालादयो जरायुजाः
खग-सर्प-सरीसृप-प्रभृतयोऽण्डजाः
कृमि-कीट-पिपीलिका-प्रभृतयः स्वेदजाः
इन्द्रगोप-मण्डूक-प्रभृतयः उद्भिज्जाः ॥

Jangamāḥ khalvapi caturvidhāḥ jarāyujāṇḍasvedajodbhijjāḥ. Tatra paśu-manuṣya-vyālādayo jarāyujāḥ, khaga-sarpa-sarīsṛpa-prabhṛtayoऽṇḍajāḥ, kṛmi-kiṭa-pipīlikā-prabhṛtayaḥ svedajāḥ indragopa-maṇḍūka-prabhṛutayaḥ udbhijjāḥ.

The mobile - creatures are also four fold -
Jarayuja - born off womb - animals, men, tiger, etc.
Andaja - born off egg - birds, snakes, reptiles, etc.
Svedaja - born of sweat - worms, insects, ants, etc.
Udbhijja - sprouting - the indra-gopa insect, frogs, etc.

Source

Suśruta-saṁhitā, Sūtra-sthānam, Adhyāyaḥ 1, Ślokaḥ 30 (6th Century BCE)

Etymology

Jarāyu + ja - womb + born

Aṇḍa + ja - egg + born

Sveda + ja - sweat (moisture) + born

Udbhij + ja - sprout + born

Indra + gopaḥ - rain + protected = the one that is protected by rain = an insect called indragopa, red or white colour insect.

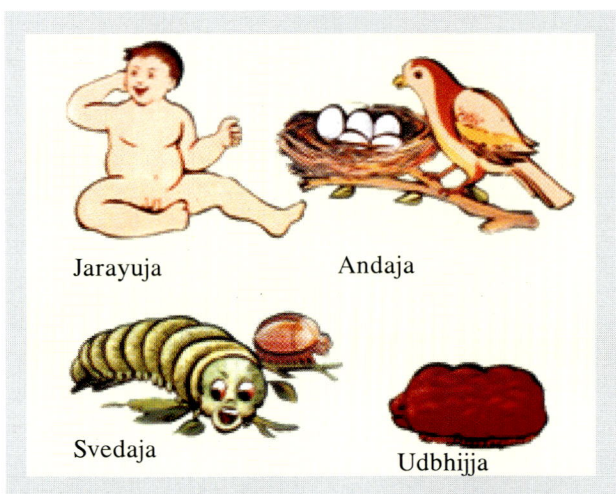

SCIENCE IN TRADITION

Gavyam

Agnihotra

Introduction

Traditions are knowledge in practice. But over a period of time, the practice could be divorced from the knowledge that brought the practice into vogue. Often the knowledge in the tradition is lost; the regression is on the following lines:

A "Rangoli" in front of the house ensures cleaning the house and provides feed for insects like ants.

	Initially it is done knowing the purpose	Conscious competence
	Later it is done without knowing the purpose.	Unconscious competence
	The edible rice powder is substituted with inedible powder or a plastic sheet is pasted in front of the house.	Unconscious incompetence
If lucky, we wonder -	Are we doing it right?	Conscious incompetence.

A correction and going back to "Conscious competence"

Complete discontinuation of the practice

We are presenting the underlying science behind some of these traditions:

- Use of Panchagavya
- Agnihotra
- Use of turmeric
- Use of copper vessel

17.1 Gavyam

गव्यं समधुरं किञ्चिद्दोषघ्नं क्रिमिकुष्ठनुत् ।
कण्डूं च शमयेत् पित्तं सम्यग्दोषोदरे हितम् ॥

Gavyaṁ samadhuraṁ kinciḍoṣaghnaṁ krimikuṣṭhanut I
Kaṇḍuuṁ ca śamayet piitaṁ samyag doṣadare hitam II

The cow's urine is (slightly) sweet, it alleviates (defects in) humours, is bactericidal, cures leprosy. It alleviates itching, is good for bile (disorder) & for the abdomen.

Source

Chāndogya-saṁhitā, Chapter 1, Mantraḥ 10 (Vedic period)

Notes

The reference to leprosy is possibly indicative of its efficacy in regard to obstinate skin diseases.

Current Relevance

The United States Patent and Trade Office has granted patent for an Indian innovation, which has proved that cow's urine can make antibiotics, anti-fungal agents and also anti-cancer drugs more effective. The patent has been granted to the Council of Scientific and Industrial Research for a product, the result of the research conducted by CSIR's Centre for Medicinal and Aromatic Plants, Lucknow, in collaboration with Gau Vigyan Anusandan Kendra, Nagpur. The innovation would help reduce the dosages of the drugs, thus cutting down on the costs of treatment and also its side effects. The tests conducted before the patent was applied for included experiments with Taxol, an anti-cancer drug. The distillate, which was produced by the Nagpur centre, was found to increase the drug's activity manifold. Taxol is used in the treatment of breast cancer. The other drugs, which were experimented upon, included ampicillin, tetracyclin and rifampicin, an anti-TB agent.*

* The Hindu (4/7/2002), U.S. Patent for Indian innovation.

17.2 Agnihotra

अग्निहोत्र एव तत् सायं प्रातर्वज्रं यजमानो भ्रातृव्याय प्रहरति । भवत्यात्मना परास्य भ्रातृव्यो भवति ।

Agnihotra eva tat sāyam prātarvarvajram yajamāno bhrātṛvyāya praharati ।
Bhavatyātmanā parāsya bhrātṛvyo bhavati ।

The one who practices Agnihotra in the morning and evening becomes (strong) like thunderbolt / diamond. Destroys enemies by himself (unassisted). His enemies remain conquered.

यावदहोरात्रे भवतः । तावदस्य लोकस्य नार्तिः नरिष्टिः । नान्तो न पर्यन्तोऽस्ति ।

Yāvadahorātre bhavataḥ । Tāvadasya lokasya nārtiḥ nariṣṭiḥ । Nānto na paryantoऽsti ।

As long as he does (agnihotra) in the day and in the night, in this world for him (there would be) no pain or misfortune. (There will be) no end to him (An Agnihotra practioner will have a long life).

Source

Taittirīya-brāhmaṇam, Aṣṭakam 2, Anuvākaḥ 5, 11 (Vedic period)

Current Relevance

On Monday, the 3rd of December, 1984, in the city of Bhopal, Central India, a poisonous vapour, methyl isocyanate, burst from the tall stacks of an MNC's pesticide plant, killing 2,000 people instantly and injuring more than 300,000. Soon after the leakage of gas, S.L. Kushwaha (45), a teacher in Bhopal, Madhya Pradesh, India, started performing his usual Agnihotra and in 20 minutes the symptoms of gas poisoning were gone from his home.

Agnihotra is the smallest form of Vedic Homa (sacrifice). This sacrificial fire is based on the biorhythms of nature. American Psychologist Barry Tathner, conducting research in Pune University, says, "Agnihotra has made many conquests so far. Today, there is not a language spoken on earth that does not number practitioners of Agnihotra."*

* Based on a report in The Hindu (7/4/1985).

Turmeric

Alzheimer's is an irreversible, progressive brain disorder that results in memory loss, erratic behaviour, personality changes and decline in thought process. The losses relate to the death of brain cells and breakdown of the connections between them.

According to the World Health Organisation, on an average of five percent of men and six percent of women suffer from the disease. There is no cure for the disease and medicines are primarily used to improve attention, reduce delusions and ameliorate cognitive dysfunction in the patients.

The studies, which were conducted on genetically altered mice, found that turmeric not only inhibited the accumulation of beta amyloid, a protein, in the brains of the Alzheimer's patients, but also broke up the existing plaques.

In other words, the studies suggested that it could be used for both treatment and prevention. As a follow-up, the scientists have now initiated measures for clinical trials with human volunteers to further evaluate its protective and therapeutic effects.

The Hindu (25/4/05), Turmeric, a potential weapon against Alzheimer's.

Copper Vessel

Waterborne diseases remain a major cause of illness and death in developing countries. Potable safe drinking water still remains a distant and expensive goal for the masses. When centralized water treatment systems are absent or inadequate, the responsibility of making drinking water safe falls on individuals and communities by default. The key factors in the provision of safe household water include the conditions and practices of water collection and storage and the choice of water collection and storage containers or vessels.

In ancient days, use of well water and storage of water in copper and brass containers were common. Microbes are destroyed through the heat and radiation provided by the sun. It is one of the traditional ideas of water treatment in this part of the world and interestingly we were able to find a microbiological basis for it - one of the researchers said. The key element is copper which acts by interfering with the membranes and enzymes of cells, eventually killing the bacteria. Pots made of brass, an alloy of copper and zinc, shed copper particles into the water they contain.

Rob Reed, a microbiologist at Northumbria University, New Castle Upon Tyne, England, found that bacteria were less likely to thrive in brass water pots than in earthen or plastic containers. The scientist, along with fellow researchers Puja Tandon and Sanjay Chhabaria, filled brass and earthen vessels with a diluted culture of Escherichia coli bacteria, which can cause diseases, such as dysentery. They counted the surviving bacteria after six hours, 24 hours and 48 hours. A similar test was carried out using naturally contaminated water. The amount of live E.coli in the brass vessels dropped dramatically over time, and after 48 hours they fell to undetectable levels.

The Hindu (20/4/05), Back to brass vessels to beat disease.

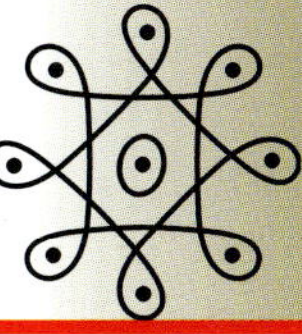

1995 The European Patent Office in Munich grants a Patent to the Department of Agriculture of the United States Government and W.R. Grace, a chemical multinational on the use of 'Neem' as an agricultural pesticide.

2000 The Patent is revoked.

2001 An appeal is made against the revocation.

2005 The appeal is turned down and finally the traditional knowledge of thousands of years is saved from being appropriated by a multinational chemical giant.

The striking features of the case are:

➢ This patent does not relate to an ancient knowledge which has gone out of vogue but a knowledge that is in vibrant use across the subcontinent in thousands of villages and towns as pesticide and as home remedy.

➢ The attempt to monopolise the knowledge was made not only by a multinational committed to the pursuit of money, but also by the Agricultural department of the Government of the United States of America, the richest country in the world.

➢ The perpetrators did not consider this attempt as untenable eventhough the history of thousand years was against them. They applied for the patent, got it from an independent agency - the European Patent Office - and also fought a legal battle to retain the right for a full decade.

➢ It is not as though this usurping was done quietly without anybody knowing about it. The multinational held on to this initiative (to appropriate to itself the traditional knowledge), despite a public outcry and the force of the Green Movement (represented by the International Federation of Organic Agriculture Movement) and the Green Party in the European Parliament for over a decade.

The case has also established a valuable legal precedence. Novelty and invention are the basis for grant of patent. "Prior use" would negate both "novelty" and "invention". **This case has recognised intellectual achievement of traditional societies as "Prior use".***

This case demonstrates the need for documenting our traditional knowledge, in the current globalised patent regime. If this experience does not shake us from our complacence and spur us into action, nothing will.

* http://www.ifoam.org/Briefing_Neem.pdf

MYTHOLOGY TO SCIENCE

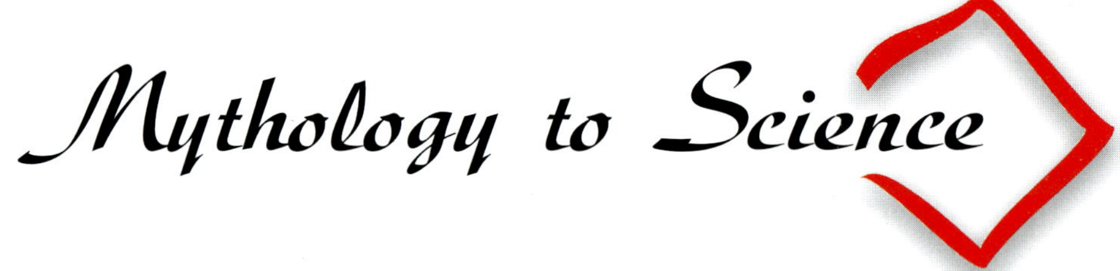

Introduction

Mythology ⟶ Science

Myth is a commonly held belief that is untrue. Mythology refers to stories of ancient legends and heroes and the study of such stories. Mythologies are expected to have veiled meanings.

The Samskrit equivalent of myth is Purana, which interestingly means that which was old and is relevant now. (Pura + Navam)

In this block we give a couple of examples of Hindu mythology which contain very interesting science in

- Cosmology
- Evolution

Very unfortunately, the only way of recognising the science in ancient texts has been after the rediscovery of the truth in the west. This book abounds in such examples.

Mythological stories contain a series of assertions, some of which have now been discovered as science. The as yet unverified truth could be postulates for future research and validation, which would go beyond merely establishing the superior wisdom of the civilisation.

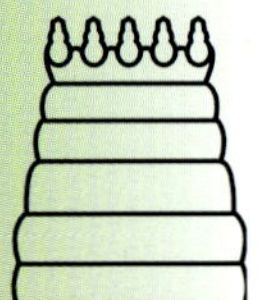

18.1 Age of Brahmā

काष्ठाः पञ्चदशख्याता निमेषा मुनिसत्तम ।	Kāṣṭhāḥ pañcadaśakhyātā nimeṣā munisattama I
काष्ठस्त्रिंशत् कला तास्तु त्रिंशन्मौहूर्तिको विधिः ॥	Kāṣṭhastriṁśat kalā tāstu triṁśanmauhūrtiko vidhiḥ II
तावत्सङ्ख्यैरहोरात्रं मुहूर्तैर्मानुषं स्मृतम् ।	Tāvatsaṅkhyairahorātraṁ muhūrtairmānuṣaṁ smṛtam I
अहोरात्राणि तावन्ति मासः पक्षद्वयात्मकः ॥	Ahorātrāṇi tāvanti māsaḥ pakṣadvayātmakaḥ II
तैः षड्भिरयनं वर्षं द्वयेऽयने दक्षिणोत्तरे ।	Taiḥ ṣaḍbhirayanaṁ varṣaṁ dvayeऽyane dakṣiṇottare I
दिव्यैर्वर्षसहस्रैस्तु कृतत्रेतादिसंज्ञितम् ॥	Divyairvarṣasahasraistu kṛtatretādisaṁjñitam II
चतुर्युगं द्वादशभिस्तद्विभागं निबोध मे ।	Caturyugaṁ dvādaśabhistadvibhāgaṁ nibodha me I
दिव्याब्दानां सहस्राणि युगेष्वाहुः पुराविदः ॥	Divyābdānāṁ sahasrāṇi yugeṣvāhu purāvidaḥ II
कृतं त्रेता द्वापरं च कलिश्चैव चतुर्युगम् ।	Kṛtaṁ tretā dvāparaṁ ca kaliścaiva caturyugam I
प्रोच्यते तत् सहस्रञ्च ब्रह्मणो दिवसं मुने ॥	Procyate tat sahasrañca brahmaṇo divasaṁ mune II

15 twinkles of the eye	=	1 kashta
30 kashta	=	1 kala
30 kalas	=	1 muhurta
30 muhurtas	=	1 day & night
30 day & nights	=	1 month
6 months	=	1 ayana
2 ayanas	=	1 year
12,000 divine years	=	4 yugas - krita, treta, dvapara & kali
	=	1 day of Brahma.

Source

Viṣṇu-purāṇam, Book 1, Chapter 3, Ślokaḥ 8-11 & 15, Vyāsaḥ (Post-Vedic period)

Notes

1 divine year = 360 human years

=>12,000 divine years = 43,20,000 human years = 1 day of Brahma, the creator of this Universe.

Western Reference

The big bang is the biggest budget universe ever, with mind-boggling numbers to dazzle us - a technique pioneered by 5th century AD Indian cosmologists, the first to estimate the age of the earth at more than 4 billion years.*

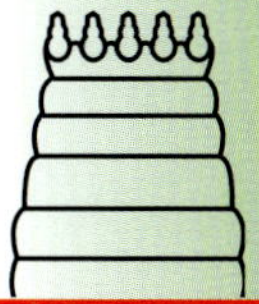

* Mr. Dick Teresi, Lost Discoveries, edn.Simon & Schuster (2003), p. 159.

18.2 Creation

तस्माद्वा एतस्मादात्मन आकाशः सम्भूतः ।	Tasmādvā etasmādātmana ākāśaḥ sambhūtaḥ I
आकाशाद्वायुः । वायोरग्निः । अग्नेरापः ।	Akāśādvāyuḥ I Vāyoragniḥ I Agnerāpaḥ I
अद्भ्यः पृथिवी । पृथिव्या ओषध्यः ।	Adbhyaḥ pṛthivī I Pṛthivyā oṣadhayaḥ I
ओषधीभ्योऽन्नम् । अन्नात् पुरुषः ॥	Oṣadhībhyo'nnam I Annāt puruṣaḥ II

From that Atman (Supreme soul) space came into being, from space wind, from wind fire, from fire water, from water earth, from earth plants, from plants food, from food man (came into being).

Source

Yajur-vedaḥ, Taittirīyopaniṣad, Brahmānanda-vallī, Aṇuvākaḥ 1 (Vedic period).

Notes

1. The above hierarchy is well appreciated when one takes into consideration the nature of the 5 elements, each inheriting the charateristics of its parent-element, as illustrated below:

	Elements		Attributes
i.	Space	-	sound
ii.	Wind	-	sound + touch
iii.	Fire	-	sound + touch + form
iv.	Water	-	sound + touch + form + taste
v.	Earth	-	sound + touch + form + taste + smell

2. The commonality of fundamental thoughts across disciplines in the Indian Knowledge System is known (Please see Life Sciences).

Time - the Indian Paradigm

The defining differentiation in the Indian thinking in regard to time and cosmology is that universe / life is in cycles and is not linear.

Scientific Rigour

Cosmology is the study of the universe as a whole, its history and origin. It is usually (but not always) based on astronomy, along with religious and social beliefs. Because it is so intertwined with general societal beliefs and attitudes, cosmology is a clue to the collective psychology of a civilisation.

Mr. Dick Teresi, Lost Discoveries, edn.Simon & Schuster (2003), p. 158.

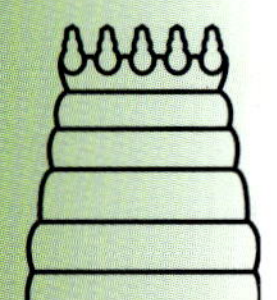

18.3 Daśāvatāras

मत्स्य: कूर्मो वराहश्च नृसिंहोऽथ वामन: ।
रामो रामश्च रामश्च कृष्ण: कल्की च ते दश ॥

Matsyaḥ kūrmo varāhaśca nṛsiṁhoSṭha vāmanaḥ I
Rāmo rāmaśca rāmaśca kṛṣṇaḥ kalkī ca te daśa II

The ten (Avataras of Lord Vishnu) are Matsya (the fish), Kurma (the tortoise), Varaha (the boar), Narasimha (the man-lion), Vamana (the dwarf), Parashurama (the axe-wielder), Rama (the king Rama), Balarama (the plough-wielder), Krishna (the flute-player) and Kalki (the evil-destroyer).

Source

Inscription, Śaṅkaranārāyaṇa temple, Mahabalipuram (5th century AD)

Notes

The first 6 incarnations represent physical evolution on to the human form

- Fish — Water dwelling
- Tortoise — Amphibian
- Boar — Animal - Land
- Narasimha — Man - Animal
- Vamana — Dwarf
- Parashurama — Fully grown man

7th to 9th deal with the social and cultural evolution of man. The evolution is evidenced by the weapons that these incarnations carry even without reference to the story.

6th - Parashurama----->Axe

Though having evolved physically, Parashurama through his life was seized by an uncontrolled anger (at the death of his mother) and his life was spent in persecuting kings. Only physically the form has become human.

7th - Rama----->Bow

Rama was the quintessential evolved human-being, who had completely overcome animal-like passions.

8th - Balarama----->Plough

The plough implies the completion of progress from being hunter gatherers to settled agriculture, with cultivated produce meeting most or all food needs.

9th - Krishna----->Flute

Fine Arts come about and flourish when there is peace and prosperity from settled agriculture and trade.

10th - Kalki is a warning about the destruction the human race is capable of bringing upon itself.

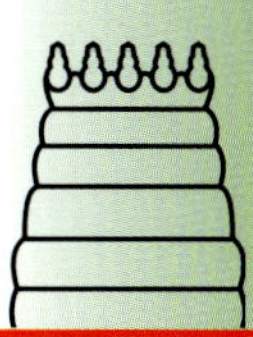

It was 1946. A young Samskrit scholar used to wait patiently on the banks of a river on solar or lunar eclipse days or on festive days hoping that somebody would throw into the river rare and ancient Samskrit manuscripts. It is the practice among some Hindu families to offer to the Ganga ancient scripts they have inherited if they feel they can no longer keep them or if there is any illness or difficulty in the house. If anybody threw any manuscripts, the young scholar had men ready to dive into the river and pick up the manuscripts. The scholar is Prof. K.T. Pandurangi who later became the Head of the Samskrit Department of Bangalore University. In his hunt for ancient manuscripts for 25 years, Pandurangi could obtain 2,500 interesting manuscripts on palm leaf, plates made of bamboo and country papers.

A collection of 2500 manuscripts made by an individual appears to be fairly large. However, it pales into insignificance when compared with the estimated number of manuscripts that are present in India today, i.e., five million, manuscripts that have been created over a period of two millennia[*].

Since the Harappan times, various societies that have evolved in the Indian subcontinent have contributed to the literary output of the Indian civilisation. This literature was created in both the oral and the written form. References to writing in early Buddhist scriptures, the Sutras, Panini's Ashtadhyayi etc., and in the accounts of Greek historians belonging to Chandragupta Maurya's time indicate that writing was practiced a couple of centuries before Ashoka's time[#]. This implies that writing has been practiced in India for over two millennia now, and would indicate a huge repository of written knowledge in the form of manuscripts that would have been created. Although it is to be expected that a significant portion of this would have been lost to the ravages of time, a fairly sizable collection is still available today.

These manuscripts span a range of subjects including Medicine, Literature, Mathematics, History, Buddhism and other Indian philosophies. For instance, the Bakhshali Manuscript, dated at 200 BCE - 400 AD, bridges the gap between the earlier Jaina mathematics and what is known as the 'Classical' or 'Golden' age of Indian mathematics (400 - 1200 AD). Some of the principal topics found in this manuscript include the Rule of Three, solutions to linear and quadratic equations, arithmetic and geometric progressions and calculation of square roots.

Manuscripts of Indian origin have been found in India and also in other parts of the world such as Germany, Britain, Italy, and Southeast Asia as well as in excavations in Central Asia. Tibetan and Chinese translations of Indian manuscripts have also been found. In India, manuscripts have been found across the country in almost all the states including Maharashtra, Rajasthan, Madhya Pradesh, Tamil Nadu, Kerala, Karnataka, Bihar, Uttar

* Mr. Siniruddha Dash, Kriti Rakshana, National Mission for Manuscripts, Dec 2005

\# MR. Kiran Kumar Thaplyal, Kriti Rakshana, National Mission for Manuscripts, Feb 2006

Pradesh, Punjab, Haryana, Jammu & Kashmir, Orissa, West Bengal, Assam and Arunachal Pradesh. These are found in Samskrit, Pali, Prakrit, Urdu, Persian, Turkish, Arabic, Hindi and other modern languages.

Within the country, manuscripts are held by various institutions and individuals. Government institutions like the Archives, religious bodies like Mutts, educational institutions like universities and individuals are the main repositories of the manuscript wealth of India. Some of the key institutions that possess a large number of manuscripts are listed below.

Sl No	Name	Location
1	Sampurnanand Samskrit University	Varanasi
2	Library of Tibetan Works and Archives	Dharamshala
3	Government Oriental Manuscript Library	Chennai
4	Oriental Institute & Manuscript Library	Trivandrum
5	TMSSM Library	Thanjavur
6	Adyar Library & Research Society	Chennai
7	Asiatic Society	Kolkata
8	Orissa State Museum	Orissa
9	Khuda Baksh Oriental Library	Patna
10	State Central Library	Hyderabad

Source: Discussion Paper, National Mission for Manuscripts, June 2002

Some of these libraries hold several rare distinctions. The Khuda Baksh Oriental Public Library in Patna, established towards the end of the 19th century as a private library, is considered to be the largest depository of Arabic, Persian and Urdu manuscripts in the Indian subcontinent. These cover a range of subjects spanning Quranic studies, Hadees literature, Exegesis, Law, Comparative Religion, Indic studies, Literature, Medicine and History. Some examples of the scientific works available here include Kitab al-Hashaish, dealing with medicinal plants and herbs. This work is an Arabic translation of the original Greek text which is not to be found anymore. Kitab al-Tasreef deals with surgery and is profusely illustrated with surgical instruments and equipment.*

As seen above, there are several centres that store a large number of manuscripts containing vast amounts of knowledge to be unlocked. However, it is estimated that the manuscript wealth that has been made available is but a small part of the total that is known to have been created as per evidence from other works. As late as 1902, Kautilya's Artha-shastra, undisputedly a work of great value in the field of polity and statecraft, was edited and published by Pandit Shyama Shastri[#]. This momentous publication was made on the basis of a single copy of the manuscript that was available in the Oriental Research Institute, Mysore. It is easy to imagine the ease with which this work may have been lost to us forever, and the number of other such works that remain unknown to us today.

Although some effort has been made to document and conduct research on these manuscripts, the bulk still remains undocumented. Instances where the traditional store houses of these

---

* Mr. Imtiaz Ahmed, Kriti Rakshana, National Mission for Manuscripts, Dec 2005

\# Mr. V.R. Panchamukhi, Kriti Rakshana, National Mission for Manuscripts, Feb 2006

manuscripts are still functional are rare. For example, Thanjavur Maharaja Serfoji's Sarasvati Mahal (TMSSSM) Library in Tamil Nadu is amongst the few medieval libraries that still function at present. An almost inexhaustible treasure house of knowledge, it was built up by successive dynasties of the Nayakas and Marathas of Thanjavur between the 16th and 19th centuries. It was made a public library in the 20th century and is maintained through grants received from both the central and state governments. The library has manuscripts in Samskrit, Marathi, Telugu and Tamil.

An interesting case is that of the "Satras" of Assam. Located in the island of Majuli in Assam, a nerve centre of neo Vaishnavite religion and culture, Satras are institutions that are akin to Buddhist monasteries. Today, there are over a score of Satras that still remain of the 64 that were established over the 16th and 17th centuries. Between them they house around 4000 manuscripts, including some rare collections of illustrated manuscripts. The main themes of these manuscripts are Religion, Medicine, Astrology and Zoology. Most are written on tree bark. The interesting thing about these satras is that the priests worship the manuscripts, not the idols of the deities. The reverence with which these manuscripts are held has ensured that they have been preserved with some degree of care over the last few centuries.

A similar instance of the importance of preservation being woven into the manuscript itself traditionally is that of Manipuri manuscripts. Manuscripts written in Meitei, which is the language most commonly understood in Manipur and used in literature in the 18th and 19th centuries, generally begin with a sacred letter to ensure that each manuscript is protected. The sacred letter is the "anji", which resembles a serpent. Significant effort is required in order to benefit from the manuscript wealth of India. The main steps involved in uncovering this wealth include:

- Documenting and cataloguing the manuscripts that are available in scattered sources across the country
- Promoting access to the manuscripts to the public - the layman and the scholar
- Conservation of the manuscripts through better awareness and training

Some of the libraries have already commenced on this mammoth task. Khuda Baksh Library in Patna has launched a project to digitise its collection. Sarasvati Mahal Library in Thanjavur regularly publishes rare manuscripts in the form of books in order to disseminate the knowledge contained in them and make it accessible to the public. These are however only the initial steps in a long journey; albeit one that is guaranteed to yield significant fruit in the form of scientific knowledge discovered centuries ago and waiting to be used today.

S.No	Samskrit word	Meaning
1.	Anushtup-chandas	A meter in prosody with 32 syllables.
2.	Aranyakas	The third part of each of the 4 Vedas elaborating various spiritualistic practices for forest (aranya) dwelling initiates in spirituality.
3.	Arjuna	The third of the five Pandava princes, an ace-archer to clear whose dilemma the Bhagavad-gita was delivered by Lord Krishna.
4.	Asuras	The demons.
5.	Ashvamedha	A part of Rajasuya ritual performed by emperors to establish sovereignty over other kings.
6.	Atharva-veda	The youngest of the 4 Vedas, the Mantras of which are intended to protect the fire sacrifices from external harm and compensate for deficiencies in the conduct of the sacrifices.
7.	Aurobindo	A revolutionary-freedom-fighter turned ascetic who practised and preached spiritual and yogic ideals, born 1872.
8.	Balarama	Elder brother of Krishna the Vishnu incarnate; a cousin to the Pandavas of the Mahabharata.
9.	Bodhayana	A sage who prepared handbooks on performance of Vedic rituals in the form of aphorisms.
10.	Bhagavad-gita	The philosophical dialogue between Krishna and Arjuna in the Kurukshetra battle field.
11.	Bhagiratha	One of the predecessors of Rama, the hero of Ramayana, known for his untiring efforts in bringing the river Ganga from the heavens to the earth.
12.	Bhartrihari	A poet and a grammarian in ancient India his principal works being Shringara-shatakam (100 verses on erotics) Niti-shatakam (100 verses on ethics) and Vairagya-shatakam (100 verses on dispassion).
13.	Bhishma	Son of Shantanu one of the earliest kings of Kuru dynasty mentioned in the Mahabharata.
14.	Brahmanas	The second part of each of the 4 Vedas directing the usage of Vedic verses in rituals.
15.	Brihadaranyaka-upanishad	Literally the big forest. Upanishad (philosophical text) forming part of Yajur-veda.

16. Brihad-samhita	Literally, the Big collection. A text that covers a whole range of subjects from astronomy to preparation of cosmetics. It was compiled by Varahamihira in 6th century AD
17. Chandogya-upanishad	Upanishad (philosophical text) forming part of Sama-veda.
18. Chaturdasha-vidyas	Literally the 14 knowledge streams. Consists of, besides the 4 Vedas, the tools for learning the Vedas -Vedangas 6, Upangas 4.
19. Daksha-prajapathi	One of the subordinates of Brahma the creator, described in Puranas.
20. Deva	An astral being in Hindu mythology.
21. Dharma-shastras	Texts that lay down canons of ethics and morals. Some of the principal texts being - Manu-smriti, Parashara-smriti Devalasmriti, Yagnavalkya-smriti.
22. Dhyana-shlokas	Verses of propitiation (on God and teacher) written usually at the beginning of a text.
23. Duryodhana	Eldest among the hundred Kaurava brothers, cousins of the Pandavas.
24. Dvapara	The third of the four yuga cycle spanning 4,32,000 years.
25. Gayatri	A sacred chant (Mantra) found in the Rig-veda attributed to sage Visvamitra.
26. Harappa	A site of archeological excavation of the Indus valley civilisation, now in Pakistan.
27. Indra	The king of the Devas, astral beings in Hindu mythology.
28. Jarasandha	An Emperor mentioned in the Mahabharata. His empire encompassed various kingdoms in the north and north-east India; an arch-rival of Krishna.
29. Kali	The fourth of the four yuga cycle spanning 8,64,000 years.
30. Kalidasa	Most famous poet of classical Samskrit literature, author of the world famous drama - Shakuntala.
31. Kanda	A chapter.
32. King Yayati	A king of Puranic fame, a distant ancestor of the Pandavas.
33. Krishna	The 9th incarnation of Vishnu. He guided the righteous Pandava princes in their fight against their cousins Kauravas.
34. Krishna-yajur-veda	One of the two versions of the Yajur-veda without a strict division of Mantras and directions into Samhita and Brahmanas. It has presently three recensions namely - Taittiriya, Maitrayaniya and Kathaka.
35. Krita	The first among the four yugas (eras), spanning 17,28,000 years.

36. Maharshi	A common noun denoting any great sage.
37. Maya	Illusion of duality.
38. Narmada	A river flowing in Western India.
39. Natya-shastra	A compendium on dramaturgy (the principles of dramatic compositions) by sage Bharata (1st century BCE). Its sweep includes dance, drama, stage management and even make-up methods.
40. Nava-ratnas	Literally the nine precious gems. It refers to the nine scholars in the court of king Bhoja, Kalidasa being the best known of these nine.
41. Panini	Grammarian par excellence who authored the famous grammatical work - Ashtadhyayi.
42. Parijata tree	A tree believed to be brought from the astral region; gives fragrant flowers.
43. Purohita	A priest. Pura + hita. Concerned with future welfare; which would be the result of the rituals he oversees.
44. Rajasuya	A Vedic ritual performed by emperors, claiming sovereignty over other kings.
45. Rig-veda	The first/oldest of the 4 Vedas. Literally the Veda in praise of the gods. The Riks that make the Samhita part of the Veda are in the form of poetry.
46. Riks	The Mantras (basic unit) of the Rig-veda-samhita, in the form of verses bound by rules of prosody.
47. Sabarmati	A river flowing through Gujarat.
48. Sage Vasishta	A Vedic sage, the preceptor of Surya dynasty. Bhagiratha, Dasharatha and Rama are some of the famous kings of this dynasty.
49. Sahadeva	The youngest of the five Pandava brothers, an expert astrologer.
50. Sama-veda	Literally, the Veda to please. Consists substantially of Rig-vedic hymns set to music. The third of the 4 Vedas.
51. Samhita	Literally a collection. The first and core portion of the Vedas containing Suktas in praise of Vedic deities.
52. Sankhya	An ancient school of Indian philosophy founded by sage Kapila.
53. Sayanacharya	A commentator of the Vedas, lived in 14th century BCE, in the present day Karnataka.
54. Shankara	Philosopher par-excellence and religious reformer who established the non-dualistic school of Hindu philosophy. (8th century AD).

55. Shatapatha-brahmana	The Brahmana of the Shukla Yajur-veda.
56. Shloka	Verse
57. Shri	A prefix denoting respect, like Mr.
58. Shukla-yajur-veda	One of the two versions of the Yajur-veda, wherein the Samhita (Mantra) and Brahmana (directions) of the text are substantially segregated. It is available in two recensions Kanva and Madhyandina.
59. Shri-vidya literature	Tantric texts dealing with the worship of goddess Shakti.
60. Stuti	Praise
61. Sukta	A set of Vedic-mantras having one subject matter most of which eulogise the various Vedic gods.
62. Treta	The second of the four yuga cycle spanning 12,96,000 years.
63. Upanishad	The final part of each of the Vedas containing philosophical thoughts to deliver the practitioners from the cycle of births and deaths.
64. Vedanta	Literally the end of Vedas - in the sense of both purpose and last part; Philosophy, the essence of the Vedas.
65. Vedas	From the root Vid, to know, meaning the text to be learnt. There are 4 of them Rik, Yajus, Sama and Atharva.
66. Vishvamitra	A Vedic sage to whom the Gayatri-mantra was revealed.
67. Vyasa	The sage who classified and categorised the entire Vedic literature. He is also known as Krishna Dvaipayana. The word Vyasa means dividing and organising and would suggest an editor. He lived around 3110 BCE.
68. Yajnavalkya	A sage to whom the Shukla-yajur-veda is attributed. His supplementary works cover various branches of knowledge including Yoga, Dharma-shastra and phonetics.
69. Yajur-veda	Literally the Veda for worship or sacrifices. The Yajus that make the Veda-samhita are in prose form. It is the 2nd of the four Vedas. It is in vogue in two forms, Krishna-yajur-veda and Shukla-yajur-veda.
70. Yuga	An era. Traditionally there are four Yugas - Krita, Treta, Dvapara and Kali, spanning thousands of years.

* Rik + Veda = Rig-veda

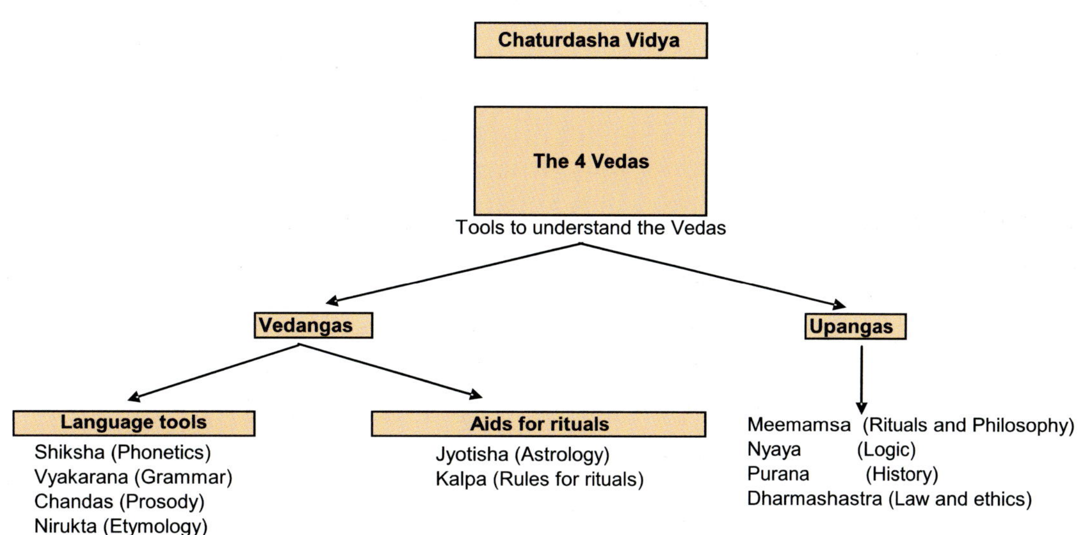
Chaturdasha Vidya
The 4 Vedas
Tools to understand the Vedas
Vedangas
Upangas
Language tools
Shiksha (Phonetics)
Vyakarana (Grammar)
Chandas (Prosody)
Nirukta (Etymology)
Aids for rituals
Jyotisha (Astrology)
Kalpa (Rules for rituals)
Meemamsa (Rituals and Philosophy)
Nyaya (Logic)
Purana (History)
Dharmashastra (Law and ethics)

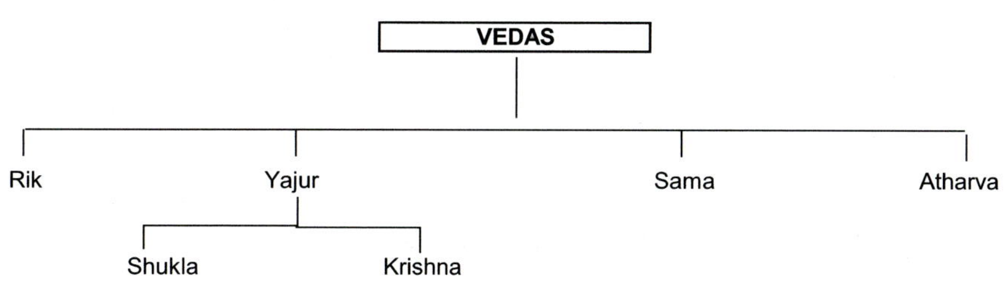
VEDAS
Rik
Yajur
Sama
Atharva
Shukla
Krishna

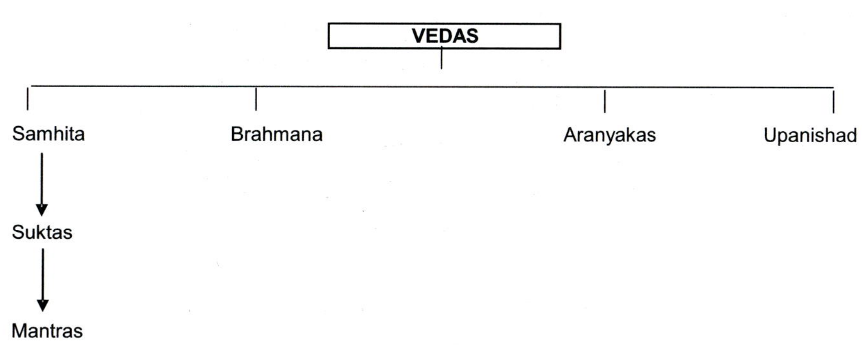
VEDAS
Samhita
Brahmana
Aranyakas
Upanishad
Suktas
Mantras

For Your Reflection

1. What does this ancient knowledge mean to us today?

i. Aryabhatiya, in 5th century AD, talked of the heliocentric theory, length of the day, etc. The same text has Shlokas which make no sense. Is it likely that there is some science in these Shlokas? Or should we wait for validation from western science?

ii. Charaka-samhita provides detailed steps on using black ants for suturing. Now that excellent suturing materials are available, is this no longer relevant? Or does this idea become a starting point for finding an organic material for suturing?

iii. To the Harappan civilisation, flooding was not a curse to be dammed. They had methodology to benefit from the flooding. They were able to see the blessing in the flood. Is there something to be said both for the perception and the methodology?

iv. Did our ancestors make no attempt to derive applications out of their knowledge? Was there no aspiration or did they fall short of this objective?

2. How did this civilisation come to posses so much knowledge so long ago?

i. Is there something to the idea of a Yuga cycle, of the world coming to an end and coming alive again in the same mode?

ii. Was there a path to knowledge different from our current practices?

iii. Is there something to the idea of divine revelation? There is the legend of a 6th century AD Vaishnavite savant Nathamuni, recovering the 4000 verses of Divya-prabandam, the Tamil Veda, by meditating on the original authors of the work.

3. Why was the knowledge not propagated?

i. Was practice seen as the only purpose of knowledge and no need was seen to enunciate the principles?

ii. Was there a great degree of apprehension about misuse, which led to even encryption of knowledge?

iii. At a point in time, was adherence to rituals (do not eat during an eclipse) and tradition (do not sleep with your head to the north) so complete that

- There was no need to pronounce the underlying science.
- That was the simplest way of ensuring total compliance.

Now there is an understandable lack of readiness to accept "handed down" wisdom. Should we work back from beliefs to reach the science which lead to the beliefs?

iv. In the case of astronomy, did the priest-class see it as their preserve and see no point in propagating the knowledge?

4. How did we lose this knowledge?

i. Did the cessation of Samskrit as a functional language result in the loss of the knowledge of which the language was the container and the vehicle?

5. Can you think of one or two things that you want to do?

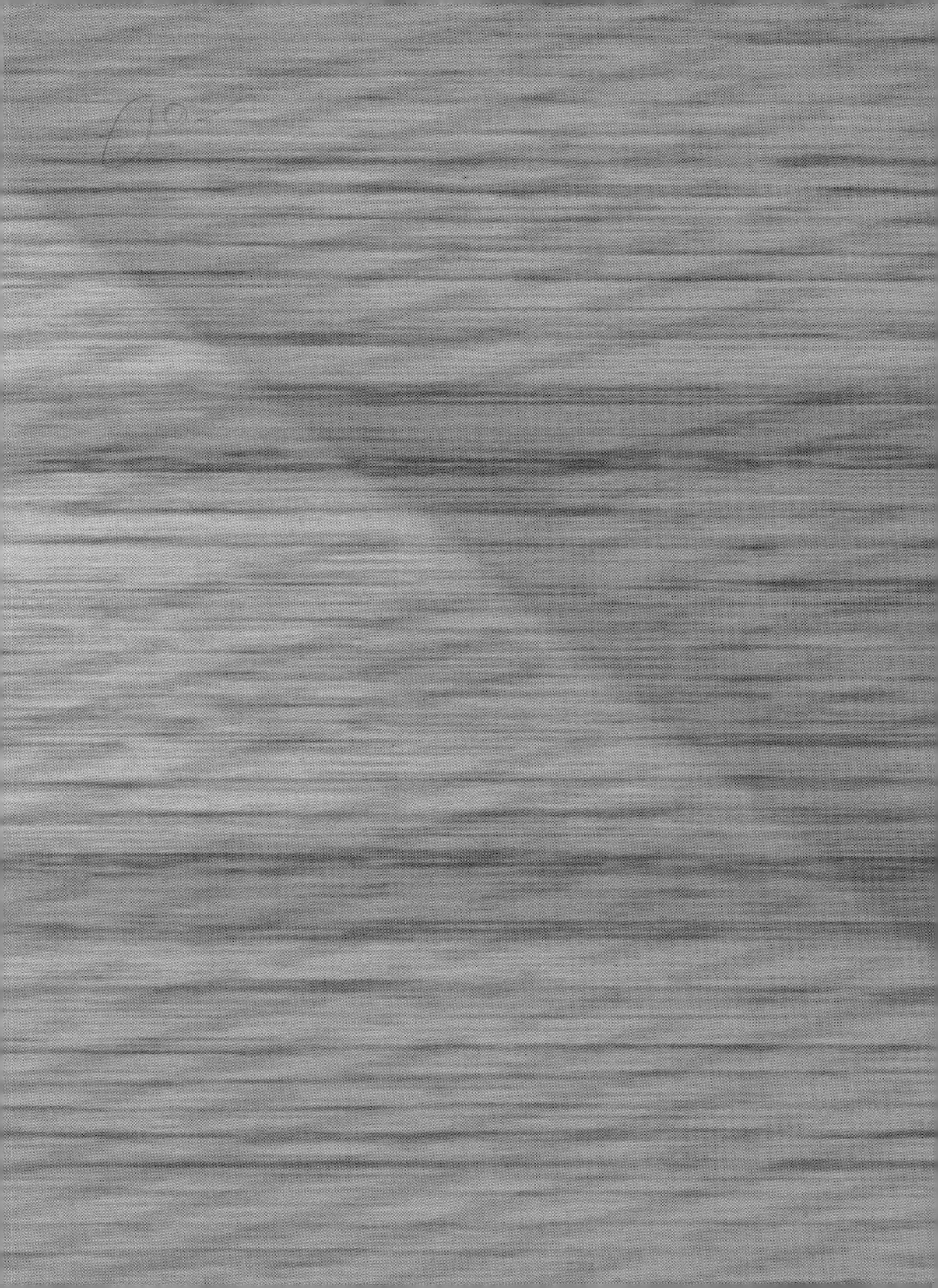